**Books are to be returned on or before
the last date below.**

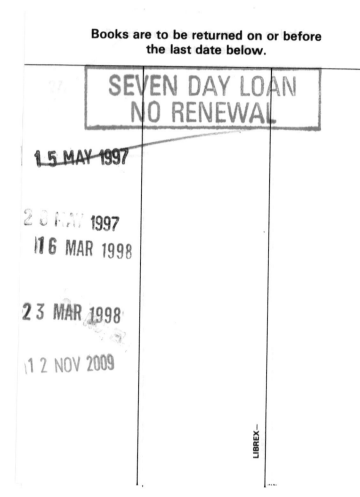

SEVEN DAY LOAN
NO RENEWAL

1 5 MAY 1997

2 3 MAY 1997
1 6 MAR 1998

2 3 MAR 1998

1 2 NOV 2009

LIBREX—

The right place:

The right place:

shared responsibility and the location

of public facilities

Bryan H Massam

Longman
Scientific &
Technical
Copublished in the United States with
John Wiley & Sons, Inc., New York

Longman Scientific & Technical
Longman Group UK Ltd,
Longman House, Burnt Mill, Harlow,
Essex CM20 2JE, England
and Associated Companies thoughout the world.

Copublished in the United States with
John Wiley & Sons, Inc., 605 Third Avenue, New York, NY 10158

© Longman Group UK Limited 1993

First published 1993

British Library Cataloguing in Publication Data
A catalogue record for this book is available from the British Library

ISBN 0–582–08116–5

Library of Congress Cataloging-in-Publication Data
A catalogue record for this book is available from the Library of Congress

Set by 8 in Times 10/12pt

Produced by Longman Singapore Publishers (Pte) Ltd.
Printed in Singapore

To my children
Alexandra Nicole and Laurent Nigel

Contents

List of figures

List of tables

Preface

The aim of this book is to provide a critical review of contemporary approaches which are used to tackle public facility location problems, and I will draw on contributions from a variety of disciplines including, economics, geography, management science, operations research, philosophy planning, political science and sociology. The search for sites for public facilities is a process of collective choice, and the literature which is reviewed seeks to throw light on components of this process. More specifically, I suggest that collective choice can be viewed as shared responsibility and hence this term is included in the title. The work falls within the field of spatial planning and it will be of particular interest to those who are concerned with improving the human condition via planning initiatives.

The political context for such initiatives is the state, as this is the basic territorial unit with the necessary political authority to raise and allocate funds for public facilities. The authority of the state also offers opportunities to regulate, control and generally manage the provision of goods and services to citizens. All states are involved to greater or lesser degrees in the management of goods and services which are consumed collectively. Even a casual perusal of the variety of states which currently exists makes it clear that terms such as the Welfare State, the minimal state or the command state, within either a federal or a unitary system, embrace considerable variations in their actual operations. In general terms it appears that politicians and citizens continue to strive for more effective, efficient and appropriate ways of improving the quality of life within a state by modifying the way collective choices are made, and goods and services are produced, distributed and consumed. The provision of so-called collective goods and services has much to contribute to the goal of improving the quality of life.

Following the seminal work on public facility location problems by Teitz (1968: 35), in which he argues that 'public determined facilities [have a] role . . . in shaping the physical form of cities and quality of life within them',

Jones and Kirby (1982: 298) remind us that 'Teitz's account of the reliance placed by the individual upon public services emphasises that it is essentially through such fixed-site resources that a welfare state is ultimately seen to succeed – or fail – and that even in relatively laissez-faire economies, such as the United States, it is necessary for the state or local state to provide a spectrum of such goods.' While it is widely recognized that the traditional Western-style Welfare States are evolving to embrace private initiatives (Day and Klein 1987a; Minford 1984; Mishra 1984), Taylor-Gooby (1991) in his review of J. Hill's (1990) book on the Welfare State notes that, *inter alia*, 'the welfare state is not unsuccessful at meeting such objectives as the establishment of a national minimum standard: state provision has not failed to advance equality'.

Day and Klein (1987a: 11) ask some pertinent questions regarding welfare. For example, 'Is responsibility for the *provision* of welfare by the state synonymous with the *production* of welfare by the state? To what extent should, or can, the welfare state be replaced by the regulatory state? What are the implications of replacing public *production* of welfare services by the public *regulation* of producers?' They acknowledge the criticisms of the left and right that argue that the Welfare State is excessively bureaucratic, paternalistic and ineffective. They go on to make the case that 'we should be asking how best to make sure that the appropriate kind of service, whether public or private, is being produced, to the right specification of quality, at the right price and in the right place for the right people' (Day and Klein, 1987a: 13). This book focuses on the search for the right place while recognizing that this locational element is just part of the total system.

Perhaps the term 'Regulatory State' is an appropriate one for the last decade of the twentieth century and as the next millennium approaches possibly the 'global public sector', albeit comprised of individual states in a variety of configurations for economic, social, environmental and political purposes, will emerge as the milieu within which collective choice problems will be addressed.

Recently N. Barry, (1990) has offered some answers to questions surrounding definitions of welfare and the part played by government in its promotion. Among other things, he argues that the growth of state welfare is directly linked to social dependency and a diminution of self-sufficiency as well as the reduction of individual choice which is a result of collectivist provision. Whether or not one subscribes to this view which purports to identify the disadvantages resulting from collectivist action, all societies are faced with location choice problems for the facilities that provide goods and services. The unfettered, unregulated free-enterprise milieu is widely recognized to be unacceptable. Now the search is on for new political paradigms, probably along the lines of the Regulatory State as mentioned earlier, which appear to combine the advantages of the market while offering sufficient protection to accommodate the views of the collectivity.

Those who examine some of the writings on modernism and postmodernism, for example Cooke (1990: 22), will observe that the 'concept of progress, [is] itself perhaps the defining characteristic of modernity', and that the breakdown of community and the nation state is, almost paradoxically, replaced by greater co-operation and the development of an 'act local, think global' philosophy.

As the 20th century *fin de siècle* approaches we seem to be confronted by change wherever we look. Debates about future directions have been raging throughout the 1980's. . . . Is the market the best mechanism for determining the allocation of all goods and services? Should the welfare state be dismantled? . . . If individuals are free to choose and benefit from the products and services of the market, do they also have responsibility towards other individuals less able to choose?

This view is discussed in an editorial comment in *The Economist* of 23 June 1990: vii, under the title 'Goodbye to the nation state?': 'Countries are getting together now as never before for good reasons. . . . As economies become more interlinked, so the people prosper. . . . Similarly, many of today's non-economic problems can best be tackled internationally. . . . More co-operation is essential.'

Cooke's book on postmodernism attempts to 'explain the problems that underlie such debates.' (Cooke 1990: 11) He goes on to suggest that: 'Postmodernists argue that modern perspectives undervalue, amongst other things, the consensus of minorities, local identities, non-western thinking, a capacity to deal with difference, the pluralist culture and the cosmopolitanism of modern life.' The ambiguity which results is captured by Cooke's assertion that 'The appeal to ideas of community and the authority of tradition is clearly a populist yet also a reactionary one.'

While emphasis is on change and evolution, and perhaps the search for Utopia continues as a dream for social thinkers, it is worth acknowledging with Dahrendorf (1958: 103) that: 'All utopias from Plato's *Republic* to George Orwell's Brave New World of 1984 have one element in common: they are all societies from which change is absent . . . the social fabric of utopias does not, and perhaps cannot, recognize the unending flow of historical processes.' Robertson (1984: 303) goes further and argues that: 'The ideal world is a "perpetuum immobile" predicated on an assumption of consensus and stability.' Unfortunately the real world falls far short of this ideal, with conflict and uncertainty typifying the milieu within which collective choice facility location problems are tackled.

The specific planning initiatives to be addressed in *The Right Place* focus on the selection of locations for public facilities. No single discipline monopolizes expertise for developing planning policies, and it is expected that the most productive work on location problems will result from co-operative efforts among scholars from different academic disciplines. At the outset I firmly endorse the view espoused by Hollis, Sugden and Weale (1985: 15) that: 'to explain how collective action problems are solved is one of the greatest challenges to social science'. Hall (1980: 187) offers a similar view, namely that 'one of the central problems of the modern world [is to explain] the way societies plan the output of public (or collective) goods'.

One of the critical elements in the production of welfare concerns the location of public facilities. Such facilities provide goods and services which are consumed collectively by citizens in *de facto* regions or *de jure* administrative units such as municipalities, townships, counties, provinces or states. Our modern world has a large number of facilities which cater to most of our needs, from the hospitals and clinics in which we may be born to the crematoria and burial grounds which receive our last remains. Our passage through life requires the consumption of growing quantities of goods and services, for example education, health care, emergency assistance (fire, police and ambulance), protection, recreation as well as heating, lighting, water and sewage treatment. Also we require facilities for storing and treating the variety of toxic and non-toxic wastes that are generated by consuming societies. Some goods and services may be provided to individuals who travel to the facilities (education from schools; health care from clinics and hospitals; recreation from parks and libraries; child care from day-care centres), or conversely they may be distributed from the facilities to consumers who may be scattered far and wide (police and fire protection; waste collection; utilities like electricity, gas and water). Communication networks comprising, *inter alia*, highways, rapid transit systems, railways and power-line corridors which link supply and demand points also present site location problems.

Typically, proximity to those facilities classed as salubrious or salutary (e.g. parks and libraries) is seen as an advantage, while the norm for noxious facilities (e.g. waste dumps) is to seek locations which are not 'in my backyard' (NIMBY). The search for appropriate collective choice planning procedures which enjoy public confidence to move the *not* (Peelle and Ellis 1986) to *maybe* (Raiffa 1985) to *yes* (McQuaid-Cook 1986) in my backyard is examined in this book. In general terms perhaps we are witnessing a shift in public facility siting processes to 'now I must be involved' (NIMBI) as a concrete attempt to increase the sharing of responsibility among all who wish to be considered as constituents of the collectivity that has to address a public facility location problem.

The search for acceptable locations for facilities attracts attention from planners, politicians and bureaucrats as well as citizens at large. While all recognize that usually there have to be compromises before a particular facility is implemented at a specific place, the route to a compromise is often not without conflict and disagreement. In this book some fundamental concepts which underlie the search process will be identified and discussed. Specifically there are three concepts which I suggest capture the basic elements of contemporary decision-making processes of collective choice which seek to provide answers to public facility location problems. These concepts are accountability, choice and consensus. Each concept will be discussed in separate chapters following an introductory chapter which examines relationships between public facilities, welfare and planning. Basic definitions will be offered in this chapter and the overall structure of the book and the linkages between the material in the separate chapters will be presented. Chapter 2 elaborates on the contexts within which location problems are defined and tackled. Emphasis is placed on the search for definitions of good planning, and comments on the important areas of environmental assessment and negotiations are included. Attention is also focused on need assessment and monitoring, inspecting and auditing as well as the generation of locational options to deal with specific planning problems. The systematic comparison of the locational options can be undertaken using a variety of formal evaluation techniques. A critique of these will be offered in Chapters 3 and 4, recognizing that location problems of public facilities are complex and involve multiple criteria and different interest groups. Chapter 3 reviews the growing fields of multi-criteria decision aid techniques (MCDA) and computer-based decision support systems (DSS), as they can be used to structure complex problems, and in Chapter 4 case studies will be presented to demonstrate a variety of MCDA and DSS. Throughout the book the term MCDA–DSS will be used to describe this body of work. Chapters 5–7 include discussions on the three basic concepts identified above: accountability, choice and consensus, together with definitions and selected examples. Finally, in Chapter 8 the possibilities for integrating the concepts with MCDA–DSS will be suggested using the notions of co-operative collective action and shared responsibility within the context of a Regulatory State.

This book contributes to the growing body of literature on the location of public facilities (Kirby 1982; L.M. Lake 1980, R.W. Lake 1987; Nelkin 1984; O'Hare, Bacon and Sanderson 1983; Openshaw, Carver and Fernie 1989; Pinch 1985; Seley 1983; Thisse and Zoller 1983; Williams and Massa 1983) by identifying the need to integrate technical and semi-technical approaches, especially MCDA–DSS, with the concepts of accountability, choice and consensus which are primarily drawn from the social science literature.

The concept of shared responsibility is suggested as an ideal to integrate and link a wide variety of literature, and to provide coherence for the development of socially acceptable collective choice planning procedures which could be used to tackle controversial and complex public facility location problems. The emphasis is on helping to improve the quality of debate by offering planning procedures which enjoy credibility because *inter alia* they are traceable and they can be closely scrutinized by the public.

Formal technical competence to understand the chapters on MCDA–DSS will be kept to a minimum, so that the concepts, principles and case studies will be widely accessible to all who are concerned about the search for the right place for public facilities. Throughout the book selected empirical examples from a variety of settings will be included to clarify the techniques and concepts, and to ensure that the material has broad appeal and relevance to practitioners as well as theoreticians.

At the outset it must be noted that I do not wish to offer a set of principles or techniques which should be used in a normative or prescriptive fashion to find the right place for a facility, rather the emphasis is on discussing concepts and techniques which might contribute to the reduction of planning mistakes and the improvement of collective choice by stressing the need to share responsibility. The important notion of planning mistakes, which is crucial in this study, will be taken up in Chapter 1.

To some the term 'responsibility' may have an attractive ring of sincerity and caring which suggests a level of decency by individuals which yield benefits to all. But why should individuals co-operate and take responsibility unless they can be made aware of the advantages of this type of behaviour or the costs of not adopting this approach? This general problem has attracted the attention of a number of scholars, for example Axelrod (1984). However, it is important to recognize that responsibility if it is to be effective must be linked to accountability. Leiserson (1964: 599) puts this succinctly: 'The term, [responsibility] in its core meaning denotes answerability, for the performance of an office, a charge, or a duty.'

A rationale for using the term 'responsibility' is partially provided by the notion that: 'As a philosophical concept, responsibility is a correlate of freedom; as a political concept, it is a correlate of constitutionalism.' (Gablentz 1968: 496). By adding 'shared' to the term I hope to reflect the linkages among the constituents in collective choice; that is, all who are involved in planning, administering, paying for and using public facilities. Further, there is a need for technical experts, who may undertake formal theoretical analyses, to work closely with regulatory agencies, legislators, inspectors and citizens, and for each to be responsible and accountable for their actions. Finally, it must be recognized that if we act irresponsibly then the consequences may be serious. The degree of severity can range from mild inconvenience to catastrophic, the former may be due, for example, to a poorly sited library that is not close to public transportation. A badly sited radioactive waste treatment facility may generate enormous adverse impacts, and some may subscribe to the views of Brown and Mikkelsen (1990) that there appears to be *No Safe Place*. In extreme cases indeed the survival of humanity may be jeopardized by selecting an inappropriate site. While clearly it is incumbent on those who make location decisions to be extremely cautious and seek with all energy and will to avoid making location choice mistakes, citizens, planners, bureaucrats and others cannot abrogate responsibility. It is imperative that if the human condition is to be improved, and recognizing that public facilities have a key role to play in such improvements, then we must acknowledge the responsibilities we bear and the need for clear lines of accountability as critical elements of collective choice. This book is written to offer a contribution to this objective.

Acknowledgements

There are a number of people in Canada and elsewhere who have provided me with encouragement, advice and information as I was preparing and writing this book. To all I offer my thanks. They bear no responsibility for the errors and omissions, or the arguments I advance.

In Canada I am particularly grateful to Mark P.A. Robinson, my research assistant at York University, for his unfailing energy and enthusiasm. I am also grateful to the 1990–91 class of graduate students in the Urban Planning Programme at the University of Toronto who shared with me their views and opinions as I lectured on the role of evaluation in planning. Among the colleagues who provided comments, papers and reports, and generally whetted my appetite to read widely about facility siting, I would especially like to thank: Audrey Armour, Ian Askew, Boris Borzic, Pat Day, Wade Cook, Rudolf Klein, Virginia Maclaren, Jacek Malczewski, Larry Phillips, Jim Radford, Ian Skelton and Nigel Waters.

I would also like to thank the Ministry of the Environment and the Ministry of Transportation in Ontario, Canada for providing me with opportunities to present seminars to government officials, and engineering and planning companies, on the use of computer-based decision support systems for informing public debate on complex location problems. I learned much from these experiences.

I am most grateful to colleagues outside Canada who invited me to visit them and spend time discussing collective choice problems and facility planning: Professor Lars-Eric Borgegård (National Swedish Institute for Building Research, Gavle and Department of Geography, University of Umeå, Sweden), Professor Derek Diamond (Department of Geography, London School of Economics), Professor Rudolf Klein (Centre for the Analysis of Social Policy, University of Bath), Dr Jacek Malczewski (Polish Academy of Sciences, Warsaw), Professor Arie Shacher (Institute of Urban and Regional Studies, University of Jerusalem, Israel), Dr Anna Vari

(Centre for Public Policy, State University of New York, Albany, USA), Professor Zhang Guo Wu (Institute of Applied Systems Analysis, University of Northern Jiaotong, Beijing, China), Dr Anthony Yeh (Centre of Urban Planning and Environmental Management, University of Hong Kong) and Professor Jia Xin Yuan (Institute of Quantitative Economics, Chinese Academy of Social Sciences, Beijing, China).

The figures were drawn by Carolyn King and Carol Randall in the Cartographic Office, Department of Geography, York University. A Macintosh IIci computer using MacDraw II was used in the preparation of the diagrams.

Financial support for research, and release time from teaching and administration during the academic year 1991–92, was provided by the Social Sciences and Humanities Research Council of Canada and the Faculty of Arts, York University. This is gratefully acknowledged.

We are grateful to the following for permission to reproduce copyright figures and tables:

A. Kellerman for fig. 4.2 (Gil and Kellerman, 1989); Pergamon Press Ltd. and the authors, W.D. Cook and L.M. Seiford for tables 3.2–3.4 (Cook and Seiford, 1984); R. Pushchak for table 2.2 (Pushchak, 1985).

1

Public facilities, welfare and planning

Every political system is prominently if not pre-eminently characterised by space.
    Ad hoc *Committee (1965)*

1.1 Introduction

The search for locations for public facilities is a problem of collective choice and this book seeks to improve our understanding of the principal components of the choice process. Examples of public facilities have been given in the Preface. In this book I argue that technical approaches which involve multi-criteria methods should be used in conjunction with certain principles which relate to accountability, choice and consensus. In sum I argue that the concept of shared responsibility can be used to integrate the methods and the principles which together comprise important components in collective choice.

Public goods and services are typically managed by governments in response to perceived and expressed needs. In general the free market is unwilling or unable to cater to the full range of needs at suitable levels for a society. Hall (1980: 187) claims that 'public goods are all those goods and services which the public are willing to pay for but which the private sector is not motivated to provide'. As mentioned in the Preface, this view is being modified as the Regulatory State emerges.

In general the goods and services that are provided from or at the facilities are paid for from the public purse. The development of public policies regarding the selection of sites for facilities involves a sharing of responsibility among individuals, including those who cast their votes, members of political parties, proponents of specific projects, activist groups who act as opponents and try to influence public opinion, those who form governments and occupy ministerial positions and those who fulfil the role of official opposition; also, civil servants, experts, professionals and others who administer the policies of governments and who provide advice on policy formulation and implementation. Planning consultants, members of boards, commissions and special bodies play critical roles in the formulation and legitimizing of location choice policies; they enjoy considerable public confidence and trust, and they have a strong obligation to be responsible. Not least of all in this list we must include those members of the media who influence public opinion by their reports on the estimates of the magnitude and importance of impacts relating to specific projects.

The nature and degree of accountability vary enormously among all who at first brush appear to have some responsibility. In a properly functioning system, as is stressed in Chapter 5 on accountability, there should be a close identifiable linkage between explicit responsibility and lines of accountability. Crises, mismanagement, accidents and catastrophes associated with poorly located and managed facilities attract attention, whereas smooth running trouble-free facilities are rarely highlighted. Vlek and Cvetkovich (1989), among others, contend that the planning and management of large-scale technological projects can be substantially improved, and that one of the key elements focuses on traceable responsibility and public accountability to complement studies of technology and risk assessment. This general assertion is also supported by the recent work by Gould (1990) on the accident at Chernobyl and it is reflected in the title of his book, *The Democratic Consequences of Chernobyl*.

In his study of the recent industrial accident at Bhopal, India, and the analysis of such crises, Shrivastava (1987: xvi) argues that 'crises occur most commonly in situations where complex technologies are embedded in communities that do not possess the infrastructure to support them'. He is of course referring to large-scale noxious facilities and he recognizes that the events that trigger crises are caused by a complex interaction of human, organizational and technological factors.

Effective responsibility demands clear lines of accountability and authority. Unfortunately such lines are often non-existent, broken, ill-defined and, in a word, poorly articulated in ways which allow clear and careful public scrutiny and prompt action. Day and Klein (1987b) provide evidence in support of this in their recent study of five public services in a region of the UK. The services they examined include: the National Health Service, police, water, education and social services. Further, for services which can surround themselves with technical knowledge, couched in terms of risk and uncertainty, it is frequently the practice to leave it to the professionals. In 1985 a private consulting firm, Price Waterhouse, in conjunction with the Canada Consulting Group Inc., were asked by the government of Ontario to undertake a study of accountability. Quoting from their final report, 'Our study was initiated by the government in response to concerns that lines of accountability were unclear, that rules were not always followed and that controls might not be adequate' (Price Waterhouse 1985: 1) A series of recommendations were made to enhance the authority and accountability relationships. Further details will be given in Chapter 5. An interview survey of representatives of the planning profession, government officials, academics and lawyers in Ontario, Canada regarding accountability and the location of waste treatment facilities in and around Toronto substantiates the view that while lip-service is often paid to supporting accountability, the lack of clear guidelines and operational definitions, as well as an extensive and widely known inspectorate, militate against a highly effective system of accountability. Details of this survey will be given in Chapter 5 when the topic of accountability is specifically addressed.

Management of public policies becomes very difficult if outputs, outcomes or consequences cannot be assessed and related to inputs. For example, Heseltine (1987) has reported on his frustrations when faced with the task in his capacity as Secretary of State for the Environment in the UK and later as Secretary of State for the Department of Defence in the British government in the late 1970s and early 1980s. He tried to address the problem squarely by introducing an accounting system known as management information system for ministers (MINIS) into the Ministry of the Environment, as a direct attempt to measure inputs and outputs, and provide information for more effective public policy-making. Others who have addressed problems of monitoring and measuring performance of public policies include Allen (1982), Carter, Klein and Day (1992), Dunn (1981), Hatry (1972) and Patton and Sawicki (1986). Obviously monitoring of the outputs is a necessary part of the management of public services, and with respect to location decisions it seems reasonable to expect utilization and satisfaction or effectiveness studies to be undertaken, within the context of *ex post* and *ex ante* impact analyses. For services which attract considerable public scrutiny due to their potential health risk, monitoring is the norm. Perhaps the best example is for the siting of facilities to store radioactive materials (Openshaw 1986; Openshaw, Carver and Fernie 1989), yet there is much controversy regarding measurements, acceptable standards, predictions, cumulative effects and the dissemination of the data to the public. In Chapter 2 I will discuss monitoring and the measurement of output as well as need.

With the growing concern about the use of public funds to support the provision of collectively consumed goods and services it is not surprising that there is increasing attention focusing on monitoring, auditing and inspecting. These are critical elements in the emerging Regulatory State, as has been mentioned earlier.

As part of the evolution towards improved provision of collectively consumed goods and services considerable emphasis is now being placed on the development and application of performance indicators as specific measures to determine as precisely as possible if society is getting value for money. An excellent review of the state of this art in the UK is provided by Carter, Klein and Day (1992), and the US literature is well presented in a series of papers and reports written by members of the Urban Institute in Washington, DC. Among the large literature on the topic let me draw particular attention to the contribution by Walsh (1991) which clearly identifies the problem of defining the quality of a service as a complement to quantity. Walsh (1991) recognizes that there are marked differences in information about quality between service providers and service consumers.

There is a need to seek ways to remove these differences if conflict is to be avoided. In a word, more emphasis is being rightly placed upon accountability, and with this in mind the use of technical methods for tackling siting problems must fit into a broader framework which embraces principles of accountability, choice and consensus as critical components of collective choice.

There is sufficiently strong evidence now available to show convincingly that the ideal location for a facility is typically a chimera, and that we are dealing with a class of problem that Hardin (1968) has characterized as a 'non-technical solution problem'. It is also clear that we can and do make wrong location choices for facilities and ideally we should strive to identify the reasons for these mistakes and ways of avoiding them in the future. By admitting publicly and frankly that there is uncertainty and risk associated with particular location options we dispel the myth that a 'right location' exists; rather the search is for the best compromise location which is most acceptable and least likely to be rejected by the various interest groups.

The distinction between risk and uncertainty needs to be made clear. Elster (1983b: 5) provides a useful summary: 'Decisions under risk are present when we can assign numerical probability to the answers to the question "What will happen?" Decisions under uncertainty imply that we can at most list the probable answers, not estimate their probabilities.'

It is incumbent upon academics and others to ensure that language on risk and uncertainty is used appropriately. Within a democratic society it is necessary that individuals trust the process that arrived at a compromise location. Unfortunately this trust is often lacking. This situation has been reported by a recent Task Force in Canada that was charged with finding a new process for dealing with difficult siting problems relating to the disposal of low-level radioactive waste in Ontario.

> In the absence of universally applied and respected procedures for handling such [low-level radioactive] waste, there has developed in the public mind a strong mistrust of, and hostility toward, waste producers and regulatory agencies . . . it is not surprising that attempts to site facilities . . . have been met with antagonism. In this particular case, low-level radioactive waste however, because the labels of radiation and radioactivity are attached, problems are compounded by a perception of risk which, while it may sometimes be exaggerated, is widely and sincerely held. (Ministry of Energy, Mines and Resources, 1987: xi)

The executive summary of the Task Force Report goes on to identify as a root cause of mistrust and hostility the current facility-siting processes which depend upon an adversarial presentation and scrutiny of options:

> On the one side stand those charged with finding a solution to burgeoning problems of waste management, prepared with their

rational technical solutions, looking to employ them in the most environmentally appropriate site. On the other side stand the potentially affected communities and residents with their concerns – their perceptions of risk, their view of inequities in the distribution of social and personal costs and benefits, their awareness of the community stigma that accompanies the unwanted facility, their feeling of loss of control over the quality of their lives and community, and their lack of trust in government regulators and waste facility operators. Neither side fully appreciates the needs, concerns, responsibilities or situation of the other; both perceive their position as eminently reasonable and responsible. (Ministry of Energy, Mines and Resources 1987: xi)

Clearly there is a need to provide a framework in which the views of each party are accommodated into a larger overarching milieu of shared responsibility. In this book I hope to offer such a framework which allows technical and formal procedures, specifically MCDA techniques and computer-based DSS, to be linked to the concepts of accountability, choice and consensus, and the whole to be incorporated into a dynamic planning process which involves monitoring the status quo, establishing need and evaluating alternative ways to cater to this need.

We cannot all enjoy the same level of advantage from the so-called salutary public facilities, for example, we are not all equally close to the park, school, library, hospital or day-care centre, neither do we all share equally the 'bads' from the noxious facilities. Our needs for the goods and services which are provided from the facilities also vary from person to person and over time. Those located close to power stations, rubbish dumps, highways, power-line corridors and the like, fear, hear, see, smell and generally suffer economic, environmental and health consequences they would prefer to avoid. In passing we should note that these consequences may be real and quite tangible or imagined, perceived or expected.

By their very nature, public facilities should provide goods and services which are available to all to enjoy to their required levels, and under general notions of justice and fairness we might assume that we should all share in the suffering of the negative effects. But this situation does not exist, and so idealistically we should find ways to reach compromises and agreements among the competing interests of individuals, so that citizens believe in the planning, evaluation and implementation process, and accept the location choices which emerge. The emphasis is on defining credible, reliable processes which allow public scrutiny and help build public confidence for the management of public facilities. Perhaps consensus-building provides the key. It is important that such processes link technical advances, for example in the field of data collection and handling, to political structures within which decisions are made, as well as bureaucratic and regulatory activities of civil servants and others (inspectors, for example), as well as the courts. All in all the search is for no less than a society in which individuals have faith and accept the hard location choices which must be made. In Chapter 2 I will provide comments on the search for good negotiation procedures which can help ensure that the final outcome is felt to be the best possible solution.

The world is becoming more cluttered with public facilities and it behoves us to ensure that we take responsibility for their selection and location. Mistakes can be very damaging. It is not sufficient or satisfactory to recite the NIMBY (not in my backyard), LULU (locally unwanted land use), TINA (there is no alternative) or NIMTOO (not in my term of office) shibboleths *ad nauseam*. Rather stakeholders must strive to develop ways to share responsibility more effectively for difficult location decisions. I argue that the concept of shared responsibility has validity as a mechanism for integrating the formal plan evaluation techniques, developed particularly in the last twenty years, and the political and bureaucratic structures within which location recommendations are generated, assessed and evaluated, and selections for implementation are made. Also shared responsibility should have a role to play in the monitoring of outcomes and the management of the production of public goods and services. We can note Berson's (1971: 283) assertion that: 'Planning is as old as the species. What has changed over time is the quality of planning . . .'. One of the aims of this book is to improve the quality of planning of public facilities by identifying some contemporary formal techniques and principles which may help to ensure that members of society feel that they share responsibility for the locations that are chosen for public facilities.

While Bracken (1981) among others has argued the case that evaluation and measurement are the cornerstones of successful planning, we should not forget the subjectivity of this type of exercise. Keeney (1981: 355), a strong supporter of the technical school of location planning, makes this case very clearly when he argues that: 'There is no such thing as an objective value free analysis. Furthermore, anyone who purports to conduct such an analysis is professionally very naive, stretching the truth, or using definitions of objective and value free which are quite different from those commonly in use.' He goes on to add that a logical systems analytical framework is needed that makes explicit the necessary professional and value judgements. With respect to transportation planning, Hutchinson (1974: 293) makes the necessary connection between so-called objective evaluation and subjective decision-making: 'It seems that if any real progress is to be made in evaluation, then the basis of the method should be some consistent theory of democratic group decisions.' The thesis of this book is that shared responsibility can be considered as a useful concept to integrate a variety of contemporary analytical tools and viewpoints about democratic society and collective choice which relate directly to public facility location choice problems.

The locational conflicts which emerge are typically discussions about tactical decisions; rarely are the conflicts, at this stage, involved with the larger strategic issues. Whereas all citizens may plead for better social services, transportation and utilities and appropriate facilities to generate and distribute power, and dispose of waste, the consequences of these strategic choices are that locational decisions for facilities must be made, and indeed some citizens will suffer greater costs and enjoy larger benefits than others. Because most public facility location problems, especially of the noxious type, rarely link closely the strategic and tactical levels of collective choice problems, it is not surprising that the public often feels cheated and aggrieved when asked to express an opinion concerning the relative merits of a small set of optional sites. Clearly there is room for improvement in the planning processes which search for sites for public facilities and I argue that perhaps such improvements may come about if they are aimed at building consensus. Ideally we might like to devise a planning process which ends in win–win outcomes for the various interest groups that comprise the collectivity, rather than the classic adversarial structure which is characterized as a zero-sum game, that is, my gains are made as you incur costs.

Consider, for example, the proposal to build a nuclear power station at Sizewell, on the Suffolk coast in the UK. The Public Inquiry into this proposal lasted 340 days, from January 1983 until 7 March 1985. It was the longest and most expensive one of its kind and in sharp contrast to those in the 1960s which lasted a matter of hours. The extraordinary length of this inquiry did not guarantee that a consensus had been achieved. Specifically the Town and Country Planning Association (TCPA) (1987: 5) of the UK made the point that 'it [TCPA] does not accept that the Inquiry has been a fair one'. A detailed set of seventeen recommendations has been proposed by the TCPA that would help to improve the planning process. Among their major points they argue that funds should be made available to allow the views of all stakeholders to be presented. Also they recognize that public policy formation and enunciation by the central government is often mixed into site-specific issues thus making it difficult for opponents. The TCPA argue that it is against public interest to restrict attention to site specific issues. Further, there is a clear need for a good secretariat who can provide full documentation to all parties without undue delays. The restructuring of an inquiry so that an adversarial approach is avoided is to be commended.

1.2   Why shared responsibility?

My current interest in shared responsibility, collective choice and spatial planning stems from earlier work on the locational aspects of public goods and services (Massam 1975, 1980, 1988a, b). Some of the work has focused on narrowly defined problems where operational solutions using formal numerical optimizing and classification multi-criteria procedures have been sought. Other papers have attempted to define location problems as complex and to offer generic problems with a view to identifying the components of such problems and the ways such components fit together. For example, following the seminal work of Teitz (1968), attention has been focused on the relationships among the number, size and location of facilities and the distribution of costs and benefits among suppliers and consumers, and on utilization patterns. Also the legal frames and political structures of a state within which public policies on such matters emerge have been examined. Among other topics measurement difficulties for determining the quality and quantity of inputs and outputs have been identified, and suggestions have been offered for judging evaluation techniques which some proponents claim will improve the quality of planning. Midgeley and Piachaud (1984: 6) subscribe to this view. They have noted with respect to social planning that:

> Although it is recognized that planning techniques have many limitations . . . , we believe that they are helpful aids to policy-making which enhance objectivity and efficiency. To reject their use is to legitimise Machiavellian tendencies and traditionalism in organisational policies and to deny the need for greater rationality in decision-making.

While I do not subscribe to their view that rejection of such techniques suggests support for Machiavellian approaches, I do believe that the development of open, traceable, decision-making processes, which use information in ways that can be scrutinized publicly, will enhance accountability and may lead to expeditious planning and the avoidance of planning disasters of the kind examined by Gould (1990), Hall (1980) and Shrivastava (1987), among others.

While this somewhat eclectic piecemeal approach to facility planning has certain intellectual appeal particularly within the realm of normative model-building and even prescription, it typically leads to frustrations because of the difficulties of relating the partial models to positive studies which seek to explain what is observed. There are also great difficulties in the area of implementation. Indeed the search for appropriate ways to examine collectively consumed goods and services is a challenge to academics, planners, politicians and of course the public. The references to Hollis, Sugden and Weale (1985) and Hall (1980) regarding collective choice problems that were made in the Preface emphasize the importance of this challenge. For ease of analytical treatment the location problems are often abstracted from society; however, I argue that there is a need to put them into the context of a state as this is the spatial unit in which consumers and producers interact with politicians in order to regulate the location of facilities. As mentioned in the Preface, there are a variety of types of states which are subsumed under the general categories of unitary or federal, and terms such as minimal, welfare or command have to be used with caution. However, I argue that the three topics of accountability, choice and consensus must be addressed no matter what kind of state provides the context for the location problem. Further, I argue that without studies of the development, evaluation and implementation of alternative plans and policies it is virtually impossible to use the normative or prescriptive models to solve practical location problems.

This book is the final one in a quartet, spanning a period of almost fifteen years, which has focused on locational questions surrounding the provision of those goods and services which are generally consumed collectively. The concept of shared responsibility is used to unite a broad body of literature of relevance to decisions about the way societies choose collectively how to provide public goods and rectify so-called lapses in the operation of the private market.

The first book, *Location and Space in Social Administration* (1975), was written to fill the gap between a social value-oriented approach to location planning and one which relies more heavily on rigorous analytical techniques. I was particularly interested to consider the notions of distance and accessibility in the evaluation of public services. I maintained that while physical proximity to a facility often relates directly to the satisfaction which an individual derives from the service which is provided, the presence of noxious facilities will become increasingly important and accessibility will be compounded by environmental concerns. I examined public awareness and its influence on utilization patterns, pointing out that although information may be available to all, comprehension varies and some people do not take advantage of facilities and services to which they are entitled. The arguments extended the seminal work of Teitz (1968). Others, for example Cox (1979), Kirby (1982) and Pinch (1985), have taken up the challenge to include social and political arguments about the state as the backdrop against which to view locational questions of public facilities as part of the study of goods and services which are consumed collectively.

An ideal world can be envisaged as one in which there are best or correct locations for public facilities and these are chosen. The second book, *Spatial Search: applications to planning problems in the public sector* (1980), offers a synthesis of the problems associated with the search for so-called best locations for public facilities. In the search for these ideal locations account must be taken of a variety of factors including construction and operating costs, utilization patterns, environmental costs and the distribution of social costs and benefits among individuals. In the definition of best, consideration must be taken of long-term and short-term effects, as well as the perceptions and preferences of individuals and groups. In an attempt to provide a general structure for tackling location problems in the public sector this book was written to offer an approach based upon the notion of spatial search, that is, the systematic consideration of alternative locations would be the key to finding a best one. Of course, the dilemma of compromise was ever-present, and the results of such rigorous analytical work on collective choice as has been done by Arrow (1951) which demonstrated the inconsistencies and virtual futility of seeking an ideal constitution hung constantly over the work.

The essential thrust of Arrow's results is captured in a summary offered by Blair and Pollak (1983: 89), namely that: 'Three widely shared objectives – collective rationality, decisiveness and equality of power – stand in irreconcilable conflict . . . there is little comfort here for those designing ideal procedures for collective choice. Nevertheless every society must make collective choices . . .'.

While it can be demonstrated using an axiomatic approach that the ideal constitution is a chimera, the general problem of finding appropriate ways to incorporate the views and opinions of individuals into a constitution remains. The dilemma facing those who seek to provide appropriate ways to tackle collective choice problems stems from the result that for certain classes of choice problem, for example the prisoner's dilemma format, the co-operative approach among interest groups will yield the best overall outcome. This is the win–win outcome sought by all negotiators! The necessary co-operation to yield such a satisfying outcome appears irreconcilable with so-called self-interest or even enlightened self-interest. This point is neatly summarized by Hollis, Sugden and Weale (1985: 15):

> Ever since the collective action problem was first identified theorists have been puzzled by the paradox that recommending the apparently rational course of action leaves people worse off than they need be. . . . The collective action problem belongs to a wider set of decision problems in which the dominant choice leaves individuals worse off than they need be.

Some comfort is provided by the writings of the philosophers Axelrod (1980) and Danielson (1986) who have tackled the general problem of choice within a prisoner's dilemma framework and specifically sought answers to the question: 'Do necessary and sufficient conditions exist which encourage egoists to co-operate in the absence of a strong central authority?' They, like Olson (1965), conclude that such desirable co-operation will result from the presence of on-going dependency relationships among the 'prisoners'. Isolation yields suboptimum outcomes, hence there is an argument for the involvement of all interest groups if the aim is to identify suitable locations. Further, as mentioned in the Preface, it is recognized that responsibility is a correlate of both freedom and constitutionalism, thus it can be seen as an important goal for planning within a democratic state.

Fisher and Brown (1988) offer a critique of the simplistic prisoner's dilemma format for a negotiation problem. As part of a large-scale project known as the Harvard Negotiation Project, they prefer an interactive process that focuses on building relationships. For location problems this essentially means the building of stable, acceptable relationships among the stakeholders. Comments on negotiation are included in Chapter 2 and a credo for facility siting which considers negotiations is given in Chapter 7.

The problem of defining and searching for the best location is complex because multiple criteria and goals must be considered. Often many individuals and groups are involved in the determination of the criteria and goals. The search process which involves the collection of information may be lengthy and costly, opinions and preferences may shift during the study, and conflicts typically arise. The scale and nature of the facility as well as the time horizon over which the search is made, the construction undertaken, and the utilization and impacts evaluated all serve to complicate the problem further. Such problems have been characterized by Churchman (1967) as 'wicked' because, among other things, they do not yield to the mathematical methods of formal decision analysis. The words 'baffling' and 'terribly difficult' have also been used (van Dyke 1964; Radford 1986; Cohen and Ben-Ari 1989).

It can be argued that given such complexity it is unrealistic to expect that a formal method could be developed to identify a best alternative. However, attempts have been made to structure collective choice decision-making procedures and to incorporate measurements of expected impacts into public siting debates. Governments and public agencies are continually faced with problems of modifying or closing existing facilities and selecting locations for new ones and planners are frequently called upon to offer advice as to the relative merits of alternative facility plans. While intuition and professional experience often serve to defend a particular choice, I argued that a stronger case could be made, and is probably more amenable to close public and professional scrutiny, if the evidence showing the advantages and disadvantages of feasible alternatives is clearly described. The fundamental aim of *Spatial Search* was to provide a critique of procedures which are used or could be used to improve the quality of the debate on the search for best locations for public facilities.

In the 1970s Berson (1971) and Prentice (1976) among others stressed the evolution of planning practice and the basic difficulties encountered in implementation. Prentice (1976: 231), has noted that: 'It is foolish to pretend that in a pluralistic society . . . one can set a target of a desired state and necessarily achieve it; in practice change is both incremental and disjointed, multi-directional and partly haphazard.' But, all this said, does it not take place within a state which embraces different degrees of conflict and consensus? The latter does not preclude the former, rather it could be argued it envelops and embraces it unless repression is evident. This assumption underlies the work offered in *Spatial Search*.

The third book, in fact a monograph, *Multi-Criteria Decision Making (MCDM) Techniques in Planning* (1988a: 11) provided an introduction, a review and a critique of MCDM techniques as used in the resolution of particular types of location planning problems. In order to discuss the utility of the techniques a formal generic planning problem was offered. Initially this was characterized as follows:

Given a set of alternative plans, each characterised by a set of assessments for selected criteria, and a set of interest groups whose opinions regarding the selection of criteria and the assessments have to be considered, provide an appropriate procedure to define the attractiveness of the alternative plans with a view to identifying the best one.

The generic problem explicitly recognizes the evaluation of options using multiple criteria and different opinions of interest groups. Alternative objectives to generate attractiveness ratings are also considered, for example:

1. Maximization of agreement among interest groups;
2. Minimization of long-term social costs;
3. Maximization of long-term social benefits;
4. Maximization of long-term net benefits; or less formally
5. Seek to build a consensus among the interest groups;
6 Seek to protect minority opinions.

In Chapter 3 details of this generic problem will be given.

The motivation for *The Right Place*, with its focus on the need to integrate formal MCDA–DSS with selected principles relating to accountability, choice and consensus within an ideal conceptual framework of shared responsibility, came from two main sources. First, the desire to find a theoretical and intellectually satisfying means to round out my previous work on planning in the public sector and the location of public facilities which would go beyond the identification of the formal and moral dilemmas and paradoxes identified by Arrow (1951), Elster (1986), Hardin (1968) and Hindess (1987) among others. Also I wanted to move away from the narrow normative approaches provided by optimization models. I had always recognized that while such normative work had certain intellectual appeal because of its neatness, tightness of argument and formal results, the assumptions which it demanded about the world left unanswered a number of pressing questions of social relevance. I am mindful of the need to find a balance between technical data analysis and practical implementation. In recent years I have examined various bodies of literature on the theories of the state, decision-making processes especially choice theories, formal decision-aid techniques particularly multi-criteria decision aid, multi-objective decision-making, multi-attribute utility theory and public choice theory, as well as plan generation, evaluation and implementation. This search embraced fields touching on law and regulations, negotiations, conciliation, mediation and bargaining. As I read widely through literature on social policy, planning and related fields in the social sciences I began to converge on the concept of shared responsibility as a derivative of collective choice as the one which may have some potential to serve my needs. I was searching for a means of integrating diverse approaches within the functional context of a state with its involvement in resolving conflicts among competing needs.

The second source of motivation stems from my wish to write a book which may be of practical use to those who are struggling with actual public facility location problems. To those I have met in many countries, for example Australia, Canada, China, France, Hong Kong, Israel, Poland, Sweden and the UK, during field visits who are dealing with specific public goods and services as they impinged on the quality of life of their citizens I wanted to do more than report further case studies. The variety of political systems I encountered, the geopolitical, financial and social imperatives as well as climatic and physical differences may suggest that the differences among the countries are such that no common ground could be found. Yet it became clearer to me that there is common ground at the level of an ideal as I had longer and more detailed discussions in each country about specific facility location decisions. I believe that the concept of shared responsibility captures the ideal, while recognizing that it is a very fragile flower especially in authoritarian countries which do not have well-established democratic and publicly accountable practices and precedents to elect responsible in-dividuals who make decisions regarding the allocation of resources for the construction, management and regulation of public facilities.

The variety of facilities I observed during my visits included waste disposal units (for household, industrial and low-level radioactive waste), health care facilities (hospitals, community clinics, rural health centres), education facilities (schools, universities and colleges), recreation and social service centres for the elderly, the very young, the handicapped and the unemployed, as well as emergency service centres, particularly fire and police stations. For each a detailed case study could be developed to describe the way that need was articulated and the process which dealt with this need to arrive at the decision to build, expand, reject or delay the construction of a facility. The justification and rationalization could be examined as well as the loci of power, authority and influence, also the nature of the types of accountability and responsiveness to pressures, political forces and environmental and economic conditions. The role of particular individuals could also be examined.

Such a set of case studies could complement Hall's (1980) collection of *Great Planning Disasters* in which he examined a set of five case studies in the 1960s which he claimed were either 'negative' or 'positive' disasters on a grand scale. The cases included the Third London Airport, the London Ringways, Concorde, the BART system and the Sydney Opera House. Hall (1980: 276) was interested to discover 'how such decisions were made, and then abandoned or continued in the face of criticism'. Following the descriptive presentations, the latter part of his book tries to interpret the material using positive and normative theory. Hall concludes that if more attention had been paid to the prescriptive material then probably 'the decision would have been taken more consciously, more rationally, with greater knowledge of likely consequences, and in the last resort, more democratically'. I hope that the use of positive or normative theory will contribute to making more responsible decisions which accept risks and uncertainty, with a minimum of regret and recrimination. This view is espoused in *The Right Place*.

In the light of the two sets of motivating forces I argue that shared responsibility can be usefully considered as a means and an end in the planning of public facilities. Shared responsibility could perhaps provide an incentive to encourage participation among individuals, and it demands the acceptance by individuals of sacrifices. The degree and nature of the sacrifices must be worked out by each society, but essentially I would argue that open debate and the careful usage of modern data-analytical tools should assist in reaching the necessary compromises which are inherent in most public facility location decisions.

More is at stake however if we consider the consequences of not sharing responsibility. Not only is it likely that the differences between the rich and the poor, the needy and the cared-for, the healthy and educated and the sick and uneducated will be accentuated, but the social consequences, tension, animosity and malaise will be of such proportions that safety and security as well as personal development will be jeopardized. Conflicts are not likely to diminish under such adverse social conditions, quite the contrary. Further, environmental damage due to ill-chosen sites for certain types of noxious facilities can have dire consequences. As environmental concerns begin to be expressed in terms of sustainable economic development, this must be matched by sustainable social and political development. There is a pressing need to seek ways to encourage co-operation and a sharing of responsibility.

Shared responsibility suggests a dynamic process and any book which deals with a particular case study is likely to become dated prior to publication; for this reason no great emphasis is placed on particular location planning problems, though selected cases are referred to for illustrative purposes. My aim is to offer a selection of material which incorporates recent advances in data collection and analysis, and relates these to the social context within which public facility location problems are posed and managed. My task is to contribute to the debate on the best way to reach the most satisfactory compromise which I argue can be considered as the consensus option, given that this implies a shared responsibility for the acceptance of the outcomes. Responsibility has to be shared among stakeholders, each bearing different types of accountability. Some of the interest groups are highly skilled professionals, others are analysts and bureaucrats, and some ill-advised lay persons; all are members of society. Ideally by persuasive argument, public scrutiny of planning procedures, open debate and responsible leadership I argue that mistakes for the planning of public facility location decisions can be reduced.

I hope that this book will make a contribution to this end.

1.3 Better planning: evaluation, measurement and mistakes

Bracken (1981) and Hatry (1972), among others, have made useful comments about evaluation and measurement as they can contribute to better planning. Bracken (1981: 292) asserts that: 'Evaluation can be regarded as the cornerstone of attempting to improve the quality of planning activities and policies', and Hatry (1972: 776) claims that: 'Without adequate measurement, so-called evaluations are likely to be little more than public relations stories by the sponsors and of minimal practical use.' It should be noted that neither author identifies the explicit need for citizens to be informed about options, be directly involved in the evaluation exercises and share in the responsibility of making hard planning choices. Sager (1981: 420) has drawn attention to the need to combine public participation with formalized evaluation procedures in order to

> link personal experience and practical insights with systematic, analytic knowledge – that is, an attempt at a dialogue between planner and affected layman. The objective is that public participation in planning should lead to a strengthening of the democratic process whereby all aspects considered significant by the participating groups are included in the analysis, and where the market prices and the weights sometimes set by experts using the evaluation method receive a local political corrective.

Heiman (1986: 135) reviews Seley's (1983) book on the politics of public facility planning and suggests that his comments on participation are abstract and stress the general right of such participation in a democracy with 'no acknowledgement of dominant social institutions affecting the form and purpose of participation'. Heiman goes on to note that:

> For too long now facility siting has been dominated by discussions of technical dexterity uninformed by careful social analysis. Without assistance from social scientists, the siting of potentially noxious land uses, even where technically feasible, has often been successfully stalled and blocked by social protest, whether informed or not. (Heiman 1986: 135)

This contemporary focus on the role of the public is perhaps a natural development of the earlier work of the 1970s in planning in which considerable emphasis was placed on formal evaluation procedures to address the concern that Rivlin (1971: 144) clearly identified, namely, 'To do better, we must have some way of distinguishing better from worse', and the response to try to measure every impact and develop numerically based evaluation procedures. A corollary of Rivlin's aphorism is the matching one that is seen posted in some public offices as an encouragement to improve effectiveness in work habits, namely: 'Things that get measured get done' (Department of Human Resources, York University, Canada, 1991).

With respect to location choice planning problems, I suggest that we should be striving towards the reduction of chances of making planning mistakes as a general strategy, rather than seeking that elusive set of techniques and principles which will yield a right answer in formal terms. I argue that if we are able to reduce the chances of making mistakes then a positive contribution will be made to the quality of collective choice and planning. I suggest that there are four generic types of planning mistakes which can be identified.

1. The *rejection* of an alternative when it should be accepted.
2. The *acceptance* of an alternative when it should be rejected.
3. The *protracted unstructured collection* of data without a clear framework for presenting the information in a way which allows decisions to be traced.
4. The *absence of detail* regarding the way that individual evaluations of impacts for alternatives are assessed by technical personnel and the public, then aggregated to support a preferred alternative.

It is naïve to suggest that the first two types of planning mistakes can be reduced if more data are collected and the study period is extended, though not infrequently this happens. Potentially such an approach feeds into mistakes of type 3 or 4.

As we look closer at mistakes this takes us into the realm of misfortune and, as Turney (1988: 11) rightly notes in his review of the controversy surrounding the work of the anthropologist Douglas (1970, 1978, 1986) that, 'when misfortune strikes, explanation and blame are inseparable. . . . Debate about causes is inextricably bound up with responsibility, even when the argument is that no one is responsible.' Douglas examines the underlying cosmology and the social context within which attitudes towards blame and responsibility are organized. Among other important contributions is her assertion that risk assessment is a social matter, not just an individual one as risk analysts persistently argue. The systemic neglect of culture is, in her view, 'so entrenched that nothing less than a large upheaval in the social sciences could bring about change' (Turney 1988: 12). While all societies select carefully those risks to which they will pay particular attention it is clear that to understand this selection process demands an understanding of moral and ethical questions. Comments on these are given in Chapter 6. The burgeoning attention that is now being given to the eclectic field of postmodernism may provide the intellectual framework for addressing the missing cultural dimension of risk and planning decisions, so clearly identified by Douglas. Certainly the field of planning has moved some way since the early hopes of some decision analysts, following the seminal work in this field by von Neumann and Morgenstern (1947) who argued that expected values of outcomes of alternatives provided a logical, rational way to judge options and select a preferred one. However, the particular characteristics of location problems for public facilities usually invalidate the use of this approach. This point is taken up in the chapter on choice (Chapter 6).

Consider a location problem cited by Keeney (1981). Two sites for a facility are being considered (A and B), and assume that the construction costs associated with A are $2.0m., while those at B are estimated to be either $2.4m. or $1.4m., with equal likelihood, i.e. 50 per cent chance of either. The expected cost of B is therefore $1.9m., whereas for A it is $2.0m. Using expected value theory, site B is preferred to A. If we are undertaking a repeated large number of location choice problems with these associated costs and likelihood values, we could argue that in the long run option B would be the better one; however, classically location problems tend to be single decisions, for a particular service, and thus in the face of A and B, with the associated costs we might reasonably argue for A on the basis of minimizing the maximum actual cost, or conversely B on the basis of maximizing the chances of minimizing the estimated costs. The use of expected values does not appear to be of use for single decisions and this view is elaborated by Radford (1986) who strenuously rejects expected utility approaches in particular, and decision theory in general, for tackling location choice problems. His preferred approach is a behavioural one which stresses strategic and tactical negotiations among the stakeholders.

Von Neumann and Morgenstern (1947) have been credited with the formal statement of axioms which form the core of modern decision theory. Kahneman and Tversky (1984: 343) have drawn attention to two of the axioms concerning transitivity and substitution. For the former if option A is preferred to B, and B to C, then A is preferred to C, and for the latter if A is preferred to B, then an even chance to get A or C is preferred to an even chance to get B or C. They note that 'there is convincing evidence that people do not always obey the substitution axiom'. Two further principles which are fundamental in so-called rational choice behaviour are referred to as dominance and invariance. Dominance demands that if option A is at least as good as option B for all evaluation criteria and better than B for at least one criterion, then A should be preferred to B. This is the condition of Pareto optimality and invariance requires that the preference ordering among options is independent of the manner in which the information about their attributes is presented.

One of the simplest and most widely used formal models that is available to compare options using scores for a set of criteria is the additive model. In essence this is based upon decision theory. Details are given in Chapter 3. If this model is to be defended then the following conditions need to be satisfied. First, that preferences for, or the trade-off for, pairs of criteria must be *preferentially independent* of fixed levels for any other criteria. Second, that *utility independence* demands that the worth of a particular criterion is unrelated to the scores on any other criterion. Further details of these conditions are given in Massam (1988a) and Keeney and Nair (1977), unfortunately they are rarely formally tested and found to be satisfied when analysts use the additive model.

The psychologists Kahneman and Tversky (1984: 343) have conducted a series of interesting empirical experiments to examine the assertion that 'two versions of a choice problem that are recognized to be equivalent when shown together should elicit the same preference even when shown separately'. They claim that their results indicate that 'the requirement of invariance, however elementary and innocuous it may seem, cannot generally be satisfied'. Phillips (1983) has taken issue with this implicit claim that behaviour is irrational, specifically he contends that the recognition of equivalence of problems may be strong in the minds and consciousness of the analysts but this is not necessarily the case for those who are faced with making the decisions. Equivalence is a subjective term, a point glossed over by some who attempt to test the axioms of decision theory. Phillips (1983) goes on to argue that it is the structure provided by an individual that determines the way information is processed and a conclusion derived. The analyst may posit a particular structure, but unfortunately this may not be the one adopted by the individual who is tackling the evaluation problem. This point reflects the position of Walsh (1991) discussed earlier, namely that producers and consumers of services frequently have different perceptions of quality. And more generally stakeholders may well have different viewpoints of expected impacts. In a word, what is rational to an analyst may not be rational to another individual; both are 'correct'.

The situation becomes more complex when we recognize the many stakeholders in a location issue, each may have a unique structure for organizing information about the impacts. Surely some are not right and the others wrong, but how is this pluralism to be accommodated? Perhaps by sharing information and seeking to share responsibility. In developing this line of argument Kahneman and Tversky (1984: 341) hold that: 'the acceptability of an option can depend on whether a negative outcome is evaluated as a cost or as an uncompensated loss.' But do citizens, bureaucrats and politicians know what 'uncompensated loss' means in practical terms? Hall (1980: 246) discusses the interactions among politicians, bureaucrats and the public, and specifically the ways their actions influence the way in which collective goods are provided. He notes, with respect to politicians:

> In general, since potential losses are perceived as much more important than perceived gains, and since fear of loss is a very potent emotional trigger to action, this kind of politics tends powerfully to maintenance of the *status quo*. The professional politicians will be particularly concerned to avoid imposing new costs on any group. For these reasons, major disturbances to the physical environment – a new motorway, a new airport – [a noxious facility] will be avoided. If, however, they cannot be avoided . . . then the professional politicians will take care to spread the costs as widely and as vaguely as possible, while concentrating any benefits very noticeably on certain groups. Fortunately, the principle of paying for particular programs through general taxation allows them to do this without too much trouble.

For a practical facility siting planning problem there is a clear case for testing these assertions using empirical data, particularly as attempts are now under way to identify clearly who bears which particular costs and who benefits, and to what extent. This search for the victims precedes compensation, and this is a useful device for easing the burden on some individuals when a noxious facility is constructed.

According to Phillips (1983) the systematic biases identified by Kahneman and Tversky cannot be justified. He criticized their work in 1973 at a conference in Rome at which he was the discussant of a paper on heuristics and biases by the two psychologists. Phillips (1983: 525) notes that: 'In particular, the view of people as "intellectual cripples", who exhibit severe and systematic biases in making judgements, is shown to be a value judgement on the part of the investigators'. Clearly even scientists do not always view the formal methods without taking sides!

Phillips (1983, 1984) offers a new approach that he calls a generative paradigm which emphasizes the role of problem structuring, in particular the subject's internal representation of the task, within which information is processed. The generative paradigm sees decision-making and the forming of judgement as a dynamic, generative process, conducted interactively between people within a social and cultural context. This view fits rather neatly into Radford's conflict resolution paradigm, and clearly it probably would satisfy some of Douglas's concerns.

Monetary outcomes and the loss of human lives are the two areas in which psychologists who study decision-making claim that reversal of preferences do result from reframing problems. Given that many location problems for noxious public facilities involve impacts on economic prosperity and health risks it is most appropriate that the framing issue be examined closely, and especially the hypotheses of Phillips need to be made operational and systematically tested. In the absence of such work it is hard to refute the empirical and theoretical evidence of Tversky and Kahneman, even though counter-arguments may be intuitively appealing.

Given that most if not all location decisions for public facilities will tend to have impacts on social welfare, and thus impinge on economic aspects of life as well as those relating more directly to health and well-being, it is important to examine this issue further. Citizens and interest groups tend to become increasingly vocal when health and economic livelihood appear to be at stake. Changes to these as a result of proposed locations of public facilities can generate strong local opposition.

Let us consider some alternative ways in which the outcome of a location policy can be described. Tversky and Kahneman (1981: 454) draw attention to a clear correlation between the statement of the outcome and responses of individuals as *risk aversion* or *risk taking*. They distinguish two phases in the choice process: 'An initial phase in which acts, outcomes, and contingencies are framed, and a subsequent phase of evaluation.' It is the first of these phases that is typically omitted from the planning process and the evaluation of siting options for public facilities. Implicitly the approach has assumed a single frame or structure if formal utility-style analysis of a numerical kind has been undertaken. Kahneman and Tversky (1984: 456) also remind us that: 'Outcomes are commonly perceived as positive or negative in relation to a reference outcome that is judged neutral.' By varying the position of the reference point it is conceptually possible to suggest an outcome is judged to be a gain or a loss, and because the value function (Fig. 1.1) is not symmetrical the perceived differences in values for an outcome are especially difficult to estimate.

One feature of some of the MCDA–DSS to be discussed in Chapters 3 and 4 is the use of reference points in the analysis. Specifically these are referred to as benchmark options, and feasible alternatives are compared to these. Preliminary results suggest that those bureaucrats who are involved in the implementation of locational decisions find the benchmark concept comprehensible and a useful one for organizing a discussion with stakeholders about the merits of alternative sites. However, if the framing of evaluation problems and the definition of reference points or benchmark options influence the perceived experiences of the impacts then 'the adoption of a decision frame is an ethically significant act' (Tversky and Kahneman 1981: 458). It is incumbent on responsible analysts to address questions of ethics.

While work proceeds on the theoretical front in order to try to determine consistencies among the biases which result from specific types of frames for choice problems, Phillips (1983) and Wooler (1987) among others offer pragmatic suggestions for helping decision-makers. Specifically they favour decision-conferencing as a structure and process for bringing together key executives and working with them to define their options, evaluate each one and assess the prospects of implementation with a view to identifying a preferred option. For decision choice problems which are in the hands of a small group of executives this approach appears to have merit. But its application to collective choice public facility location problems remains to be explored. In the chapter on choice (Chapter 6) an elaboration of these points is given.

Mechanistic approaches to the study of public choice using voting

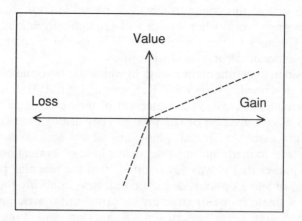

Fig. 1.1 A hypothetical value function

methods, for example, simply count support and opposition as providing a measure of popularity or acceptance. However, such models typically lack appreciation of compliance and the consequences of accepting an option or rejecting another. Some models allow the candidates, that is the alternatives, to be ordered and votes may be transferred to search for the one that enjoys greatest support. The implicit assumption is that the alternatives which are being scrutinized have been described accurately and fairly. But precisely what does this mean? If the options for a location decision, for example, are a set of sites for a facility, then a fair description of each should indicate the distribution of costs and benefits. While many would probably support this view, it is clear that it is the ways in which the distributions are described that can strongly influence the preferences of individuals, and hence their voting patterns, and ultimately the numerically determined acceptability of a project. Chapter 6 takes up the discussion on voting as a means of collective choice.

As noted earlier, it has been suggested that similar impacts can be framed in different ways. However, if Phillips's view is adopted then the corollary is that different impacts can be presented to separate stakeholders, each with a unique frame, and similar preferences can emerge. Indeed a difficult situation arises, both for the analyst and for the member of the public who is keen to examine the nature of the impacts, and to participate actively in providing opinions and preferences. Hollis, Sugden and Weale (1985) among others, have demonstrated that suboptimal outcomes can result from rational actions of individuals who seek to maximize their individual benefits. This paradox is troublesome as it implies that optimum collective decisions are not necessarily best achieved by consulting individuals. Detailed examination of this phenomenon, which manifests itself rather neatly in the classic prisoner's dilemma game, has been undertaken by some philosophers including Axelrod (1984: 68), who concludes: '. . . co-operation can emerge from . . . individuals, as long as these individuals have even a small proportion of their interactions with each other'. As noted earlier, it appears that dependency is a necessary condition for co-operation. The form of the dependency, the nature of the co-operation and the definition of sufficient conditions need to be examined for cases within their particular cultural, spatial, political and historical contexts. All these points touch on views of consensus which are taken up in Chapter 7.

1.4 Beyond case studies, towards principles and concepts

In this final section I want to identify a generic facility siting planning process and suggest selected concepts which lie at the heart of the decision-making activities which make the process realistic. As mentioned earlier, it is not my intention in this book to examine in detail a series of case studies and so describe the motivations, influences and outcomes of decisions by individuals as they influence the site selection process. Neither is it my task to offer specific studies on the roles of institutions such as government departments, planning agencies, commissions and boards of inquiry or instruments, for example compensation packages, mitigation measures, public hearings or zoning regulations. Rather I wish to discuss three selected concepts which I suggest lead us to ask key questions about facility siting, particularly questions which pertain to concerns about the avoidance of mistakes and the desire to improve levels of responsibility in collective choice. All these concepts are receiving close scrutiny by those who are currently tackling facility siting problems and it is timely that they be reviewed.

It is generally agreed that a generic planning process, which can be applied to many site location problems for public facilities, can be characterized as comprising four basic components which are shown schematically in Fig. 1.2. The components are linked by evaluation, assessment and appraisal exercises which in turn are motivated by decisions in the light of perceptions of the current situation, and of course the context for such perceptions plays a significant part in making the process function. If we adopt the earlier view that the Regulatory State is a meaningful context, then accountability is stressed and appreciation of consensus and choice is needed. Further, I argue that the context should take account of the state of art of formal procedures such as MCDA and DSS, hence this information technology has a role to play.

On occasions certain independent principles which appear to have merit for guiding policy-making are in conflict. A. Weale (1990, personal communication) and his colleagues at the University of East Anglia (UEA) have suggested a set of four principles which they argue would improve the quality of health care planning as an example of a social policy problem area. He notes that while it is unlikely that deep disagreements of moral theory could be resolved by the unanimous acceptance of specific principles,

Instead they [the group at UEA] recognized the plausibility of an

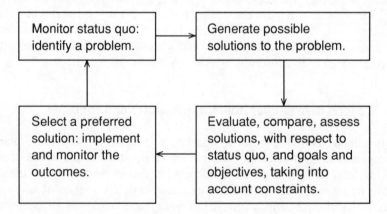

Fig. 1.2 Generic planning process: four basic components

intermediate stance for applied ethics proposed by some bioethicists. According to this stance a wide variety of moral theories, utilitarian and deontologist, religious and secular, left wing and right wing, could agree on the *prima facie* importance of four, potentially conflicting, principles: respect for autonomy, non-maleficence, beneficence and justice.

Autonomy not only implies self-rule, but also the capacity to reason and deliberate, and base actions upon plans and envisaged outcomes. Weale (1990, personal communication) goes on to argue that:

> A development of the notion of respect for autonomy occurs in the idea of democratic consent. Just as autonomy recognizes the scope for self-determination at the levels of individuals, so the principles of democracy incorporate the idea of self-determination at the collective level of society. The existing mechanism of representative government is an imperfect method of eliciting consent from citizens. Nonetheless it is an important principle that whatever policies are agreed they should be supported by a broad consensus of those engaged in the finance, provision and delivery of health care.

I suggest that implicit in this principle is the notion of shared responsibility albeit as a Utopian concept. With respect to the principles of non-maleficence and beneficence, the former appears to be virtually self-evident, though with respect to the siting of noxious facilities there is much debate about the magnitude and importance of certain impacts. For the latter the notion is, from a utilitarian perspective, the search for an optimum location to maximize utility. This Pareto optimum arrangement continues to elude practitioners. The principle of justice is often invoked to satisfy claims as to what is felt to be due and what others should yield by virtue of recognition of their duty. The adjudication of rival and incompatible claims is intricately involved in the system of justice and the rule of law, and of course this varies among states. Credibility and acceptance of decisions of the courts are necessary conditions for a democratic system of government. With respect to site location conflicts, resorting to the law to seek a just solution implies faith in the maxim, *ubi jus, ibi remedium*, that underlies the rule of law. The academic lawyer Dworkin (1985: 3) has drawn attention to the possibility that for certain classes of problem presented for judicial opinion it is conceivable that it is not possible to assert that there is a clear answer as to right or wrong. He reminds us that we should not expect that resorting to the rule of law will yield the 'right answer'. Specifically he argues that:

> Anglo-American lawyers have on the whole been skeptical about the possibility of a 'right answer' in any genuinely hard case. If lawyers and judges disagree about what the law is, and no one has a knockdown argument either way, then what sense does it make to insist that one opinion is right and another wrong? Surely, so the common view runs,

there are only different answers to the question of law and no right or best answer.

B. Barry (1990: 1) has identified two principles of distribution which he claims, if honoured by institutions, will characterize a just society. However, it is not explicitly stated if such principles, namely *compensation* to counteract the effects of accidents and *personal responsibility* such that the voluntary acts of individuals result in final outcomes of social arrangements, are more than necessary conditions. Barry goes on to note that 'the application of these two principles of justice would always have to be modified by the operation of a principle of expediency, which is I believe accepted in every society. According to this, which I'll call the principle of common advantage, an inequality is justified if it works to the benefit of everybody.' (Barry 1990: 1) This can be viewed as a subtle restatement of Pareto optimality.

While the search continues for principles to help guide collective choice to ensure that just and efficient outcomes result, it must be noted that practitioners continue to demand rules, regulations and practices which they can follow for administrative purposes. Also there is a need to have procedures which can be explained to citizens without resorting to abstract arguments, and perhaps not least of all which satisfy politicians as not detracting from their power and influence, which they might claim are needed to reflect the views of the constituents whose views they represent and for whom they feel responsible and to whom they are accountable.

One set of practical principles has recently been enunciated by the Canadian Task Force on siting low-level radioactive waste facilities. Implicit in this set of principles are some of the notions which have been referred to above, though unfortunately no formal linkages have yet been developed. Five principles have been defined and they are listed as follows:

1. Volunteerism;
2. Partnership;
3. Compensation;
4. Right to select;
5. Non-compromise of safety of health and environment.

If these are applied to the siting of a noxious facility, for example a waste dump, then the principles can be elaborated as follows:

1. Volunteerism – a community should volunteer and have the right to opt out as the process continues.
2. Partnership – a community should be a partner in defining and solving managerial problems relating to the facility.
3. Compensation – a community should receive compensation to offset unmitigable impacts and to enhance local benefits.
4. Right to select – a community should have the right to select from given

technical options and impact management measures the ones it finds acceptable.
5. Non-compromise – the agency that is responsible for implementation must ensure that health and environment compromises do not occur.

A discussion on the practical difficulties that have been encountered in the application of these principles to the low-level radioactive siting problem in Ontario, Canada, has been offered by Armour (1991). She concludes that this innovative process appears to be working well and enjoys public confidence. However, it must be noted that the process is still at a fairly early stage.

If we consider a salutary facility then these principles as they stand would have to be modified. A suggested set of five principles that could be applied to the problem of finding a site for a salutary facility are given below. The words in italic indicate the changes from the principles for locating a noxious facility.

1. Volunteerism – a community should volunteer and have the right to opt out *or in* as the process continues.
2. Partnership – a community should be a partner in defining and solving managerial problems relating to the facility.
3. Compensation – a community should *contribute* compensation to offset *local benefits*.
4. Right to select – a community should have the right to select from given technical options and impact management measures the ones it finds acceptable.
5. Non-compromise – the agency that is responsible for implementation must ensure that *the more affluent communities do not benefit unjustly by acquiring salubrious facilities and that compensation adjustments are fairly distributed*.

Obviously the implementation of the principles will demand operational definitions of the general concepts, but it is hoped that as a starting point such a set of principles could be enunciated and agreed to as initial statements. An elaboration of these principles in the style of a credo is being attempted in the USA and details are given in Chapter 7 in the discussion on consensus.

In this book I argue that if we wish to improve the quality of planning, and especially if we wish to reduce the chances of planning mistakes, then we should seek to enhance the generic process by examining collective choice procedures; and further, that to understand the process by which sites are selected demands that attention be focused on decision-making, I put forward the proposition that such decision-making embraces, *inter alia*, the three linked concepts of accountability, consensus and choice. Those who seek to be involved in the site selection process as non-elected individuals must inevitably make choices about their positions for or against options.

Those elected or appointed individuals are responsible for making choices for which they can be held accountable. Together these two groups interact within a legal and political system which in a democratic society typically is characterized as consensual. The stability of the system requires that, even though there are winners and losers, consensus as a principle obtains.

According to Day and Klein (1987b: 1),

> accountability is one of the fashionable words of our time. Over the past decades, new institutions and new techniques have been developed in the service of accountability. . . . Accountability is not merely seen as a crucial link in the chain between governor and governed: effective democracy, it is argued, implies a system which ensures that the former are accountable to the latter . . . accountability is all about the construction of an agreed language or currency of discourse about conduct and performance, and the criteria that could be used in measuring them.

While it is almost meaningless to say that the ideal planning process for a site selection problem is one in which accountability is maximized, it is appropriate that the lines of accountability are publicly recognized and the notion has general credibility. There is a clear need to link accountability to responsibility.

Choice lies at the heart of decision-making and planning, and while so-called rational choice has been heavily criticized as too simplistic to capture the subtleties of incommensurate trade-offs, it is clear that with an increase in the public scrutiny of siting plans for public facilities, citizens, regulatory agencies as well as politicians are increasingly keen to ensure that alternatives are assessed systematically with respect to goals, objectives and planning targets and that evaluation and choice processes are as traceable as possible. This is not to say that the choice problem has to be, or can be, reduced to a numerical manipulation exercise, but rather that the process enjoys credibility and is one in which members of society have confidence.

Cohen and Ben-Ari (1989: 1) in a lengthy commentary on 'hard choices', remark that:

> Human action is ordinarily oriented to a plurality of values, none of which can be fully realized without injury to some others. . . . Situations of value incommensurability present themselves . . . as difficult moral dilemmas and are often referred to in the literature as 'hard choices'. These choices are not amenable to rational solutions.

Hindess (1988) among others has taken issue with rational choice analysis, he argues that human individuals are only one set among a collection of actors and second, he suggests there is a need to examine processes of deliberation which play such a critical role in actors' decisions. A further dimension to the debate on choice and action can be added by challenging the proposition of Hume that action can only be motivated by desire. Indeed it is clear that the story of choice as elaborated in Chapter 5 is broad yet critical to our understanding of ways in which site planning mistakes can occur.

With respect to the third concept, namely consensus, I suggest that it can be viewed as a means to an end. It is more than the absence of major dissent, disagreement, discord and conflict. As a positive feature of a dynamic participatory democratic society, consensus represents a degree of congruence which embraces individual positions and opinions to allow a collectivity to function. But to function with what degree of harmony, effectiveness or equity? Building a consensus can take time and resources, and there are opportunity costs. Some see consensus as an end in itself, offering a measure of collective harmony which does not diminish the integrity and dignity of individuals, but as noted in Chapter 7 not all share this view. In very general terms Healey, McDougall and Thomas (1982: 103) assert that the purpose of planning is 'to encourage a new consensus based on interpersonal relations'. I suggest that implicit in this is the notion of shared responsibility.

In order to improve location planning it is my assertion that we should not only examine these three concepts, but importantly we should seek to link them to advances in evaluation and monitoring, especially through the recent work in multi-criteria decision aid (MCDA) techniques and computer-based decision support systems (DSS).

Since the 1970s there have been significant advances in the development of MCDA techniques as applied to the evaluation and classification of alternative sites for facilities. More recently these advances have been incorporated into computer-based DSS which explicitly require preferences, opinions and attitudes of the users to be formulated in ways that allow interactions between humans and computers.

In summary I argue that all these elements – accountability, choice, consensus as well as formal techniques like MCDA–DSS – viewed within the context of a Regulatory State provide a basis for achieving the ideal condition of shared responsibility for tackling public facility location problems. The next chapter will elaborate on the components of complex location problems as further contextual information.

2

Complex location problems

Inspection is one of the hallmarks of a truly democratic regime.
    Hartley (1972)

2.1 Complex location problems, environmental assessment and good planning

That the search for the right place for a public facility is complex is well established and need not be laboured. However, it is worth noting that the complexity is not without structure, and it is the recognition of this that gives legitimacy to adopt a systematic approach to the generation of alternative locations for a facility and the defence of a preferred option. Further, the planning process, if it is to be credible, has to allow examination and evaluation of the alternatives with a view to considering the perspectives of the interest groups who will enjoy the benefits or suffer the consequences associated with specific location decisions. The material presented in Chapter 1 attests to the complexity of the site selection problem, and the roles in contemporary facility siting exercises of important concepts like accountability, choice and consensus, also MCDA techniques as incorporated into computer-based DSS.

Typically the legislative and regulatory framework which has been developed in most Western states to legitimize the planning process for tackling site selection problems of large noxious public facilities falls within the scope of environmental assessment. Other states are under pressure to follow this route. For this reason the first part of the chapter includes substantial comments on some theoretical and practical aspects of environmental assessment. While some emphasis will be placed on the Canadian situation a narrow perspective will be avoided.

With respect to site selection planning for salutary facilities the emphasis tends to be placed on accessibility assessments of alternative sites with respect to the spatial distribution of demand. Of course, factors other than distance to potential clients or customers are considered, for example land costs and evolving demographic patterns.

This long section on environmental assessment will be followed by a briefer section (2.2) which highlights some principles concerning negotiations among the various interest groups. Such negotiations are critical to the implementation of environmental legislation as applied to facility siting, and if negotiations result in stable acceptable outcomes then it can be argued that the goal of achieving effective shared responsibility has been reached.

Section 2.3 will focus attention on the problems of measuring, monitoring and inspecting existing or proposed arrangements for the provision of public goods and services. I argue that this task of performance assessment must be closely related to the determination of needs, and the evaluation of the effectiveness of planning decisions. Section 2.4 deals specifically with selected aspects of need assessment and section 2.5 discusses some recent literature which has as its focus the concept of integrated evaluation.

Radford (1988) outlines the four main characteristics of complex location choice problems which he argues make them unamenable to solution by formal decision analysis procedures such as mathematical programming or expected utility analysis. Indeed Churchman (1967) suggested that it is the 'tamer' variety of problem which lends itself to treatment by decision analysis, whereas complex problems, as discussed in Chapter 1, are 'wicked', to use his phrase. This unfortunate quality, though daunting, is not a sufficient reason for either trivializing and manipulating the problems to fit into the 'tamer' category or for resorting to exhortations about the impossibility of offering reasonable advice on strategies and tactics for tackling such problems. It is important to remind ourselves what is meant by the term 'tackling the problem'. In the context of this book I refer specifically, as outlined in Chapter 1, to the reduction of location choice mistakes and the search for acceptable solutions which ideally involve the accountable sharing of responsibility.

The four characteristics of complexity as identified by Radford (1988) are:

1. The absence of deterministic and complete information about the set of options, impacts and interest groups;
2. The difficulty of assigning numerical ratio values to indicate the relative attractiveness of options for all the criteria;
3. The possibility that each interest group may have more than one objective against which possible outcomes are compared and the objectives may be in conflict;
4. The fact that different interest groups are involved in the search for a preferred site and that they may have different perceptions about the problem and the different objectives that affect their preferences for outcomes.

The collection of papers in Faludi and Voogd (1985) give some hints on the use of formal evaluation procedures for tackling complex policy problems and specifically Hill's (1985: 9) essay recognizes the need to avoid simplifying problems to make them fit into predetermined decision analysis methodologies. He notes that:

> the real world of planning and policy-making is a far cry from . . . simplistic assumptions. Administrative bureaucracies and political decision-making bodies can be varied in extent of their power and control, perception of their responsibility, extent to which they are able to act in accordance with the public consensus, extent of their accountability, and so forth. It therefore appears hasty to assume away all this complexity in order to adopt a pure formula for arriving at an optimal decision in the public interest . . . on the contrary, it seems essential to take note of the complexity and try to take it into account in developing approaches and tools for the evaluation of alternatives.

The Right Place is a direct response to Hill's plea.

The search for approaches to address complex decision situations embraces the seminal work of March and Simon (1958) on the principle of bounded rationality which yields what they call a 'satisficing' solution. Such a practically reached solution may fall short of a formal optimum. Further development by Lindblom (1979) and Braybrooke and Lindblom (1963) recommends a complementary procedure for dealing with ill-structured decision situations which they refer to as 'disjointed incrementalism'. In essence they commend the consideration of alternatives which are only incrementally different from the status quo; a heuristic approach is sought. However, with respect to facility siting problems, in general the category of problem is not of this type for basically a site is chosen or rejected. Etzioni (1967) is credited with combining so-called rationalistic–comprehensive and incremental approaches to yield a 'mixed-scanning' strategy which begins with a broad review of the issues behind the more narrowly defined siting problem which is the subject of later analysis. One of the merits of using a DSS for tackling a complex problem rests with the claim that a poorly structured problem can be accommodated. This will be elaborated in Chapter 3.

Radford (1986, 1988) attempts to move beyond decision analytical methods by elaborating on strategic and tactical approaches, but for public facility location style problems it is left to Friend and Hickling (1987) to introduce the intriguing concept of 'responsible scheming'. They argue that a strategic choice approach to planning which embraces evaluation within a humanistic participatory heuristic framework may help 'in preparing people for responsibilities in the world of complex decisions'. Their work is an outgrowth of the seminal work by Friend and Jessop (1969) which sought to link the use of operational research tools within the political and bureaucratic framework of local municipal government in the city of Coventry.

Humphreys and Wisudha (1987) provide a comprehensive survey of approximately sixty tools for structuring and analysing decision problems within a general framework that describes ways of handling decisions effectively in situations which initially appear to be unstructured, as they are new and essentially non-repetitive. They argue that many organizations, including government agencies, have great difficulty tackling such problems using traditional decision analysis approaches because of the *complexity* (too many conditions, constraints and consequences that must be considered simultaneously), the *uncertainty* (related to the objectives and preferences of those concerned and external conditions) and the *lack of information* about the degree of complexity, the uncertainty and the problem-solving methods available. As mentioned in Chapter 1, Phillips (1984) has argued that an appropriate approach to such complex problems should involve requisite decision modelling, specifically he argues that, it is necessary to involve all those who are in some way responsible for aspects of the decision in the development of the requisite model. The process of building the model is iterative and consultative, and when no new intuitions emerge about the problem, the model is considered to be requisite. I share his view of the role of responsibility in the process of facility siting. For practical facility siting problems in the public sector it is difficult to envisage this ideal end-state condition ever being reached. Rather we can observe a dynamic interactive negotiation process as leading to outcomes which it is hoped are acceptable. Comments on good negotiations are provided in the section 2.2. While the characteristics of the complex problems defined by Humphreys and Wisudha (1987) are generic, it appears that the context for their class of problem is provided by a hierarchical organizational structure, following the ideas of Jaques (1990), which contrasts with the multi-faceted structures that characterize the milieu within which public facility location problems are posed, defined and eventually solved.

Useful as conceptual approaches may appear to be as devices to provide some order to decision-making, they fall short of the desires of participants in multi-party situations who seek advice on finding acceptable sites in which consensus is maximized, the potential for error is minimized and their sense of fairness is unoffended.

The study of environmental legislative instruments such as laws, regulations and policies as well as *de facto* practices can tell us something of no small importance about the collective conscience of a society and the way specific facility siting problems are tackled. The actions and reactions of politicians and civil servants as well as the initiatives of groups and individuals reflect both public policy positions and private dreams. Conflicts among politically strong and weak parties, majorities and minorities are the norm in practice. From a theoretical standpoint following Dawes, Delay and Chaplin (1974), for example, drawing on the ideas of Lloyd (1833), the strong, richer party will continue to dominate the weak. While Dawes,

Delay and Chaplin (1974) and Hardin (1968) subscribe to the so-called rationality of such public choice or collective action behaviour within the narrow confines of an axiomatic framework, it is clear that co-operation and conscious sharing of responsibility, as promoted by Axelrod (1980, 1984) among others, have advantages for all parties. The philosopher Danielson (1986, 1988) is attempting to develop a rational framework that encompasses notions of egotism, ethics and utilitarianism. Such challenging work might help provide a theoretical basis for asserting that rational behaviour by individuals can lead to a set of relationships such that co-operation is practised and everyone wins, or at least everyone will appreciate the justification for a particular outcome and not harbour resentment. Site location problems for public facilities demand such a framework for collective choice to replace the long-standing zero-sum game structure.

Within the realm of public policy-making site location problems and environment impact assessment often draw upon the concepts, ideas and models of science. When accidents occur which generate damage to the environment it is all too easy to point the finger of responsibility at the scientist, but surely there is a vital burden of accountability that must be shouldered by elected politicians and public civil servants as well as professional scientists. This point has been recognized by Grima *et al.* (1986). There is a clear mandate for a credible and widely available information system which gives a realistic, balanced and socially responsible interpretation of scientific objectivity. With respect to risk analysis Megaw (1985) demonstrates statistically, using lifestyle risk data, that the farm worker who lives, for example, in a small community near Toronto, Ontario and is employed on a small mixed farm is in a very high-risk occupation compared to a globe-trotting sales director who travels 40 000 km a year by air and is a steady drinker who lives near to a nuclear power station, for example Pickering, Ontario; 'he incurs very little risk by living in Pickering' (Megaw 1985: 3). Facetiously, of course, we could remark that such a traveller, in fact, can hardly be classed as living near Pickering! But this aside, following the arguments of Dooley and Byer (1982) there is a need for greater public awareness of this type of work on risk analysis so that prejudices, perceptions and policy are founded on sound data and analysis, not hearsay and rhetoric. In a word I argue that we can learn much about how a society functions and specifically how complex public facility location problems are tackled by examining environmental assessment practices in which matters of short-term economic efficiency and effectiveness, often with widespread benefits, confront highly localized costs and issues of social equity, political expediency and sentiment.

The need to examine environmental impacts for facility location projects has increased in recent years, due to a large extent to two major factors. First, the nature of the impacts caused by noxious facilities, for the risk of irreversible damage to the environment, which includes the human species, by accidents, seepage or pollution from facilities can be catastrophic; and second, there has been a significant increase in public awareness concerning accidents which supports the view that removal of environmental insult far away from a population centre is no guarantee that the negative effects will not in due course be felt by all, albeit in a different form perhaps after quite a lapse of time. The effects may be insidious and the links through components of the environment not easy to identify. An attempt to apply the tool of cross-impact analysis to simulate a complex environmental system has been made by Vizayakumar and Mohapatra (1989) who show how KSIM, which is a qualitative cross-impact technique, can be used. Such a tool can help inform debate about the variables which need to be considered in an environmental assessment and the linkages as well as the consequences of changes on the outcomes.

With respect to questions of equity, Miller (1987: 60) has examined Rawls's (1971) second principle of justice which holds that 'social and economic inequalities are to be arranged so that they are . . . reasonably expected to be to everyone's advantage.' Specifically he examines the case of radioactive waste, and the siting of a facility to handle such material clearly has equity ramifications. The case for compensation is clearly made to ensure the principle is not violated, and different schemes are examined specifically as to whether they are seen as bribes because 'it is not fair' or 'it is not safe'. Also Miller stresses the need to consider the distributive effects of any compensation package and whether a waste agency should consider retrospective compensation.

In September 1988 the British Prime Minister, Margaret Thatcher, spoke to the Royal Society about environmental problems. She suggested that 'protecting the balance of nature was one of the greatest challenges of the late 20th century' (*Observer*, 2 October 1988). Nigel Haigh, a leading observer on environmental policy-making, especially in the European Community (EC), is quoted as saying, after Mrs Thatcher's speech that: 'now environmentalism is official', as it had reached the political agenda of the Prime Minister, he added: 'Up till now being an environmentalist in Britain has been like being a Christian in Rome when his religion was proscribed . . . all progress has been by subterfuge and incremental, with Government trying to play down in case anybody notices' (*The Independent*, 29 September 1988).

The analysis of environmental impacts can be defined as a process which involves the identification, description, measurement and classification of causes and effect. The causes are any action of a proposed project or policy which has an effect upon the environment, and it is these effects which are the environmental impacts. Primary and secondary, as well as higher-order impacts typically occur and their incidence can be felt at some distance from the site of the project. The primary impacts are effects on the biophysical and socio-economic elements of the environment that arise as a direct consequence of a project or policy, whereas the higher-order impacts result from the interdependent relationships among the elements comprising the environment. Shopley and Fuggle (1984) also note that 'environmental impacts are a by-product of human activities undertaken to meet the physical and emotional requirements of man'. Implicit in this is the notion that humans are part of a global ecosystem and if we subscribe to a systems view then perhaps as we realize the environmental folly of some of our activities so we will seek to curb our requirements. This is the optimistic view shared by those who drafted the early legislation and tried to put in place the regulations to administer environmental assessment activities. Munn (1975: i) has summarized the purposes of environmental assessment: 'Environmental impact assessment is an activity designed to identify and predict on man's health and well-being of legislative proposals, policies, programs, projects and operational procedures, and to interpret and communicate information about the impacts.'

In 1969 the US Secretary of the Interior, Roger C. B. Morton, introduced a piece of environmental legislation, the National Environmental Policy Act (NEPA), which has been emulated by many countries. He prefaced an important report on the conduct of environmental impact assessment (Leopold *et al.* 1971: i) for this legislation with the words which have been repeatedly echoed:

> Man cannot survive on this planet without utilizing its natural resources prudently. Every human action affects the world around us in some degree and the full effect is difficult to assess because of the complex relations among living and non-living things. Under the circumstances, one can neither expect to restore the entire past nor preserve the entire present for future generations. However, all can and should strive for a proper balance between resource development and maintenance of pleasant surroundings.

The aim of NEPA was to ensure such a balanced approach.

The United Nations Conference on the Human Environment which was held in 1972 reflected growing public concern and the wish for action. Munn (1975) has reviewed this conference and he acknowledges the long history of practical responses to various kinds of environmental insults. The burning of coal was recognized as a significant generator of air pollution in London as early as the fourteenth century and regulations were introduced. This action can be seen as a significant early step in the emergence of the Regulatory State referred to in Chapter 1. Those responsible for producing 'pestilential odors' were taxed through capital penalties and such measures were recommended by a number of commissions as a means of combating air pollution. In the eighteenth century William Blake (1757–1827) wrote of England's 'dark satanic mills'; however, it was not until 1863 that the Alkali Inspectorate was set up with the first comprehensive legislation to control emissions from factories. Almost 100 years later the Clean Air Act (1956) was passed in response to the deathly smog of 1952 which led to over 4000 deaths in London. Governments are beginning to react more promptly and in some cases take a commendable proactive stance.

On the North American continent it was in 1912 that President Theodore Roosevelt took steps to set aside land for national parks, and to preserve wilderness areas and natural ecosystems. However, while piecemeal regulatory measures were being introduced in most industrialized countries to protect the environment, no systematic legislation was introduced until the passage of NEPA on 1 January 1970. This landmark Act has been widely recognized as the first comprehensive legislation to integrate detailed environmental assessment into planning, to involve careful scientific estimates of the nature and magnitude of impacts and to take into account the social importance of such impacts.

In the UK in the early 1970s the Secretary of State for the Environment appointed Catlow and Thirlwall (1976: 1) to study and report on the subject of environmental impact assessment. After two years of study their report appeared and they noted:

The growth of the environmental movement has been one of the more striking features of the 2nd half of the 20th century. It has its origins in the revolt against industrialism and technical progress typified by the romantic writers in the 19th century. Their philosophy was part nostalgia for a past which they regarded as a golden age and part a questioning of the values of their own age with its ideals of a better society brought about by technological and scientific advance.

Recently Whitney and Maclaren (1985: 1) reviewed the Canadian scene and reiterated the point that:

Environmental impact assessment is one of the more innovative concepts introduced by governments in recent years. It is innovative because, for the first time, an institutionalized decision-making process has been established to evaluate the impacts of development on the biophysical and socio-economic environments. . . . Environmental impact assessment is also innovative (in most jurisdictions) in that it recognizes a role for the public (as distinct from experts and bureaucrats) in assessing the kind of environmental quality that is to be preserved or enhanced.

Great expectations were shared by all those involved in setting up Acts and regulations in the 1970s to ensure that sound environmental impact studies were undertaken, and the results incorporated into public policy formulation. However, we should be under no illusions and think that the mere passage of an Act can ensure the right balance between economic growth and environmental protection. When the Canadian Ministry of the Environment was formed in 1971 'a sprawling department with diverse responsibilities' was produced according to Woods (1986: 128) who goes on to note that: 'Among its components was what is now the fisheries department, along with waste disposal groups, water study and environmental impact agencies, Canadian wildlife survey, forestry units, and the weather monitoring establishments.' This made it an enormous new department with over 12 000 employees on staff but 'it was still a junior portfolio, with little clout in cabinet', and that surely is where it counts! Some of the difficulties which still beset the Ministry are identified in the following passage:

Historically, the Ministry of the Environment has had to function with formidable handicaps. In some respects it's a no-win game. Differing jurisdictions make it difficult to take decisive action on many environment problems. Air and water pollution are typical examples. Quite often these issues end up in court and take years to resolve. Then there is the political reality of the portfolio. The attitude of Canadian politicians (with the possible exception of the NDP) towards the environment is an even greater handicap than the jurisdictional dilemma. Politicians have traditionally paid lip service to the quality of the environment, but when it comes to the crunch and the question is clean air or jobs, short-term economic considerations win every time. (Woods 1986: 128)

Professor Kenneth Hare, the eminent Canadian environmental scientist, has drawn attention to the fact that the federal Ministry has an incomplete set of powers since the British North America Act assigned resources of all kinds, for example land, water, wood and soils, to provincial governments (Woods 1986). The ex-secretary of the Arctic Resources Committee, Vincent, adds another perspective that: 'The real problems came with the energy crisis. The real environmental questions today are about trade-offs between industry and the environment. And that's when the government retreated to such an outstanding extent' (Woods 1986: 134) In a series of papers edited by L. G. Smith (1987) an attempt is made to demonstrate the important contributions to environmental assessment practice and policy-making which the discipline of geography can offer. The aim is to move beyond a mere catalogue of legislative and procedural provisions for environmental assessment to produce an evaluation on the nature of such policies, with a view to classifying Canadian provinces. The results suggest a diverse arrangement which is summarized in Table 2.1.

According to Smith (1991) this classification is intended to indicate the relative adequacy of EIA provisions across the country. It is interesting to compare this classification with the views offered by Conacher (1988) who notes that with the exceptions of Prince Edward Island, New Brunswick and Manitoba, all the other provinces have statutory requirements for environmental impact assessment (EIA). Pushchak (1985) offers a simple classification of the types of legislative instruments used in each province. This is shown in Table 2.2.

Table 2.1 Smith's classification of provinces

Class 'A' province	
Newfoundland	Strong, clear legislation
Saskatchewan	Committed to the environment
	Strong public participation
Class 'B' provinces	
Quebec	Same basic strong points as 'A' but have
Ontario	problem areas with legislative loopholes and
New Brunswick	political exemptions
Class 'C' provinces	
British Columbia	Primary energy oriented
Alberta	Complicated (convoluted) procedures
	Multi-level bureaucratic overlap
Class 'D' provinces	
Nova Scotia	Government policy takes place of legislation
Manitoba	Little actual impact assessment, instead have
	environmental protection legislation
	No single Ministry responsible for environment

Source: Smith (1987).

According to Couch (1985) the content and format of environmental impact statements (EISs) are similar in all jurisdictions; however, confusion is added by the claim of Beanlands and Duinker (1983: 2), who reviewed thirty Canadian EISs, and found 'in general, the EIS's lacked a recognizable investigative design within which ecological relationships could be studied. Rarely was there a central conceptual or analytical theme to guide the collection and interpretation of data.' It has been asserted by Marshall *et al.* (1985) that EIA in Canada is often applied as a reactive activity only marginally related to the process of integrated regional or sectoral planning or facility siting. Beanlands and Duinker (1983: 2) in their detailed review of Canadian EIA practices, claim that 'from a scientific perspective, the basic dilemma is that environmental impact assessment is the result of public pressure and political motivation: its origins cannot be traced back to either the requirements or outputs of science'. The inevitable conclusion as suggested by Conacher (1988), is that the 'so-called shotgun approach' has prevailed. And while this has gone some way to placate concerned groups and individuals, and is perhaps a not unreasonable initial reaction by government to public pressure, the credibility of environmental assessment in Canada is now severely questioned.

At the federal level, the Environmental Assessment and Review Process (EARP) deals with the physical and biological aspects of development proposals: air, land, water, plants, animals and people. The EARP was established by the federal Cabinet in 1973 and adjusted by Cabinet decision in 1977. On 22 June 1984 the process was strengthened and updated when the Environmental Assessment and Review Process Guidelines were issued by an Order in Council (1984) under the Government Organization Act 1979. The authority for the process is provided by this Guidelines Order, but

Table 2.2 Provincial approaches to environmental assessment, 1980

Province	Use specific Act	Use other environmental legislation	Use EA policy or admininstration procedure
BC		✓	✓[a]
Alberta		✓	
Saskatchewan		✓	✓[b]
Manitoba			✓[b]
Ontario	✓		
Quebec	✓[c]	✓	
New Brunswick			✓[a]
Nova Scotia		✓	
Newfoundland	✓[c]	✓	✓[b]
Prince Edward Island			✓

[a] For public projects.
[b] Underway.
[c] Being considered.

Source: Pushchak (1985).

Canada's Federal Environmental Assessment Review Office (FEARO) does not have the power to ensure the implementation of recommendations arising from the review process. This has given rise to concern and the matter is currently being addressed by the federal government. Attention can be drawn to the absence of any clear legislative basis for the federal EARP and the continued weakness of its bureaucratic position. Smith (1987) consigns federal provisions for EIA into the lowest, Class D, category in Table 2.1.

In an editorial in *The Globe and Mail* of 27 January 1992 under the title: 'Sharing responsibility for the environment', it is claimed that constitutional jurisdiction in Canada over environmental matters is both federal and provincial. This has led to problems as to who should review specific projects, and the Supreme Court has recently ruled and affirmed the right of the federal government where projects impinge on matters under federal authority. Of course this general assertion remains to be fully tested but the editorial comment notes that 'the language of the ruling appears to give the federal government broad latitude'. Mr Justice Gerard LaForest wrote: 'the environment as understood in its generic sense, encompasses the physical, economic and social environment touching several of the heads of power assigned to the respective level of government . . . quite simply, the environment is comprised of all that is around us and as such must be a part of what activates many decisions of any moment'.

And while we might wish to endorse Conacher's (1988: 339) claim that 'Canada implements some of the world's most enlightened environmental management procedures', perhaps this speaks less well of Canada as a well-regulated state than it does of the poor position of the rest of the world. Within Canada there are significant variations in statutory and discretion requirements. The assessments have been primarily descriptive and impacts presented in disaggregate style with limited integration of risks and predictions within a strict scientific framework. Also, trade-offs are notoriously difficult to determine and incorporate systematically into an EIA in ways that allow close scrutiny, explanation and repeatability. The results have rarely, as yet, been included systematically into formal public facility siting planning, but this is changing, especially for recent waste management facility siting exercises.

An optimistic positive view of this phase of recent Canadian history on environmental assessment might suggest that Canada has set in place legislation, regulations and practices that take a very broad view of the environment, beyond the biophysical elements comprising land, air, water, flora and fauna, to include social aspects, and to open up a debate not only in response to expressed public pressure, but also to orchestrate a public debate and seek consensus on the search for the right balance between growth, development and environmental preservation. The journey continues in search of better, more effective environmental assessment practices which can be included in collective choice planning processes.

During the last fifteen years there has been a considerable amount of activity in Canada, the U.S.A., Australia and the EC, among other jurisdictions, to come to grips with environmental assessment legislation and related procedures as part of the emergence of a Regulatory State. We might expect that a sizeable body of expertise has been built up and that difficulties are successfully being overcome. This is too naïve an assumption.

Since 1970 hundreds of EISs have been completed in Canada (Duinker 1985) and close to 20 000 have been prepared in the USA under the requirements of NEPA. The state of New South Wales in Australia has witnessed almost 1 000 EIAs since the passage of their environmental legislation over a dozen years ago.

Within the context of the EC, a Select Committee of the House of Lords in the UK heard evidence in the 1980–81 session on the draft directive concerning the assessment of the environmental effects of certain public and private projects. The aim of the directive was 'to introduce a common procedural framework to ensure that environmental factors are adequately considered by the planning authorities of Member States in decisions concerning the authorization of certain development projects' (HMSO 1981). It was suggested that the assessment would involve the co-operation of the developer, the planning authorities and the public. Further, possible alternatives for the achievement of a planning objective should be examined in terms of the potential effects on the environment and the assessment should take account of measures required to minimize adverse impacts on the environment.

The preamble to the draft directive claims that 'a significant disparity between measures in force in the various Member States with regard to the assessment of environmental effects may create unfavourable competitive conditions and thereby directly affect the functioning of the Common

Market' (HMSO 1981). As European integration continues following 1992 this is clearly undesirable. On 1 July 1987 the Single European Act came into force and gave the EC Treaty a chapter on the environment for the first time. The European Year of the Environment (EYE) was launched on 21 March 1987 to promote public awareness of the environment. A definitive guide to European environmental legislation, directives, regulations and decisions has been produced by Haigh (1987) in which almost 200 items are dealt with. In many EC countries there appears to be a renewed interest in environmental issues. Whether governments and the public have the will to see meaningful controls implemented, only time will tell.

Specifically with respect to the Canadian situation, Whitney and Maclaren (1985) have argued that 'innovative though the concept of EIA may be, its practice has, for the most part, been pedestrian and governments have spent as much effort sidestepping the procedures that they have set up as they have spent implementing them'. Pushchak (1985) claims that only in a limited number of cases has the EIA procedure been instrumental in forcing the consideration of potential environmental consequences of large public projects before irreplaceable natural resources have been lost. The case of the proposal in 1980 by Eldorado Nuclear Ltd to build a refinery in the Mennonite community of Warman, Saskatchewan is cited as an example of a project that was halted by the EARP because of the possibility of the damaging impacts on the distinctive and cohesive social environment. Pushchak (1985: 75) suggests, however, that the Warman case is not typical, rather that 'in the majority of cases, the EIA process has either been applied to projects too small to warrant a costly assessment or has been arbitrarily applied or, in some cases, not applied to large-scale projects'.

The approach to EIA in Canada is one which is highly flexible and much less binding than in the USA. Pushchak (1985: 79) goes on to argue that: 'This has proved to be politically fortunate, since the widespread and vocal popular concern for environmental quality which created the demand for EIA procedures has declined considerably.' We wonder if events in the early 1990s would substantiate this 1985 claim – possibly not, and there now seems to be a mixed interest and concern about environmental damage especially as governments and citizens are preoccupied with economic recession and the need to create jobs.

Smith (1989), drawing on the work of Whitney and Maclaren (1985), has compiled a categorization of weaknesses that characterize current EIA practice in Canada. This is shown in Fig. 2.1.

A content analysis of thirty final EISs was used to derive these conclusions. The sample included a wide range of projects from waste disposal to offshore hydrocarbon development, over the period mid-1970s to 1987. Smith (1989: 28) concludes that 'No significant pattern existed on either a temporal or a topic basis: just as many poor EIS existed in 1986 as in 1976.'

Finally, I identify a set of five major issues which I believe capture the major problems that have been associated with attempts to implement

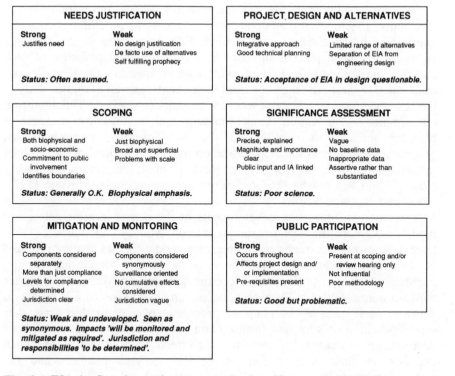

NEEDS JUSTIFICATION	
Strong	**Weak**
Justifies need	No design justification
	De facto use of alternatives
	Self fulfilling prophecy
Status: Often assumed.	

PROJECT DESIGN AND ALTERNATIVES	
Strong	**Weak**
Integrative approach	Limited range of alternatives
Good technical planning	Separation of EIA from
	engineering design
Status: Acceptance of EIA in design questionable.	

SCOPING	
Strong	**Weak**
Both biophysical and	Just biophysical
socio-economic	Broad and superficial
Commitment to public	Problems with scale
involvement	
Identifies boundaries	
Status: Generally O.K. Biophysical emphasis.	

SIGNIFICANCE ASSESSMENT	
Strong	**Weak**
Precise, explained	Vague
Magnitude and importance	No baseline data
clear	Inappropriate data
Public input and IA linked	Assertive rather than
	substantiated
Status: Poor science.	

MITIGATION AND MONITORING	
Strong	**Weak**
Components considered	Components considered
separately	synonymously
More than just compliance	Surveillance oriented
Levels for compliance	No cumulative effects
determined	considered
Jurisdiction clear	Jurisdiction vague
Status: Weak and undeveloped. Seen as synonymous. Impacts 'will be monitored and mitigated as required'. Jurisdiction and responsibilities 'to be determined'.	

PUBLIC PARTICIPATION	
Strong	**Weak**
Occurs throughout	Present at scoping and/or
Affects project design and/	review hearing only
or implementation	Not influential
Pre-requisites present	Poor methodology
Status: Good but problematic.	

Fig. 2.1 EIA in Canada: performance evaluation (*Source*: Smith 1989)

environmental assessment into site planning decisions to inform collective choice and so contribute positively to the development of a Regulatory State which encourages shared responsibility as a maxim of behaviour. A summary of these issues is given below. They have been organized sequentially with the view that the most important issues should be addressed first.

1. Better science to measure impacts and predict risks and relationships among components of the environment (Beanlands and Duinker 1983);
2. Need to integrate EIA into broader regional and sectoral planning efforts (Conacher 1988);
3. Need to make clear the lines of authority, responsibility and accountability in the preparation of the EIAs and their use in making planning decisions (Beanlands and Duinker 1983);
4. Reduce the number of exemptions (Fitzgibbon 1987);
5. Improve the involvement of the public in hearings and prior stages (Shrybman 1986).

While for large-scale (often noxious) public facilities, such as waste dumps, airports, power stations and the like, there is legitimate concern which focuses on environmental impacts, for smaller perhaps, salutary facilities such as libraries, fire stations, day care centres and primary health care units, the focus for analysis rests on access to potential clients and questions of effectiveness and equity. For these reasons considerable emphasis has been placed, in building a case for good planning of such facilities, on the development of models which measure the distance and time which separate the facilities from their clients, as well as on the study of the size and shape of the *de facto* or *de jure* service districts. This literature on distance minimization model-building and accessibility maximizing planning models often relies on the wide variety of mathematical programming family of location–allocation models developed in the fields of operations research and geography. Reviews of this literature are widely available and will not be repeated here. See, for example, Massam (1975, 1980) and Rushton (1975).

A number of interesting developments of the classic location–allocation models have been made. For example, Gregg, Mulvey and Wolpert (1988) have demonstrated a stochastic optimization model for tackling the problem of selecting sites for new social services or policies for closing existing facilities which specifically consider estimates of future demand, together with economic criteria. They recommend an interactive choice model in which at each stage of the planning process, a planner or decision-maker selects potential sites for new facilities and for closure. The impacts of these decisions are evaluated. It is clear that the effectiveness of such an approach depends on close co-operation among the analysts, planners and the politicians. There is a need for effective sharing of accountable responsibility. One particularly interesting feature of this model which fits into the context of this book concerns the incorporation of general errors in the evaluation. Specifically the analysis includes two types of possible errors, namely underusage and overusage estimates into the planning objectives. The model is applied to a set of empirical data for Queens borough public library system in New York City. Using the World Bank's general algebraic modelling system (GAMS) as the basic model this work shows clearly how fundamental deterministic location–allocation distance minimizing approaches can be modified to deal with economic considerations and to incorporate judgements of planners and others within a stochastic framework. This is a clear advance over the earlier deterministic models.

The general problem of relocation of fire, police, library and school facilities in a large urban area, such as New York City, with shifting demands over time has been examined by Dolan, Wolpert and Seley (1987). They recognize that planning inferences drawn from static analyses of demand, public expenditure patterns and distribution of facilities are subject to serious error. The authors argue for a dynamic approach to examine service allocations. Gains and losses of facilities as well as population changes in neighbourhoods are analysed. The analyses consider the educational levels of the target populations and criteria that relate to poverty levels and the needs of children, old people and ethnic populations.

Among the major findings it is concluded that as the needs of the population evolve because the supply patterns, namely the location of facilities, remain fixed so inequities are manifest. This maldistribution of facilities is troublesome and detracts from the development of stable acceptable public facility location decisions.

Problems relating to the location of services extend beyond urban areas, for example, Richard, Beguin and Peeters (1990) examine fire protection in the Belgian rural province of Luxemburg. A variety of demand situations are characterized, to include road accidents, fires in private homes, in public buildings and in agricultural buildings, forest fires and ambulance calls. Data for a five-year period (1976–80) were collected and also response times for the existing fifteen fire stations. Three classical location–allocation models (*p*-median, *p*-centre, set covering) were used on a set of 908 demand points and 99 possible supply points to consider both equity (*p*-centre) and efficiency (*p*-median) considerations. Different normative results are generated by each model, yet it is clear that by having available a clear set of data, objective repeatable analytical tools and a set of results in terms of outcomes, the policy-maker is likely to be in a strong position to present to the public the pros and cons of alternative siting planning and as a consequence help build confidence and improve the level of information for tackling difficult site selection problems. Obviously the location–allocation models must be closely integrated into the plan evaluation process if they are to reduce the chances of making planning mistakes.

One fundamental element in this confidence-building exercise concerns the involvement of the public. Katz (1989) provides a good review of the innovative work in Denmark between 1969 and 1975 which reformed planning processes in that country which had among other objectives the desire to have meaningful citizen participation with a view to improving the quality of life of citizens. Katz (1989: 982) contests the view that 'the general consensus that the planning reform in Denmark has achieved its objectives'. With respect to his case study in West Zealand he claims that participation levels were extremely small and highly institutionalized at the early stages of planning, but at the later stages when implementation was under way public reactions erupted.

If a meaningful sharing of responsibility is to be obtained it is necessary for citizens to be actively engaged in facility siting exercises from the outset. It must of course be recognized that the so-called optimum locations suggested by location–allocation models do not always satisfy all the interest groups, as inevitably some clients will be further from the facilities than they would like. Within the general context of the principles of fair negotiations, which will be discussed in section 2.2, it is argued that workshops, teaching sessions and the open sharing of information provided by a traceable style of analysis can help to build a co-operative milieu within which all parties learn to share responsibility, and alienation is kept to a minimum. In chapters 6 and 7 on choice and consensus I will deal with the use of decision-conferencing as a means to achieve stable acceptable negotiated settlements.

2.2 Some comments on negotiations

The process of negotiation should result in an outcome which is regarded as good by those involved in the development and presentation of arguments for stakeholders. Specifically Susskind and Babbitt (1987) have characterized a good negotiated outcome as one in which a set of four conditions is generally satisfied; namely the outcome should be seen as fair, efficient, wise and stable. These can be elaborated as a set of attributes:

1. Negotiations should yield benefits at least comparable to those derived by unilateral actions.
2. All joint gains should be realized, that is gains in which no party loses.
3. Legal obligations and planning regulations should be demonstrable by public officials.
4. The outcome should be perceived as just and no party should end up feeling cheated.
5. With respect to future negotiations it is hoped that a current settlement will have a positive effect.
6. Knowledge, data and other formal information should be used to the greatest extent possible.
7. The final outcome should be reached expeditiously and effectively in terms of cost, compared to any other means of resolving the dispute, for example via arbitration.

Richards (1989) examines strategies that have been adopted in the province of Manitoba to deal with conflicts in the siting of a hazardous waste management facility in such a way that proponents and potential host communities can jointly investigate, in an open fashion, options and consequences. The aim is to build consensus and to share responsibility among citizens. Local citizens are represented on a community advisory committee which, *inter alia*, has responsibility for co-management. Information is publicly available and participation by potential host communities is without obligation. The process which has been developed is making a serious attempt to dispel the view that the implementing agency has already chosen a site and the public meetings are mere publicity campaigns. So far this process seems to be enjoying a measure of respect which is in marked contrast to siting processes in some other jurisdictions which have been characterized as adversarial and highly confrontational. Armour (1988a), Emond (1987) and Kemp (1990) offer preliminary reviews of the necessary conditions to change confrontational siting processes into more co-operative ones which implicitly reflect effective sharing of responsibility. The former tends to result from the process which Williams and Massa (1983) characterize as a progressive increasing of scope from a broad geographical area and range of factors to a short list of discrete sites and highly specific evaluation criteria. The features of the co-operative approach which can be envisaged as commendable features of a Regulatory State stem from principles of volunteerism and open sharing of information as typified by the process outlined by the Siting Task Force that was discussed in Chapter 1 and which will be presented as a credo in Chapter 7.

Kemp's article stands apart from many on siting as he specifically moves away from technical considerations to look at the context within which public policy is formulated and opposition groups emerge. He concluded with the assertion that: 'What is needed is a more careful analysis and consideration of the vocabularies of motive which lie behind public opposition to plans for radioactive waste, and to take them into account before further decisions are made.' (Kemp 1990: 1257)

According to the *Interim Guidelines on Environmental Assessment* in Ontario (Environmental Assessment Branch 1989: 2), 'The Environmental Assessment Act is about good planning.' A set of five principles has been defined as necessary to achieve successful planning under this Act, and I suggest that the term 'successful' embraces the principles of fairness, efficiency, wisdom and stability that have been discussed above and as such encompass the concepts identified in section 1.4. Further, it is hoped that successful planning incurs a low probability of a planning mistake. The five principles aim to:

1. Ensure that the planning process is a co-operative venture which involves all the affected parties and that early consultation with the affected parties is essential.
2. Ensure that a reasonable range of alternatives is identified and considered; this set should include alternatives to any specific undertaking that is proposed as well as the status quo, do-nothing option.
3. Identify and consider the effects of each alternative on all aspects of the environment. This should examine effects on the natural or biophysical environment as well as social, economic and cultural conditions that influence the life of individuals or a community.
4. Explicitly evaluate all the alternatives in the light of their advantages and disadvantages developed through a net effects analysis. These include the effects remaining after mitigation or enhancement has been taken into account.
5. Ensure that the environmental assessment accurately represents the process that was followed in a clear fashion to guarantee that the process can be traced and scrutinized publicly.

Fisher and Ury (1981: vi) in their study of negotiations ask, 'What is the best way for people to deal with their differences?' They recognize that negotiation is a fundamental human activity involving communications 'designed to reach an agreement when you and the other side have some interests that are shared and others that are opposed'. Of course typically public facility location problems involve more than two well-defined opposing parties, though as the planning process unfolds the various interest groups may converge as protagonists and opponents. A method of so-called *principled negotiation* (PN) has been developed at the Harvard Negotiation Project to replace the more forceful hard line approach or softer approach in which one party makes concessions rather readily to avoid personal conflict, but ends up possibly feeling exploited and bitter. The PN approach searches for mutual gains, and when interests are in direct conflict then the resolution should be based upon some standard which is independent of the will of the contesting parties. A set of three criteria can be used to judge a negotiation process. First, a wise agreement should result if at all possible. The agreement should be efficient; further it should enhance or at least not diminish relationships between the parties who might well have to meet again on a future conflict.

Fisher and Ury (1981) argue that PN or *negotiation on the merits* involves four basic elements, each can be expressed as a principle and together they can be seen to comprise a set of necessary conditions for a good negotiated outcome. The elements include:

1. People: individual personalities, egos and emotions must be separated from the issues and the problem.
2. Interests: avoid focusing on stated positions, rather concentrate on trying to determine and deal with the underlying interests.
3. Options: before deciding on a course of action generate a wide variety of alternatives which possibly yield mutual gains.
4. Criteria: objective standards should be employed to determine results.

Reasonable as these may sound in the abstract, we can wonder why negotiations break down, mutual co-operation does not occur and principles are not readily employed. These points represent many realistic facility siting problems as the empirical literature attests, yet perhaps with the increasing awareness of books like Fisher and Ury's *Getting to Yes*, and Axelrod's *The Evolution of Co-operation*, possibly some progress is being made. Whereas Fisher and Ury (1981) and Fisher and Brown (1988) seek to deal explicitly with practical negotiation situations, Axelrod (1984) offers a theoretical prisoner's dilemma framework for a conflict and seeks to identify the conditions to achieve a win–win outcome in collective choice. Basically, he argues that four simple suggestions be taken into account, namely:

1. Do not be envious.
2. Do not be first to defect.
3. Reciprocate both co-operation and defection.
4. Do not be too clever.

Further elaboration on these points to enhance the chances of achieving mutual co-operation argue for making the future more important relative to the present, changing the perceived pay-offs to the players and teaching the players values, facts and bargaining skills. It is worth pointing out that there are ethical questions involved in negotiations and these are touched on in Chapter 6 on choice. It seems clear that more workshops and teaching sessions are needed to encourage the scrutiny of negotiation processes and the development of strategies and tactics so that, through shared responsibility, wise negotiations are concluded. Perhaps the key recommendation of Axelrod (1984: 126) is embraced by his expressed desire that co-operation can be improved if we 'enlarge the shadow of the future'; possibly this can be taken to mean that we should increase awareness of the negative effects of not co-operating and focusing on narrow short-term maximizing tactics.

Given that the costs of non-co-operation and unprincipled negotiations may be very high, it is fair to say that in some circumstances incentives to improve negotiating styles do exist. It is also worth asking the question: why negotiate? The aim, put simply, is to produce an outcome that is potentially better than would result from not negotiating. With this in mind negotiation strategists often use the term 'best alternative to a negotiated agreement' (BATNA) as representing a standard against which a proposed agreement could be compared. Within the context of environmental assessment as applied to a site location problem the standard that is frequently used is the status quo option, or the do-nothing alternative.

Consider the problem of comparing three alternative locations for a low level radioactive waste facility. This general problem has been structured as a teaching game on negotiations, bargaining and conflict resolution by Susskind and Babbitt (1987) under the title RADWASTE II. Six parties are involved in negotiations concerning the three optional sites – A, B and C – which each satisfy a set of basic siting criteria. This noxious facility is not wanted by any of the three communities. The fourth party, an environmental coalition, has hired an independent consultant to examine the impact statements concerning the siting criteria and flaws have been discovered. However, they have accepted the EIS of the state which yields site A as the most preferred one. The waste generators as the fifth party have an interest in the negotiations and their preferred site is C which has advantages in terms of expense and hence user fees. The final party in the negotiations is the Governor who is motivated by political crisis to keep public opposition and costly delays to a minimum. She believes that if a site is selected by consensus this will have distinct advantages. However, because of long-standing personal ties with the community near A, her clear preference is for either B or C.

In summary, these specific positions yield the following patterns of support for the three sites:

Site A: supported by: B

                        C

                        Environmental coalition

Site B: supported by: A

C

Governor

Site C: supported by: A

B

Governor

Waste generators

The rules of the game state that five votes are needed for an acceptable win so even site C with four out of six votes has insufficient support to be adopted. The Governor takes the initiative at the end of the first round of negotiations to circulate a memorandum reminding the parties that a site could be imposed by the Public Management Authority (PMA) and to help avert this while keeping to the spirit of consensus a compensation package is offered. This would be withdrawn if the PMA acted unilaterally.

Within the context of principled negotiations the parties now begin to explore some critical underlying issues which may persuade them to reconsider their positions. Specifically shared arrangement control procedures, source reduction, upstream pollution as well as different compensation packages are suggested and scrutinized until a compromise outcome is determined. It is hoped that principles of fairness, efficiency, wisdom and stability will remain intact. The use of voting procedures to deal with collective choice problems of this kind is discussed in Chapter 6.

The use of a simulation game can be very instructive to illustrate the consequences of not adhering to the general principles of good negotiation and the adverse consequences of unreasonable, obtuse, dogmatic or insipid negotiating styles and position bargaining, rather than focusing on the issues as suggested by Fisher and Ury (1981), as well as Raiffa (1982) who recognizes that negotiation is both an art and a science. A mediator can play the critical role of helping each party identify the critical issues. These points are taken up in Chapters 6 and 7.

2.3 Measuring, monitoring and inspecting

According to Day and Klein (1990: 1) we now have 'the age of inspection.' They draw on their extensive experiences in the UK and their close familiarity with the operations of the Audit Commission and the Social Services Inspectorate which were set up in the 1980s to scrutinize, report, regulate and to complement the long-standing Health Advisory Service. Inspection and auditing must be seen within the context of state regulation and the point has already been made in Chapter 1 about the emerging Regulatory State. Further, inspection necessarily must be linked to accountability, for without inspection is it possible to know what is going on? Are levels of compliance, outcome or performance reaching legislated or acceptable levels? And if not what can be done? And who is responsible?

The point has been made most forcefully by Hartley (1972: 447) who asserts that 'strict inspection is one of the hallmarks of a truly democratic regime'. Inspection according to Day and Klein (1990) is seen as a key instrument in accountability, and the current interest in the field should be judged as a reflection of the current evolution of the public provision of goods and services that is replacing 'provider paternalism' by greater accountability to consumers. Accountability is the focus of attention of Chapter 5.

The study by Day and Klein (1990) of the three inspectorate agencies in the UK that are concerned with senior citizens suggests a need for greater co-ordination of their efforts and convergence of methods and styles. A common widely accepted set of performance indicators incorporated into a data management system is required. It is also noted that public opinion needs nurturing and it is insufficient to suggest that forms of inspectorates should be dealt with only by the so-called professionals.

Some ten years ago the Government of Ontario suggested that if municipalities in the province could improve their productivity by only 5 per cent then an annual financial benefit of over $225m. would be realized (Ministry of Municipal Affairs and Housing, Ontario 1981). Such an assertion had popular appeal especially as it was couched in terms which suggested that there should not be a diminution in the quality of services provided. This type of financial claim caused a surge of interest in the search for methods to measure efficiency and effectiveness of the services provided by municipal governments and attempts were made to develop sets of performance measures. The government of Ontario has developed a set of guidelines for monitoring official plans; this document was published in 1982 and its general premises have relevance for facility siting. The link between the development of a plan or the selection of a site for a facility and its implementation is provided by a monitoring system which 'continuously reviews the relevance of the assumptions on which the plan is based and evaluates the effectiveness of the policies and the subsequent decisions to achieve the plan's objectives' (preface). While a strong case is made for monitoring, the guidelines suggest that the monitoring agency 'begin slowly and carefully', while recognizing the exercise is 'a learning process' and should be complementary to existing decision-making practices. Clearly the aim is to encourage monitoring by developing a consensus as to its utility.

Macmillan (1987) offers a critical analysis of the terms 'efficiency' and 'effectiveness' as applied to non-market organizations. He clearly identifies the problems of measuring the impacts (labour of different kinds, land, capital goods, rates, rate support grants etc.) which provide a multiplicity of outputs of public goods and services. He goes on to argue that as there is no theoretical optimum performance, thus denying the notion of marginal economic analyses, 'the only basis for comparison is the performance of other local authorities. But authorities differ widely in the conditions under which they operate.' (Macmillan 1987: 1511) A review of a technique known as data envelopment analysis (DEA) which focused on the problem of measuring the relative efficiencies of decision making units within non-profit organizations is presented. One of the leading public agencies that is exploring DEA is the Department of the Environment in the UK. While trial problems appear amenable to manipulation by this innovative linear programming model it is recognized that the technique's novelty and apparent complexity militate against its rapid incorporation into facility planning procedures. The message seems clear, namely there is overriding need to ensure that technocrats work co-operatively and in harmony with bureaucrats in the development of evaluation tools. The development of user-friendly computer-based DSS, as described in Chapters 3 and 4, is a step in the right direction.

A wide variety of approaches for measuring and monitoring have been developed, reviewed, tested and criticized in the pages of journals such as *The Canadian Journal of Program Evaluation* and *Evaluation Review: a journal of applied research*. The search continues for the appropriate combination of formal methods for the collection of numerical data on inputs, outcomes and workloads which can be combined with statements of preference and perceptions of citizens about the quality of services and their expectations, and the whole incorporated into the prevailing bureaucratic matrix and political system so that those who currently provide the services do not feel threatened by the results of evaluation exercises.

Patton and Sawicki (1986) and Dunn (1981) offer detailed carefully organized reviews of the state of art of procedures for monitoring and evaluating policy outcomes, and they draw particular attention to the differences between *ex ante* and *ex post* exercises. While the latter examine the existing levels of outcomes the former focus on the problem of predicating future effects. And it is within this context that it is worth noting the assertion that for many public facility siting exercises benefits are often overestimated while costs are underestimated, a point that has been made in Chapter 1. Dunn (1981) compares and contrasts four approaches to monitoring – social systems accounting, social experimentation, social auditing and social research consultation – as well as a wide variety of complementary statistical and graphical techniques. He concludes that monitoring does not have clearly distinguishable sets of procedures and 'many of the same techniques are therefore appropriate for each of the four approaches' (Dunn 1981: 332). Among the most important techniques must be included: graphical and tabular displays, index numbers, interrupted time-series and control-series analyses, as well as regression–discontinuity analysis.

But no single technique can stand alone. Patton and Sawicki (1986) make the important point that the final step in policy analysis involves monitoring, evaluation and feedback. These are the critical features of an open facility siting planning process. They go further, and while reviewing a variety of methods, drawing in part on the well-known and very useful taxonomy of evaluation models produced by House (1980), which focus on experimental designs, they also indicate that there is a need for evaluation techniques which are quick and easy to implement. For it is the latter which will probably enhance the chances of incorporating the results into future planning, especially if programme staff are closely involved in the monitoring exercises and do not view themselves as bureaucrats who fill out data forms for others to use, possibly in a way which might threaten job security. This is an important aspect of monitoring which is too often overlooked; DSS can be viewed as complementary to evaluation techniques and they are generally easy to use as is discussed in Chapters 3 and 4.

The initiative to attempt performance measurement has occurred in many jurisdictions in a number of countries and progress has been made to seek formal ways to monitor the quantity and quality of services provided, to audit delivery systems, to check on the levels of service delivered and to examine the relationship between predicted or expected levels of output and actual or realized levels. An excellent review of this work is provided by Hatry (1991: 1) and he bases the growing interest in accountability and performance measurement on two assumptions.

1. Government agencies are there for the welfare of their citizens – whether the public agency provides environmental protection, garbage collection, water supply, public safety, transportation, health and social services, parks and recreation, housing, or whatever.
2. Government services should be judged on how well they provide their services; that is on the quality of these services. Each level of government should be judged, whether: (a) the government is responsible for *delivering* the service, or (b) the government agency *funds* the service.

He goes on to claim that the 'New wave of decentralization and democracy in many countries is a marvellous opportunity for these countries.' (Hatry 1991: 1) Hatry provides support for the view that the Regulatory State is emerging. Also, it is clear that the results of performance analyses can provide useful information to address matters of equity. Individuals, groups or regions, for example, which appear to have higher or lower levels of service can be identified systematically and attempts made to redress unacceptable differences.

Closely linked to all this work has been the development of inspectorates to oversee the quality of service provided, and most recently in the UK assessments of the effectiveness of such inspectorates for services like health care and education. With respect to hard services provided from public facilities, for example, power and water, it is a relatively non-controversial matter to inspect, monitor and audit the output. However, with respect to the social services, especially health care and education, it is far from easy to define mechanisms which are broadly accepted, well understood and stand up to close scrutiny. A review of this literature is given in Massam (1980). In passing it should be noted that there is a considerable debate on the difficulty of finding the precise relationship between quantity and quality of output. This point has been well made by Nijkamp (1989) with respect to the difficult task of developing evaluation indicators to describe features of the built environment which could be classed as part of a society's cultural–architectural heritage. At a more prosaic level we have the example of work by Skaburskis and Bullen (1987) which seeks to estimate the price effects of a waste landfill site in the city of Kitchener, Ontario. Using data for the mid-1980s and a multiple regression model they concluded that a $90 000 house would retain its value as long as it was at least 1500 m from a landfill site. However, a similarly valued house would lose about $5000 if it happened to be within about 60 m of the dump. Also, a downwind location for a house could cause a further loss of approximately $2000.

A useful discussion on some theoretical problems associated with selected evaluation methodologies is provided by Alemi (1987). Specifically trade-offs are discussed between (a) Bayesian and traditional statistics, (b) decision and cost–benefit analysis, and (c) anthropological and traditional case studies. The purpose of the article is to make evaluators aware of the implicit trade-offs associated with the selection of a particular subjective or an objective method. While some evaluators may look for the right method, a more satisfactory view is to accept that such an ideal does not exist and to be aware of the advantages and disadvantages of a chosen methodology. These should be presented for public scrutiny.

In the process of undertaking an *ex post facto* evaluation or monitoring exercise it is possible to rely on either objective or subjective assessments of the outcome. The former tends to focus on so-called hard data, for example the distances travelled, number of visits to a facility, number of times the service is provided, together with some indicators of effectiveness and equity. On the other hand the subjective data reflect attitudes, perceptions and opinions, particularly with respect to the quality of the service which is provided from the facilities.

A recent study by Day (1987) has examined relationships between perception or subject assessments of air pollution and selected measures of personality for a sample of residents in the Junction Triangle, an older inner-city neighbourhood in the city of Toronto, Canada. This district is characterized by proximity of industry and housing and growing concerns by residents and others about the adverse environmental conditions on level of health. On 6 April 1982 a major chemical spill provoked the closure of three schools and seven people were hospitalized. For nine days, the source of the pollutants could not be identified, but eventually Nacan, a local chemical industry, admitted responsibility. The concerns of the residents can give rise to a variety of behavioural responses, for example stay and do nothing, stay and become involved in local anti-pollution activities, or move. Day (1987) argues that personality measures can be used to classify individuals and to understand their responses. From a facility siting perspective it is suggested that this type of work can assist in the development of mitigation and compensation packages which address the concerns of citizens while recognizing that individuals have different personalities and needs. This type of work fits into the larger field of hazard research which, according to Mitchell (1984: 37) is concerned with 'the totality of factors which generate, sustain, exacerbate or mitigate those characteristics of natural and man-made environments that threaten human safety and emotional security and material well-being'.

Day (1987) found a lack of involvement in local anti-pollution activities by citizens while at the same time they had a high level of awareness of the pollution crises. He maintains that there is possibly a consensus of opinion that 'the government' is actively dealing with the problem, yet there seems to be an absence of a significant sharing of responsibility for the task. The application of a battery of tests to measure personality traits and statistical analysis did not reveal significant findings. So while we might recognize that individuals have different perceptions of the control they may or may not have over close potentially hazardous sites, it is unclear precisely how these can be measured and linked in a meaningful way to enlighten facility siting planning exercises to enhance participation so that the final outcomes are seen as the result of legitimate collective choice.

While most evaluation, monitoring or auditing exercises focus on objective or subjective assessments of outcomes a useful approach is to place work into a broader context by asking citizens to express opinions about trade-offs. This sort of work can be particularly useful for further planning of public facilities. An example of this trade-off approach is provided in the study by Atkinson (1981) that involved interviewing 1600 residents of metropolitan Toronto and seeking their views about trade-offs between taxes and services. In general the survey suggested that more Toronto residents would prefer to pay more taxes to obtain better services, rather than vice versa. In particular one borough, York, has the highest proportion of respondents who favour tax hikes, and this underscores the relatively poor quality of services in this borough as perceived by residents. I argue that this type of trade-off survey offers a distinct improvement in *ex post* monitoring over a survey that does not offer respondents sets of choices.

With respect to environmental monitoring it has been recognized in Ontario that without having in place an effective system to ensure compliance and guarantee that commitments and conditions of approval are satisfied, the goals of the province's Environmental Assessment Act are unlikely to be met. A review of this Act is currently under way by Ministry officials and a critical focus of attention rests on the development of improved monitoring procedures. While expressions of need abound ultimately it is a resource question and one which tests the political will of the provincial government to allocate money to hire staff for expanded operations.

In the early 1970s Hatry (1972) had already identified the fact that there was a renewed interest in productivity assessment in the public sector in the USA, supposedly because of a national concern over rising prices without apparent rises in output. He argued that productivity measurement would not only help identify problem areas and priorities for improvements but perhaps more significantly determine the rate of progress towards targets or goals and help to establish and implement employee incentive schemes. Clearly, without some attempts to monitor progress there will be a lack of the necessary feedback information to be incorporated into future planning exercises.

In simplistic terms it is suggested that productivity means relating the amounts of inputs of a service to the outputs. However, as Hatry (1972: 783) reported, and the situation has hardly improved in recent years, 'the state of the art of productivity measurement for local government services is disappointing'. Hence there has tended to be a continued emphasis on the measurement of the more traditional workload type of measurements. He goes on to stress that 'Single, readily available, physical measurements, tempting as they may be, should be viewed with a jaundiced eye.' (Hatry 1972: 783) One of the classic studies on productivity measurement provided the basis of these comments by Hatry.

More recently Hatry, Millar and Evans (1984) have offered a set of evaluation criteria in order to provide a classification of the relative importance of a project for funding approval. The demand for such an approach stems directly from the fact that the cost of providing all the facilities that are demanded exceed the available budget. A discussion of the criteria, which can be grouped into the following categories: fiscal, health and safety, community economic, environmental and social, distributional, public support, deferral, risk and uncertainty, broader interjusdictional and multi-project effects, is provided by Levy (1991). Wisely, he avoids offering any formulaic suggestions as to precisely how each criterion is to be measured. It is perhaps sufficient to say that there is a need to be able to explain publicly which data have been used in order that the analysis can be traced and replicated. The overall aim of the exercise is to ensure credibility for the difficult exercise of defining and defending an ordered list of priorities for a set of projects. Steiss (1978) offers a general priority ordering from urgent, essential and necessary to desirable, acceptable and dependable. However, we are left with the difficult task which is brushed over lightly by Levy (1991) in the following quotation. 'When projects have been evaluated by these [Hatry, Millar, Evans: 169] criteria, they can be *ranked* [italics in original] or sorted into various categories.' We are left to wonder precisely how the ranking and sorting are to be conducted. I suggest that MCDA techniques and DSS as reported in Chapters 3 and 4, can help to tackle the problem of ordering facility siting projects.

2.4 Social need assessment

The basic reason why many public facilities are provided is that they cater to social needs. It is therefore appropriate to turn attention to this topic. One of the seminal papers on this topic is provided by Bradshaw (1972: 640) in which he recognizes that the history of the provision of social services is essentially 'the story of the recognition of social needs and the organization of society to meet them'. York (1988) considers need assessment as a critical aspect of human service planning, and he acknowledges the important conceptual work of Bradshaw which is complementary to Maslow's (1954) hierarchy of needs which begins with those relating to physical conditions, then safety and so on to embrace belonging, self-esteem and self-actualization or self-fulfilment. It is contentious to assert that an individual necessarily proceeds in sequence through this hierarchy or that several levels cannot be pursued concurrently. When all is said and done for facility planning and siting, generic comments on need assessment have to be converted to data collection exercises usually via a census or questionnaire survey in order to provide a set of scores or indicators which are felt to be related to needs. Also, of course such scores represent performance levels of existing facilities and as such are explicitly required in any monitoring exercise.

In general terms Bradshaw identifies four separate definitions of need which are recognized by administrators and researchers. First, *normative* need as defined by an expert as a desirable standard against which existing provision can be judged. Second, *felt* need as equated to a want and as such is generally an inadequate measure as, *inter alia*, it is severely influenced or limited by the perceptions of individuals. If this type of need is turned into action then *expressed* need is identified. For example, for a new health care facility, lengthy waiting lists or extensive travel times to existing facilities provide an expression of this type of need. Finally, *comparative* need is identified by examining the characteristics of those who receive a particular service, and if those with similar characteristics do not receive a service, then it can be claimed that they are in need. A taxonomy of the intersection of the four types of need is developed by Bradshaw (1972) in order to provide a systematic framework for precise determination of service requirements. He argues that if social policy-making, and hence facility planning, are to be more than a matter of political hunches and academic guesswork then solid frames are needed. At the outset it must be recognized that there are difficult methodological problems which have to be faced, specifically with respect to the search for information from potential clients as to their requirements (i.e. their expression of need) and combining criteria which are treated as independent indicators of need into final scores of need which can be used for practical planning exercises. It should also be recognized that the separate indicators may not be statistically independent.

One of the most ambitious schemes in the USA that is being developed to measure need for health care via a priority rating approach is provided by the so-called Oregon formula. In general this type of formula for rationing health care services is advocated as 'the only effective way to control health care costs' according to Relman (1990), who goes on to argue that as funds are not available to cater to all the health care needs of an ageing population some kind of need assessment rationing procedure will have to be developed. However, he clearly recognizes that 'to be seen as fair and therefore have a chance of acceptance by the public and the medical profession, a rationing plan needs to have medical and ethical, not simply economic justification'. In the case of Oregon this search for a fair method for determining need and rationing is causing quite a debate among the various interest groups who, in general, subscribe to the view propounded by Schwartz and Aaron (1990) in their critique of the scheme that the procedure for assessing need must measure costs and benefits at the level of the particular circumstances of individuals. Such an approach, which tends to place a heavy burden of responsibility on the individual physician to make the hard allocative choices, militates against a uniform formula for deriving a rating of priorities.

A useful balanced review of the Oregon procedure is provided in a series of articles by McBride (1990), Welch and Larson (1988) and Dixon and Welch (1991). A review note by Klein (1991) in the *British Medical Journal* generated a number of letters in reply in the same journal, later in the same year. In essence Oregon is developing a formal method of measuring need for health services and to set priorities for particular categories of health condition. The method is based on a cost–utility formula which, they claim, incorporates public attitudes and values. Implicit in this is the notion that it enjoys public support, however, this is debatable as reviewers point out.

In 1987 Oregon passed legislation to withdraw Medicaid coverage for organ transplants in order to transfer resources to an extra 1500 poor women and children. This political and resource allocation decision represented a need classification, however, Dixon and Welch (1991) argue that there was limited input from the public or health professionals prior to the decision. The Senate Bill (SB 27) was drawn up by Kitzhaber who claimed that such an allocation would help to make hard choices more rational and open to public scrutiny. An eleven-member Health Services Commission was charged with drawing up a ranking methodology which must include input from the public. Before the Bill was passed a demonstration project was presented for scrutiny, and focus groups were asked to rank services. According to Dixon and Welch (1991) 'each focus group ranked the services in order of effectiveness of the treatment using a consensus methodology'. The details of this methodology are not given. Further refinements were undertaken to take into account a set of principles involving the trade-off between length of life and quality of life, efficiency and equity as well as the cost and benefit of the service. It is worth noting that the commission soon rejected the consensus approach because it lacked specificity, and hence would not lend itself to public scrutiny, traceability and replication. By early 1990 a preliminary priority list was made public. Flaws relating to inaccurate cost and effectiveness data were identified. A further attempt was made to develop a consensus-building approach and to blend this with views generated from public meetings and hearings.

In summary, it is clear that this is a firm political decision to address a very difficult need assessment problem in the critical area of health care and while criticisms of the Oregon formula are not lacking, the status quo of using professional judgement and intuition seems less than satisfactory, while an alternative process still escapes definition and implementation. Other jurisdictions especially in the UK are examining closely the Oregon experiment. Perhaps it should be seen as breaking new ground in the assessment of social needs and providing a procedure to allocate scarce resources in a way which is seen as wise, fair and stable. These conditions which I identified earlier in this chapter are important ones within the context of negotiations and collective choice in a Regulatory State.

Let me now turn to some methodological questions concerning the determination of need for a social service drawing on work reported in Massam (1991a). Specifically, I will discuss four different technical procedures for analysing the relative importance of a set of five indicators which relate to the need for day-care facilities in Ontario. The procedures include two pairwise comparison techniques, a simple ranking method and Metfessel point allocation. A critique of the utility of each will be offered and recommendations made to help in the collection and analysis of data to assist in the formulation of public policy on matters relating to the analysis of indicators of need with a view to using them for the allocation of resources. One of the principles enunciated in a report on day-care by the Ministry of Community and Social Services of Ontario (1987) is the explicit statement that 'services must respond to individual, cultural and regional needs'.

Prior to the search for specific sites for day-care facilities it is often appropriate to consider the allocation of resources from a central agency to a spatially defined district and then within this district to map the distribution of children, together with the transportation system to seek those locations which are most accessible to receive the new resources. As mentioned in Chapter 1, this latter problem is often tackled using a location–allocation model as reported by Holmes, Williams and Brown (1972), for example for Columbus, Ohio or by mapping the supply situation on to a demand pattern, as has been done by Kanaroglou and Rhodes (1990) for the city of Waterloo, Ontario. Specifically they provide evidence to support the view that if equity is a prime consideration then licences for new facilities should be strongly influenced by locational criteria. This represents a zoning tactic to generate an appropriate supply to match a given spatial demand pattern.

Consider a region that is divided into sub-regions and for each of the latter data relating to several indicators of need for a social service are available. Attempts to develop formal procedures for handling these data with a view to determining a single measure of need for each sub-region have been made by Bosch-Domenech and Escribano (1988), Stevens (1989) and Skelton (1990), among others. Much of their work has focused on the search for weights for the indicators so that scores for each indicator for each sub-region can be combined in a linear model to derive an overall index of need for each sub-region. The allocation of financial resources among the sub-regions is then determined on the basis of the need index for each sub-region. The adoption of this approach for allocating resources is based on the view that the methodology is sound and any technical procedures that are used can be scrutinized publicly, and hence decisions regarding the use of public monies are made in a way that is clearly accountable.

While in general all these claims are meritorious we should not overlook the fact that such a methodology places no direct emphasis on trying to determine the effectiveness of the allocation of resources among sub-regions. Specifically, marginal effects of investments are not examined, neither is attention focused on the definition of specific planning goals, objectives and targets for the social service under examination. Further, it should be recognized that different opinions may exist about the relative significance of indicators. At least four distinct interest groups can be identified: parents of children who use or would like to use day-care facilities, providers who administer day-care facilities through ministerial policy-making, those who work at the local level in day-care and citizens at large who, as taxpayers, contribute to the public purse and, as voters, elect politicians to establish *inter alia* social policies, including policies relating to the provision of day-care facilities. These points about interest groups have been made by Truelove (1989). It appears that in general little progress has been made since Bradshaw (1972: 643) noted that: 'The research worker is still faced with difficult methodological problems and the policy maker has still to make complex decisions about the categories of need [that] should be given priority.' In 1989 Stevens claimed that:

> Despite the large amount of money which is allocated to social service agencies . . . there has been little systematic investigation of the information and procedures which . . . funders employ to arrive at their decisions. However, with publicly-accountable funders . . . there is a strong feeling that the pattern of their allocations should reflect the need for services in the community in some objective fashion. (Stevens 1989: 1)

Stevens proposed a multi-attribute utility procedure to derive a score to reflect the priority for a particular need *vis-à-vis* a total set of needs for a range of social services. This work focused on Winnipeg and dealt with the problem of allocating resources among competing social service needs. The judicious use of MCDA techniques and DSS can address the problem of incorporating the views of different interest groups into a formal multi-attribute analysis as will be mentioned in Chapters 3 and 4.

In order to give a specific focus to the Ontario study reported here a set of five indicators drawn from the work of Skelton (1990) and Truelove (1989) will be used. These indicators refer to the need for day-care services, though both Truelove and Skelton draw attention to the debate on the relative importance of each indicator. The specific problem that is to be examined is to test and evaluate alternative formal methods for collecting opinions from a set of subjects about the five indicators. The opinions will be used to determine the relative importance of each indicator. For the purposes of testing each methodology opinions from a group of sixteen fourth-year undergraduates at York University, Ontario were used. The data were collected in 1990.

The five indicators identified by Truelove (1989) as the critical ones for determining need in Ontario for day-care services within a spatial unit are:

1. Number of existing places;
2. Number of children less than six years of age;
3. Percentage of lone parents;
4. Percentage of women (18–60) in the work force;
5. Average household income.

It is suggested that once the subjects have deliberated on the problem of considering the relative importance of the five indicators they will attempt to transfer their opinions to an analyst using the instrument provided by the analyst. In this study four different instruments were considered. The subjects were asked to comment on the ease with which each could be used and to offer opinions regarding the utility of each one for collecting and summarizing preferences for the indicators. One of the purposes of the study was to compare the procedures to see if consistent results for the indicator weights are given. Each instrument uses a separate procedure, thus:

1. Ranks;
2. Metfessel allocation;
3. Pairwise comparison – nine-point scale;
4. Pairwise comparison – five-point scale;

The first procedure yielded a ranking of the indicators from most to least important. The full set of 16 opinions generated a 5×16 matrix which was analysed using a median ranking method of Cook and Seiford (1982) to yield a consensus ranking. A review of literature on methods for deriving a consensus from rank data is given in Massam (1988a) and a discussion on the general topic is given in Chapter 7.

The second procedure (Metfessel) allowed a ratio scale to be created by asking each subject to allocate a total of 100 points among the set of 5 indicators. The larger the allocation of points the more important the indicator. The consensus weights for the indicators were calculated from the sum of the allocations to each indicator. The third procedure offered a pairwise comparison matrix of the form shown in Fig. 2.2. Each subject was required to place a value in each cell to indicate the relative attractiveness of one indicator with respect to another. For example, if x_1 was deemed to be 'very much more important' than x_2, then a score of 9 is placed in the cell

(x_1, x_2). The reciprocal value 1/9 is placed in the cell (x_2, x_1). The completed matrix is known as a positive reciprocal matrix and, following the procedure developed by Saaty (1980), it can be analysed to yield a set of weights for the indicators. The analysis determines the normalized principal eigenvector for the positive reciprocal matrix, and to use this as a set of weights to reflect the relative importance of the indicators. Shim (1989: 161) offers a good review of Saaty's analytic hierarchy process (AHP) and he argues that: 'Today, AHP is perhaps one of the most important decision analysis techniques for multiple objective decision making.' This view is elaborated in Chapter 3 when the method is judged against other MCDA techniques. In Fig. 2.2 the weights shown are derived from the values in the matrix. Given that sixteen such sets of weights are derived, that is one for each subject, I have used the totals to produce a set of weights for the indicators.

Finally, the fourth methodology uses a matrix of the style shown in Fig. 2.3. This matrix can be analysed to identify clusters of subjects who have similar sets of opinions regarding the pairwise comparisons of the indicators. An example of such an analysis for measuring groups who share similar opinions has been presented by Lootsma, Meisner and Schellmans (1986).

The first three methodologies seek to indicate the relative importance of the indicators with a view to using these values in a formal model that will yield an overall score for need for each sub-region. At the outset three general observations can be made. First, do we have consistent results for the opinions using ranks, Metfessel and the positive reciprocal matrix? Second, we should recognize that the rank procedure yields a scale which intrinsically does not have cardinal properties. It is these properties which are used to generate legitimate weights for the indicators and to generate a score for a sub-region using a general linear model of the form

	I_1	I_2	I_3	I_4	I_5	Weights*
I_1	x	9	4	2	3	41.8
I_2	1/9	x	2	1/5	1/3	6.4
I_3	1/4	1/2	x	1/2	1/5	6.8
I_4	1/2	5	2	x	4	28.7
I_5	1/3	3	5	1/4	x	16.2

$I_1 ... I_5$: indicators of need

*   : normalized principal eigenvector

Fig. 2.2 Hypothetical pairwise comparison matrix

IS	very much more preferred	much more preferred	equal	much less preferred	very much less preferred	TO
I_1						I_2
I_1						I_3
I_1						I_4
I_1						I_5
I_2						I_3
I_2						I_4
I_2						I_5
I_3						I_4
I_3						I_5
I_4						I_5

$I_1 ... I_5$: indicators of need

Fig. 2.3 Pairwise comparison of indicators

$$S_i = W_a q_{a1} + W_b q_{b2} + \ldots W k q_{kn}$$

where S_i is the score for sub-region i, W_a the weight for indicator a and q_{ai} the quantity of this indicator a, in sub-region i, given a set of weights $a, b, \ldots k$, for a set of indicators $a, b, \ldots k$, and a set of sub-regions $1, 2, \ldots n$.

In general the ordinal values should not be treated as a set of weights, 1,2,3,4,5, etc., from least to most important. Hence a different sort of method from the linear additive model is required. Cook and Kress (1992) note that the search for a suitable formal method for handling this problem continues, though lexicographic ordering (Massam 1988a) is a recognized general method. Unfortunately this does not allow trade-offs among the criteria and hence has limited practical utility. The subjects suggested in a group discussion that a ranking of indicators was quite easy to produce and it served as a useful starting point in the allocation of points as demanded by the Metfessel procedure. However, there was a consensus that they were less comfortable with this latter method as reflecting their overall opinions than the AHP procedure. Cook and Kress (1992) support the view that the AHP is easy for a subject to complete. The third observation concerns the aggregation of opinions. Clearly if all subjects generate data which are identical then the aggregation exercise is trivial and no conflicts emerge. This is rare and the search for procedures to aggregate individual opinions into a group value has a long history as will be discussed in Chapters 6 and 7 on choice and consensus. In this study the data which were summarized in a matrix of the style shown in Fig. 2.3 were analysed using cluster analysis to identify groups of subjects with similar sets of opinions. For this set of data two broadly distinctive groups were identified. One contained four subjects and the balance of twelve comprised the second group.

Analysis of the data that were collected using a matrix of the style shown in Fig. 2.3 was undertaken using Ward's minimum variance cluster technique. This generated groups of subjects with similar sets of opinions regarding the pairwise comparison of the five indicators. Given a set of five indicators there are ten pairwise comparisons, hence the matrix in Fig. 2.3 has ten rows. Following the procedure outlined in Lootsma, Meisner and Schellmans (1986), the comparisons scored are shown as follows:

x_i IS	+4	+2	0	−2	−4	TO:x_j
	very much more preferred	much more preferred	similar	much less preferred	very much less preferred	

Hence for each subject a column of scores was derived to indicate the preference profile for each of the ten pairwise comparisons. The complete set of data comprised a matrix 16 by 10, given that 16 subjects expressed opinions. It was this matrix that provided the basic input for the cluster analysis. Examination of the results shown in Table 2.3 indicates that, beginning with the grouping of subjects 7 and 18, who have identical profiles, as we move up the hierarchy two fairly distinct clusters can be identified, namely (5, 15, 14, 16) and (1, 2, 4, 8, 7, 18, 11, 10, 17, 9, 13, 3, 12, 6). The full set of clusters is shown in Fig. 2.4. For the purposes of this section and to demonstrate the general utility of this type of analysis I will only consider the disaggregation of the group into two clusters. Specifically, after examining the results for the total set of sixteen subjects, attention will be turned to an examination of the results for each of the two clusters identified here. With respect to a practical problem it could be instructive to follow this strategy to identify subjects who have similar profiles, and to use this as information in the process of mitigation and compensation as part of the exercise of building an acceptable consensus so that a public policy enjoys legitimacy and credibility. Perhaps one way to proceed, for a planning practitioner, is to examine the preference profiles for representatives of the interest groups identified in the introductory section.

Table 2.3 Ward's minimum variance cluster analysis eigenvalues of the covariance matrix

	Eigenvalue	Difference	Proportion	Cumulative
1	28.7	17.2	0.46	0.46
2	11.5	1.3	0.18	0.64
3	10.1	5.5	0.16	0.80
4	4.6	1.5	0.07	0.88
5	3.0	1.0	0.04	0.93
6	1.9	0.7	0.03	0.96
7	1.2	0.6	0.01	0.98
8	0.5	0.2	0.00	0.99
9	0.3	0.1	0.00	0.99
10	0.1	—	0.00	1.00

Root mean square total – sample standard deviation = 2.5
Root mean square distance between observations = 11.2

Number of clusters	Clusters Joined			Frequency of new cluster	Semi-partial R-squared	R-squared
17		7	18	2	0.00	0.99
16		10	17	2	0.00	0.99
15		4	8	2	0.00	0.98
14		9	13	2	0.01	0.96
13		14	16	2	0.01	0.95
12		3	12	2	0.01	0.93
11	CL17		11	3	0.01	0.91
10	CL11	CL16		5	0.02	0.88
9	CL12		6	3	0.03	0.85
8		5	15	2	0.03	0.82
7		1	2	2	0.03	0.79
6	CL15	CL10		7	0.04	0.74
5	CL6	CL14		9	0.05	0.69
4	CL7	CL5		11	0.07	0.61
3	CL8	CL13		4	0.11	0.49
2	CL4	CL9		14	0.13	0.36
1	CL2	CL3		18	0.36	0.00

A summary of the ordering of the indicators using the rank data, Metfessel scores and Saaty's (1980) analysis is given in Table 2.4. It is clear that for the aggregate data the overall ordering is highly consistent for the first three indicators (3,2,1) and for the other two there is slight disagreement as to whether 4 is preferred to 5, or vice versa. As mentioned earlier, generally it is inappropriate to assign weights to an ordinal scale, though this certainly is not unknown even though it flies in the face of conventional mathematical logic. If the weights 5,4,3,2,1 are assigned to the indicators in the order in which they are ranked and the scores normalized so that, for the five indicators, they sum to unity, then a direct comparison

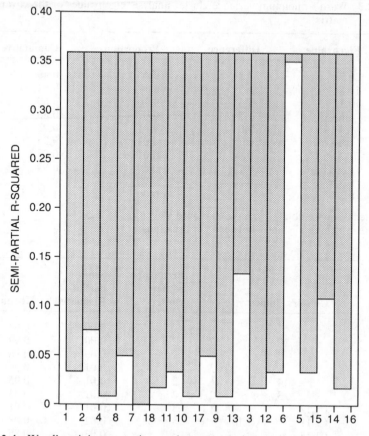

Fig. 2.4 Ward's minimum variance cluster analysis

with normalized weights for the Metfessel data and the Saaty analysis can be made. A summary of the three sets of weights is given in Table 2.4, and among other things it is clear that the rank weights do not correspond satisfactorily with those derived from the other two methods. Specifically indicators 3 and 2 should be accorded almost equivalent weights of about 0.25 and indicator 1 about 0.2, with indicators 4 and 5 somewhat lower values.

With respect to the disaggregate data and using only two clusters, it is clear that the larger cluster of twelve subjects shares a consistent ordering of the indicators $(2 > 3 > 1 > 5 > 4)$, whereas for the smaller group there is a lack of consistency. The results are shown in Table 2.4. For the larger group heavy emphasis is placed on the first three indicators (2,3,1), and a more limited weight is given to 5 and 4. For the small group approximately one-third of the total weight is assigned to indicator 4. Separate discussions with members of this group after the analysis made it clear that they felt that the key indicator of need for day-care in a sub-region was 'percent of women in the workforce'. There was also a measure of consensus that 2 was fairly unimportant, but there was disagreement on the significance of indicators 1,

Table 2.4 Ordering of five indicators of need

	Ranks		Metfessel		Saaty	
Aggregate data						
I_3	5	0.33	I_3 0.24		I_3 0.25	
I_2	4	0.26	I_2 0.23		I_2 0.25	
I_1	3	0.20	I_1 0.22		I_1 0.18	
I_5	2	0.13	I_4 0.15		I_5 0.17	
I_4	1	0.06	I_5 0.13		I_4 0.14	

Disaggregate data

(4)			(12)			(4)		(12)		(4)		(12)	
I_4	5	0.33	I_2	5	0.33	I_4	0.25	I_2	0.26	I_4	0.35	I_2	0.30
I_3	4	0.26	I_3	4	0.26	I_3	0.23	I_3	0.25	I_5	0.28	I_3	0.26
I_1	3	0.20	I_1	3	0.20	I_1	0.17	I_1	0.24	I_3	0.21	I_1	0.22
I_2	2	0.13	I_5	2	0.13	I_5	0.17	I_5	0.13	I_2	0.12	I_5	0.12
I_5	1	0.06	I_4	1	0.06	I_2	0.16	I_4	0.12	I_1	0.04	I_4	0.10

5 and 3. We should of course note that formal analysis of the preference and opinion data only searches for patterns, it does not seek to convey the impression that there is agreement among individuals unless such agreement is contained within the data.

All the four procedures appeared to be straightforward to use according to the consensus of opinion of the subjects, and hence probably not too complex to be employed in data collection even with subjects who do not have a sophisticated background in quantitative methods. The requirement that an evaluation procedure be easy to use has been made earlier in this chapter and it will be stressed again in Chapters 3 and 4. However there are some significant features of the procedures which are worth noting. First, the ranking method should not be used to generate weights for indicators, but it may be a useful preliminary step towards the application of the Metfessel scheme. Second, Cook and Kress (1992) among others, claim that subjects are more willing, able and competent to provide pairwise data of the sort found in Fig. 2.2 or Fig. 2.3, than in providing a complete set of weights, for example, using the Metfessel scheme. The evidence from this study suggests that these procedures generate comparable results, and given that the Metfessel scheme yields weights directly without any complex numerical analysis to derive the principal eigenvector of a matrix, as required by Saaty's method, it is probably preferable. Further, in the course of discussions with the subjects it was suggested that Metfessel scales could be part of discussions among interest groups as they seek to examine the scales produced by separate groups to try to find a consensus.

The analysis of the data using the cluster methodology can identify in a systematic fashion groups of subjects who share common preference profiles. In the generation of a public policy it is often useful to be able to identify such groups in order to enter into direct negotiations involving mitigation and compensation with representatives of such groups. However, we should keep in mind the views of Sager (1981) when considering the practical utility of formal evaluation procedures. Specifically, he argued that in any evaluation exercise citizens are particularly interested in the final outcome of their expressions of opinions about disaggregate indicators of costs, benefits and need. If we follow this view then the exercise of collecting opinions lacks a sound basis in any social theory concerning equity, as the emphasis is probably on maximizing self-interest by weighting indicators on the basis of selection of the ones with the lowest values for the sub-region in which the subject resides, and hence generating a high value for need. This is a general problem of collective choice as will be mentioned in Chapter 6.

Truelove (1989: 166) has reviewed a selection of literature on measures of equity and draws attention to the view of Alonso (1971) that 'it is extraordinary that there has been so little technical discussion of a concept so central to political economy'. Truelove (1989: 166) opines that 'perhaps this is because of the traditional concern of public administration with process rather than with outcomes'. Surely a link between process and outcome can be made in a way which accommodates concerns about equity, recognizing that this is a principle that surely lies at the heart of resource allocation of a public good or service.

There is another argument which is worthy of consideration, and this stems from the principle of the 'veil of ignorance' as propounded by Rawls (1971). This principle, which is grounded in his notion of justice, rests on the view that if subjects do not know precisely which benefits will accrue to them as individuals as a result of expressing a particular set of opinions and preferences then their preferences are expressed 'justly' so as to maximize the benefits to those who are most needy. Self-interest manifests itself on the assumption that those who are least well-off should benefit most because any particular subject may in fact be in this category of deprivation and among the least well-off. It can be argued that the expressions of opinion will generate a set of indices which it is hoped will be broadly acceptable to the various interest groups so that the allocation of resources follows a process which is derived from systematic involvement of individuals and analysis of preferences in ways which can be scrutinized publicly. It is perhaps this general procedure which, it can be argued, is the appropriate one for the development of social policy for the allocation of resources in support of a public service.

Finally, I suggest that while it is important to develop and test formal methodologies for deriving indices of need, in order to identify those that are easy for subjects to understand and which are internally consistent and logical, it is also vitally important to ensure that the preferred methodology is based on principles of social theory, such as justice, equity, effectiveness and efficiency, which are seen as legitimate and appropriate in the context of a Regulatory State that seeks to encourage shared responsibility for complex problem solving. For this reason I suggest that in the development of indicators of need for sub-regions in a jurisdiction such as a province like

Ontario with respect to a social service, it is reasonable to use all four formal procedures to complement economic and related analyses of the distribution of marginal costs and benefits from the addition of resources to a sub-region. In a word the use of formal procedures should only be undertaken if they have credibility, and are believed by the stakeholders who bear accountable responsibility to assist in public debate by their contribution to improving public scrutiny of recommendations and policy decisions.

2.5 Integrated evaluation and implementation

In the final analysis it is important that if a variety of evaluation approaches and needs assessments are undertaken they have to be integrated. Alterman, Carmon and Hill (1984) have used the concept of 'integrated evaluation' in an attempt to demonstrate how such integration could occur. They recognize that evaluation research has a long history yet they argue that too often the results have not been of significant use to decision-makers who are primarily concerned with implementation. This lack of co-operation and sharing of information is likely to change as greater use of modern technology such as DSS, which is easy to apply, becomes more widespread. Clearly there is a need to link *ex post* and *ex ante* monitoring and auditing exercises with the goals and needs of those decision-makers who have responsibility for planning new facilities and for modifying or closing existing facilities. The concept of integrated evaluation is elaborated by the authors to embrace basic features which support the use of the goals achievement matrix that was originally developed by Hill (1968). This type of matrix forms the basis of ones used in MCDA and will be discussed in Chapter 3. Monitoring, combined with a review of the procedures by which policy decisions are arrived at, is combined with data on input costs and measures of outcomes. The aim is to have a better understanding of cost-effectiveness. Finally it is necessary to involve all stakeholders, not only decision makers at an early stage if an acceptable outcome which enjoys wide support is to be identified. Alterman and her colleagues at Technion in Israel recognize that no single set of techniques will be sufficient to avoid all criticisms, but that the development of formal techniques for evaluation should be accommodated within a broad framework to include political and managerial realities as well as views of individual citizens as consumers.

The link between evaluation techniques and decision-making as related to EIA by using integrative concepts has been made by Fuggle (1988) and Lang (1990), among others. With respect to experiences in South Africa, Fuggle reviews integrated environmental management as defined by the Council for the Environment (1988) as comprising four basic stages: proposal generation, assessment, decision and implementation, and he argues that such a management system represents a distinct improvement over the more traditional EIA approaches which have been widely developed and which seem to interfere with expeditious decision-making, rather than enlightening or informing it.

The concept of integration was identified as a critical one and it provided the theme for the conference of the International Association for Impact Assessment (IAIA) that was held in Brisbane in July 1988. Among the numerous contributions which stressed the importance of integration thus echoing Fuggle's point, the President of the IAIA noted that integration could be divided into technical, consultative and institutional aspects. Another contributor to the conference (R. Buckley) suggested a further set of four main aspects to integration, all of which he argued are equally important: space, time, economics and administration. Such vague statements are not very helpful, probably it is better to focus on the contribution of integration to improving welfare, as surely this is the ultimate goal of evaluation exercises. The different emphases of social and natural scientists served as a reminder that integration with a view to promoting both good science and socially responsible outcomes is not without difficulty.

In 1983 and 1985 the Banff School of Management in Canada organized seminars on integrated approaches to resource management, and while the focus did not specifically address facility siting problems it is implicit that tackling such problems demanded the integration of technical, consultative and co-ordinative functions in the plan generation, evaluation and implementation phases. Lang (1990) provides a synopsis as follows:

(a) *technical* – to balance economic, social and environment considerations within resource development planning;
(b) *consultative* – to consider the views of affected parties and include them before final commitments are made;
(c) *coordinative* – to link public and private agencies who are responsible for planning and implementation.

Between these two seminars an important conference was held at the Banff School in 1984 which focused specifically on facility siting. The details of the papers, most of which were offered by private companies, who typically act as proponents for facility planning and representatives of government agencies, are included in the two-volume *Proceedings* (Environment Canada, 1984). One of the three themes of this conference focused on *regulation*, public interest and decision-making to complement *methods* for routeing and siting and *elements* of the process. These latter two themes concentrated attention on technical approaches and current methodologies for data collection and management. Implicitly the emphasis was on developing tools that would improve collective choice within a Regulatory State that wished to promote welfare.

One very important aspect of facility siting must deal with the generation of options against which the current arrangements can be compared. A straightforward description of proposal generation has been offered by

Fuggle (1988: 11): 'Proposal generation is concerned with formulating a proposed action, as well as viable alternatives to this action for meeting some purpose or need.' The strict application of a formal technique such as sieve mapping, site screening or the use of potential surfaces, trees, lattices and advanced mathematical procedures like Markov chains may have certain appeal on grounds of rigour and objectivity according to Batty (1974), but it is debatable as to whether such tools alone can be sufficiently credible so that proponents can justify their choice of feasible alternatives at public meetings and hearings or in front of environmental assessment boards and the like. The analysis of the results of needs assessments can generate proposals for specific facility siting exercises.

According to a report on economic and environmental principles related to implementation studies that was published in 1983 by the US Water Resources Council a set of four criteria should be considered in the generation of alternative plans. The criteria refer to completeness, effectiveness, efficiency and acceptability, and brief comments on each are provided as follows.

1. *Completeness:* all necessary investments or other actions must be included, recognizing that actions relating to other planning activities must be considered.
2. *Effectiveness:* an assessment of the specific extent to which a proposal alleviates a defined problem.
3. *Efficiency:* an assessment of the cost effectiveness.
4. *Acceptability:* an assessment of the degree of compliance with laws, regulations and practices.

It seems imperative that while proponents may be charged with the task or assume responsibility for providing an initial set of alternatives or options, the planning process is usually sufficiently flexible to allow further options to be considered prior to selection of a preferred option and the phase of implementation. There is generally a desire to be expeditious and move the process towards a resolution and to balance this against the efforts needed to build consensus and handle conflicts to ensure that the final preferred option is drawn from a reasonable set of feasible options. Formal legislation, such as the Environmental Assessment Act of Ontario, for example, requires alternatives to be defined explicitly and evaluated by the proponents. This practice is gaining common currency.

The need for a well-defined set of options is a prerequisite for the majority of MCDA–DSS, as it is this set which characterizes the solution space. Explicit is the assumption that the preferred site for a facility will be drawn from this set. Finally, it should be noted that the set of alternative sites for a facility, while generally viewed as feasible ones, can include some hypothetical or benchmark options which serve as reference sites against which practical feasible alternatives can be compared. The use of such reference sites will be included in the discussions offered in Chapters 3 and 4 which focus explicitly on MCDA–DSS as they are used for tackling facility siting problems.

3

Multi-criteria decision aid–decision support systems: reviewing the field

3.1 Introduction

In the last two chapters I have identified and described the major components of the milieu of the Regulatory State within which public facility location problems, as specific examples of collective choice problems, are posed and tackled. This and the next four chapters will deal specifically with techniques and concepts that can be used to help address these problems. Chapters 3 and 4 focus on formal work which is based on MCDA–DSS and this is complemented by a review of literature on the three concepts – accountability, choice and consensus – which are fundamental to successful collective choice within a Regulatory State.

At first blush it might appear that the formal approach assumes that facility planning is merely a technical matter which can reduce the problem to a set of impact scores, and that arithmetic manipulation of these scores will yield the right answer. This is a mistaken view. I argue that the formal methods to be discussed in Chapters 3 and 4 can be used to help collect and organize information in such a way that assumptions can be scrutinized and goals and objectives made as clear as possible to all parties who are involved in the planning process, and in general these methods should improve accountability. Typically the results of the formal methods appear as a classification of options. Whether the option that appears at the head of the list is actually implemented depends on the credibility that the method enjoys in the opinions of the legislators, regulators and other stakeholders. This impinges on the notion of consensus as will be discussed in Chapter 6.

This chapter will offer an introduction, a review and a critique of a selection of MCDA–DSS as they can be applied to the general problem of classifying alternate sites for public facilities and helping to identify a preferred option. In summary I argue that MCDA–DSS allow information on planning goals and objectives to be formulated as evaluation criteria which can be incorporated into a legitimate planning framework that takes account of opinions of interest groups. Now MCDA–DSS are being used in conjunction with spatial information systems and this new field is referred to as spatial decision support systems. Reviews of this literature are given by Armstrong *et al.* (1986) and Densham and Rushton (1988). Fedra and Reitsma (1990) note that there is considerable potential for co-operative research involving both geographic information systems (GIS) and MCDA–DSS especially if good visual displays of alternatives and impacts are made available to decision-makers. They go on to claim that:

> GIS and DSS have a lot in common, but they also can complement each other in many applications. Merged with simulation and optimization models, and artificial intelligence/expert systems technology, they are important building blocks for a new generation of useful and usable 'smart' information technology supporting planners, managers and decision makers. (Fedra and Reitsma 1990: 187)

Some researchers, for example Henderson (1987), have argued that DSS and related systems, such as expert systems, should encourage organizations to transform radically their style of management. However, with respect to facility siting problems it seems that the most useful single purpose of MCDA–DSS is to contribute to making the planning process clearer and more traceable. It appears unlikely that radical changes to planning procedures in the public sector will occur through the use of MCDA–DSS. As mentioned above, the field of artificial intelligence is closely linked to MCDA–DSS and according to Chalmers and MacLennan (1990: 1) 'significant progress was made in the process of problem solving, in non-algorithmic programming and in cognitive science as a consequence of the intellectual energy generated at Dartmouth'. They are referring to the founding conference on artificial intelligence held at Dartmouth in 1956. Their annotated bibliography of approximately 150 pages, which reviews recent work on the use of expert systems in geography and environmental studies, identifies clearly the uncertainty which surrounds the claims as to the utility of artificial intelligence and expert systems for tackling environmental impact assessment (EIA) problems. They conclude on an optimistic note by claiming that, 'Premature papers have become less frequent, and the promise of useful incorporation of knowledge into computer systems is being increasingly realised.' However, there are as yet few examples of the direct application of this new technology to facility siting problems.

It is suggested by Armstrong *et al.* (1990: 341) that there are three kinds of knowledge which must be incorporated into any computer-based spatial or locational DSS: 'factual knowledge about the environment that is relevant to the problem being examined, specific rules that decision makers use to solve problems in their problem domain, and knowledge that locational analysts have of locational decision-making principles and of optimization algorithms useful in solving locational site problems'. They argue that interactive knowledge-based DSS (KBDSS) can be constructed to tackle practical facility siting problems. Among other things, we must acknowledge the important contributions of this team of researchers who are not only focusing on actual problem-solving, by looking at school location issues in Iowa, but perhaps more importantly they are engaged in a debate on the fundamental principles underlying complex public facility location problems, and the need to sort out such principles and algorithms prior to launching into applied work. A review of this work appears in Rushton *et al.* (forthcoming).

A review by Alter (1980) of fifty-six DSS clearly indicated the wide variety of approaches and the lack of clear boundaries that separate DSS from any other computer-based system for handling information of use to managers. In a word the field has grown like Topsy. An article by O'Sullivan (1985) attempts to put some order into the literature by stressing the need for evaluators and clients to work closely together. She draws on the ideas of Keen and Scott-Morton (1978) and Anthony (1965) which sought to categorize organizational decisions – the latter author recognizes three categories: operational decisions that seek to ascertain if tasks are effectively and efficiently carried out; management decisions that seek the effective use of resources and strategic decisions that seek to define policies and objectives.

Before MCDA–DSS are used to tackle a specific site selection problem it is appropriate that test cases be conducted, using small empirical or hypothetical data sets with a view to building confidence among those who must make the siting decisions. There is a strong role for workshops to help build the necessary consensus which precedes the acceptance of MCDA–DSS into facility planning. Criteria for judging the worth of a particular MCDA–DSS are given later in this chapter.

There are a variety of computer models that can be used for tackling facility siting problems. One of the most popular and best known is the urban data management software package that has been developed in the United Nations Centre for Human Settlements (Robinson 1983). This software enables, *inter alia*, the solution of a semi-structured location problem and at the same time it allows decision-makers to be involved in the process of solving the problem. Furthermore, the package can be used to tackle multi-objective location problems situated in a fairly complex decision-making environment.

Horn *et al.* (1988) have presented a prototype of a system called the interactive territory assignment package. Although this system has been primarily used to plan administrative districts, it can also be used to solve locational planning problems. Since this software enables the solution of a locational problem to be identified with the participation of decision-makers it can be considered as a DSS.

While the overall objective of MCDA–DSS for our purposes is to improve the quality of collective choice, and hence implicitly the reduction of planning mistakes, much remains to be done to link the efforts of theoreticians who seek to develop algorithms and deductive arguments, with the work of practitioners who are faced with actual location choice problems.

An attempt to review literature on MCDA–DSS and link theory to practice is provided in the monograph *Multi-Criteria Decision Making (MCDM) Techniques in Planning* (Massam 1988a). The recently created journal *Location Science* (Pergamon Press, Oxford) hopes to provide a forum for theoreticians and practitioners to exchange ideas, and the newsletter *Locator*, published by the College of Locational Analysis, the Institute of Management Science and funded by the Faculty of Business, University of Alberta, Canada serves a similar purpose. In February 1991 volume 1 of the newsletter *Spatial Decision Support Systems* appeared (Department of Geography, University of Tennessee), and the contents provide evidence that suggests closer co-operation among all who are interested in tackling facility location problems using MCDA–DSS and related technology.

In 1990 the Ministry of the Environment in Ontario, Canada sponsored a workshop on the use of a selection of MCDA–DSS for assisting in the preparation of environmental impact statements (EISs) concerning a variety of public facilities, such as waste disposal facilities, highways, etc. A report summarizing the workshop presentation has been prepared: 'Computer-based Decision Support Systems (DSS): their role in environmental assessment' (Ministry of the Environment, Toronto 1990).

A review of the literature on MCDA–DSS suggests that to a large extent the formal techniques have been developed in operations research, though other fields including social psychology, regional science and business management offer significant contributions. Elam, Huber and Hurt (1986) offer a systematic review of DSS literature for the period 1975–85 on the basis of a carefully organized examination of over 200 articles published in 20 refereed journals. They begin by noting that the concept of DSS was introduced by Gorry and Scott-Morton (1971) in their seminal paper on 'A framework for information systems', and that the field has grown rapidly with particular emphasis on applications to practical problems; however, the authors are somewhat critical of the heavy emphasis that has been placed on studies based on single cases at the expense of efforts to test systematically and develop new DSS.

An extensive list of over ninety journals reporting MCDA work has been compiled by Hwang and Yoon (1981). In 1972 the first international conference on multi-criteria decision making (MCDM) was held, and Zeleny (1984) has suggested that it was at this meeting the new, previously unorganized, field of MCDM was officially launched. A summary of the papers is given in Cochrane and Zeleny (1973). The decennial MCDM meeting was held under the auspices and sponsorship of the American Association for the Advancement of Science in Washington DC. It is clear that the field is growing rapidly and has wide-scale appeal, as is evident from even a casual glance at the 1700 references listed in the source book edited by Zeleny (1984), and perusal of the two special issues on MCDM which were published in 1986 in the *European Journal of Operational Research*. In a review article Vincke (1986) documents convincing evidence to support his claim that the research in this field has been one of the fastest growing areas of operational research in Europe during the last fifteen years.

Some researchers, for example Taylor and Taylor (1987), Spezzarro (1986), Keen and Scott-Morton (1978), McLeod (1986) and Massam and Malczewski (1990), argue that MCDA–DSS can be viewed as a category of planning technique which is embraced by managerial support systems. Most MCDA–DSS are based on formal mathematical models of the optimization variety (DINAS, for example, as used by Massam and Malczewski 1990) or on multi-criteria classification techniques (DAS, for example, as used in Massam 1991b). Both DINAS and DAS will be discussed later in the chapter. However, a number of authors (Brill 1979, Liebman 1976; Brill *et al.* 1989) have clearly pointed out that the role of MCDA–DSS models in decision-making is to provide 'intuition, insight, and understanding which supplements that of decision-makers' (Brill *et al.* 1989: 3), rather than formal answers to tightly structured choice problems. It is clear that tightly structured problems, for example of the optimization variety, typically assume away important elements of collective choice, in particular the views and opinions of individuals. Proponents of MCDA–DSS, for example Humphreys and Wisudha (1987), argue that the views of individuals can be incorporated into the evaluation exercise if the formal models allow the individuals to interact with the computer-based models. Obviously though for very practical reasons the number of individuals who are able, willing and available to do this is limited. Perhaps the best we can hope for is that interest groups will be represented by individuals who participate in decision conferences that use MCDA–DSS. This topic will be discussed in Chapter 6.

Following these introductory remarks, section 3.2 will set the scene for understanding why MCDA–DSS have an important role to play in collective choice and facility siting exercises. Section 3.3 will include basic descriptions of the data requirements and the underlying principles, and section 3.4 focuses on a discussion of selected MCDA–DSS. I will avoid providing details of algorithms which may detract attention from obtaining an appreciation of the basic principles and assumptions. I argue, however, that some detail must be provided so that the analyst, planner or interested decision-maker is not left with just a list of references without appropriate operational definitions or practical applications. The application of selected MCDA–DSS to two types of facility siting problems will be given in Chapter 4. The first problem deals with the location of primary health care centres in a rural region in Zambia and the second considers the problem of finding sites for waste transfer stations in the city of Ashdod, Israel.

3.2 MCDA–DSS and related fields

The study of MCDA–DSS embraces a variety of related topics, for example multi-attribute decision-making (MADM), multi-attribute utility theory (MAUT), multi-objective decision-making (MODM) and public choice theory (PCT). Authors who have reported on these topics include Keeney and Raiffa (1976), Zeleny (1982), Thiriez and Zionts (1976), Bell, Keeney and Raiffa (1977), Nijkamp (1979), Nijkamp and Spronk (1981), Rietveld (1980), Hwang and Yoon (1981), French *et al.* (1983), Voogd (1983), Linstone (1984) and Fandel and Spronk (1985). Nijkamp and Spronk (1981: preface) suggest somewhat optimistically that 'multicriteria analysis appears to be becoming a new mode of thinking for decision-making, planning theory, choice analysis and conflict management'; however, they add the important caveat: 'it occurs too often that those designing new techniques . . . are hardly aware of the varying needs and desires of the potential users of these techniques'. Bell, Keeney and Raiffa (1977: v) admit that 'the analytical tools that were developed to aid decision makers facing complex problems originally addressed only single-objective problems . . . the artificiality and restrictiveness of that approach for most real world problems has led to the development of various methods for handling multiple objective problems'. A note of caution and realism has been added by Batty (1985) in his article in *Rationality in Planning* edited by Breheny and Hooper. Batty indicates that formal rational models may be too restrictive in dealing with complexity for they tend to impose order where there may be none.

In the 1970s decision analysis was offered as the preferred rational way to tackle a whole range of choice problems and specifically Bell, Keeney and Raiffa (1977: 9) suggested that 'the aim of decision analysis is to decompose a problem into two parts: one to indicate the probabilities of different possible consequences of each alternative and the other to evaluate the desirability of those consequences'. This seems a perfectly reasonable and sensible way to proceed as long as all the necessary data can be obtained and there is agreement among all parties regarding the alternatives and their consequences, however, rarely are these demanding conditions ever fully satisfied. These points are elaborated in Chapter 6.

It seems clear that the distinctions among the four areas, MODM, MADM, MAUT and PCT, while conceptually significant, are probably less important when we consider that they are all related to the generic collective choice facility planning problem which can be stated thus: Given a set of M plans for a public facility, and for each an evaluation on a set of N criteria, for a set of G interest groups, classify the M plans in such a way as to identify their relative attractiveness so that agreement among the interest groups is maximized.

The generic problem identified above comprises two problems. The first has been characterized by Stewart (1981: 46) in the following way: 'The problem facing the decision maker is thus to select an alternative such that the collection of criteria values ($_jS_k$, $j= 1, 2, . . . N$) is preferable to that of any other alternative. Where S_k is the utility, attractiveness or score for plan k given a set of N criteria.' The second has been stated by Cook and Seiford (1978: 1723) thus:

> Consider the problem in which each member of a committee provides an ordinal ranking of a set of . . . projects. Any one member's ranking is considered equal in importance to the ranking preferred by any other member. The problem is to determine a compromise or consensus ranking that best agrees with all the committee's ranking.

Massam (1984) and Rietveld (1984) have shown that the structure of these two problems is very similar. Rietveld (1984) indicates that in the case of the collective choice problem nothing is known about the relative importance of individuals (note that Cook and Seiford assume equality is the norm), whereas for the evaluation problem some information on the relative importance of criteria is generally available. In fact it appears to be very difficult to derive any good formal definitions of satisfactory weights for criteria, as interest groups clearly have their preferred weighting schemes which reflect their preferences and priorities only in terms of the final outcome.

According to Sager (1981) it can be shown that *ex ante* weighting of attributes and goals has logical weaknesses which follow from assumptions of rational choice under uncertainty. Who would willingly agree on a set of weights *ex ante* and risk that their preferred alternative was replaced by another which they perceived to have inappropriate consequences? It is probably preferable for the planning process to include meaningful participation of interest groups in order to attempt to build a consensus regarding a preferred plan. Conflicts cannot always be avoided, therefore they must be managed. The concept of consensus will be discussed in Chapter 7.

3.3 Components of MCDA–DSS problems

It is clear from an examination of the generic collective choice facility site planning problem outlined above that there are three major components which must be considered: first, the alternative facility siting plans, second, the criteria which are used to evaluate the plans, and third, the interest groups. I will begin by focusing on these three components and consider the ways they can be combined as a set of matrices in which data can be recorded. This will lead into a discussion on the scores and values in each matrix, and a review of selected procedures for standardizing these scores. The rationale for such an exercise will also be given. At this stage I will introduce the notion of benchmark plans; also I will stress the need to recognize explicitly that errors are likely to occur in the estimation of the scores.

One of the major areas of concern for those using MCDA–DSS techniques rests with the problem of deciding how to select criteria and how to deal with them. Should they be ordered from most to least important? Should they be weighted? If so, then what rules should be used to derive the order or to assign the weights? These and related questions focusing on the treatment of criteria will be dealt with in this section.

Let us consider a set of M alternative facility plans $P_1, P_2, \ldots P_M$, a set of N criteria $C_1, C_2, \ldots C_N$ and a set of L interest groups $I_1, I_2, \ldots I_L$. These three components can be combined and presented as a series of matrices as shown in Fig. 3.1. These matrices are sometimes referred to as evaluation tables, options tables or impact or achievement matrices; terms such as priority matrix and appraisal matrix have been used by Voogd (1983) to

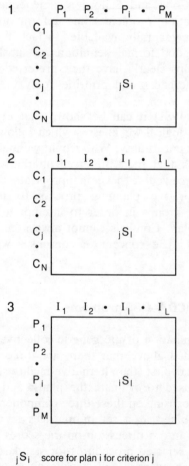

$_jS_i$ score for plan i for criterion j

$_jS_l$ score for criterion j for interest group l

$_iS_l$ score for plan i for interest group l

Fig. 3.1 Three major components

describe matrices 2 and 3 respectively. The terms 'exact value matrix' and 'preference matrix' have been used to describe matrix 1 (Massam 1980). The latter suggests that the data in the matrix have been derived from a technical assessment without any direct consideration of the views of the interest groups, whereas the information in the former matrix gives an indication of the importance of the data from the perspective of an interest group. We might distinguish between these views by using terms such as magnitude of impact and importance of impact. These terms are used in the environmental impact matrix that was developed by Leopold and his colleagues at the US Geological Survey in the early 1970s to help with the implementation of the National Environmental Policy Act that was referred to in Chapter 2.

The criteria conventionally focus on economic, social and environmental factors; however, this list could be extended to include mitigation measures and implementation difficulties. The plans may represent alternative locations for a particular type of facility, or different strategies for tackling a particular problem, for example expansion of existing sites or closure. Clearly the alternatives are dictated by the specific problem under investigation. The interest groups or the stakeholders may be composed of producers, operators and consumers as suggested by Lichfield (1970) or proponents and opponents. The task of defining interest groups or publics who should be involved directly in facility siting is not easy. Ultimately selection is a political act which seeks to balance the rights of minorities to be heard with the rights of the majority whose representatives have responsible, legitimate power during their term of office. This touches on matters of accountability, choice and consensus – topics that will be addressed in Chapters 5–7. According to the principles on public involvement that have been outlined in a manual prepared by the US Department of the Interior (1980: 1): 'Effective public involvement requires not only that specific regulations be met . . . but also that activities are carried out within the spirit of public involvement.' Public involvement is seen as a process by which individuals, organizations, agencies and the like are informed, consulted and included in decision-making.

Prior to the analysis of a data matrix it is necessary to determine the scores in cells; these are shown as $_jS_i$ (score for plan i for criterion j), $_jS_e$ (score for criterion j for interest group e) and $_iS_e$ (score for plan i for interest group e). A superscript t could be added to each of these, for example $_jS_i^t$, to indicate the score during a certain time period or at a particular point in time. This is an important dimension when plans are assessed in terms of their long-term and short-term effects. It should also be recognized that the information shown on these matrices can be combined into a single table or diagram. Three examples of this are shown in Fig. 3.2.

Attempts to analyse the three-dimensional matrix (1) shown in Fig. 3.2 have been offered by Massam (1986), and Jaakson (1984) has used the second type of matrix (2) in his application of a technique called planning assistance through technical evaluation of relevance numbers (PATTERN). This second matrix is referred to as a relevance matrix.

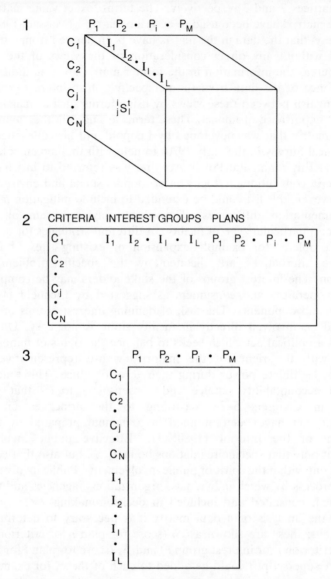

Fig. 3.2 Combinations of plans, criteria and groups

Among the three components perhaps the most important one is the set of interest groups, for it is from this set that the specifics of a proposed plan are generated, one or more options may be offered and opposition may arise, also one group may be charged with bringing about a final settlement. This can be referred to as the collective choice solution which ideally is a stable acceptable outcome. We can identify three types of interest groups. First, those who express the need for a planning exercise or who recognize an opportunity for development – the proponents. Second, those whose lives will be affected either positively or negatively by the actions of the proponents, and third, those who have the legitimate responsibility for mediation, arbitration or sanctioning the actions of the proponents or opponents. This third group may also have the implicit authority to protect those who do not overtly support or object to a specific plan. For example, their concern may be to enhance the public good. These three types of interest groups may each try to assess the range of planning options available, as well as the criteria which they feel reflect suitable indices to make judgements on the relative merits of the options given their particular objectives. As well, it is clear that the interest groups will seek to understand each others' views and to estimate ways to ensure particular outcomes.

This first stage which can be viewed as an initial step in consensus-building involves the organization of information as a set of matrices. This provides a useful framework for handling the debate on the identification of options, criteria and interest groups. Perhaps no further formal analysis of the information in these matrices is undertaken in the plan evaluation process, and the debate on the relative merits of each option is undertaken within a negotiations framework in which each of the interest groups seeks to present its case as forcefully as possible, while avoiding unsatisfactory outcomes and recognizing that delay has a price. If, however, detailed analysis of the options is seen to be an important part of the planning process then we must look further at these matrices and consider how the scores in each one can be derived and used.

Once it is decided that a particular matrix is to be examined the next task is to obtain scores for the cells. In this section brief comments on the four major types of measurement scales for such scores will be given. I will then consider the problem of standardizing these scores so that the values are commensurate. Basically the disadvantage of this approach is that the units of measurement – costs, jobs, noise levels, etc. which probably have fairly clear meaning and significance for an interest group, are converted into dimensionless units which do not have a specific attribute with a recognizable name. On the other hand, by converting all the different sorts of impacts on to a standard scale there is some legitimacy in accumulating the scores on a single scale, and if this scale is in monetary units then the final score for each plan potentially has significance for the interest groups. This assumes that the unit is the critical variable on which decisions are based. While we might try to standardize scores in order to make the criteria commensurate, it would be naïve to suppose that simple arithmetic operation on the new numbers will yield the right or even acceptable solution. What we might hope for perhaps is that the standardization procedure can yield values which we can then use in a classification exercise and add to this a series of sensitivity tests. It is this latter operation which is a vital part of using MCDA–DSS.

The four measurement scales which can be used for the scores in the matrices are:

(a) ratio;
(b) interval;
(c) ordinal;
(d) nominal.

The characteristics of each of these are discussed in standard texts and the details will not be repeated here. See for example Voogd (1983).

The ratio scale contains most information, as a basic point of departure, an origin is given and the magnitude of the measurement units; the nominal scale provides categorical information, and as such it is hard to use for comparative purposes. A mistake frequently made in the analysis of a matrix is to assume that an ordinal scale has the same properties as an interval scale. This point has been forcefully made by Nowlan (1975) and the case is reviewed in Massam (1980). As a general rule, whenever numbers are placed in a matrix a declaration of the scale should be made so that all ambiguities are avoided. This will improve accountability. Ordinal scales are frequently used by planners and care must be taken to ensure that simple arithmetic operations are not conducted using such scales. The rationale for this rests on the notion that the ordinal scale does not give details of the magnitude of differences; ratio and interval scales contain such information. We should also avoid using geometrical approaches for analysing ordinal data; for example, it is not legitimate to draw a graph and claim that the data on the axes exhibit only ordinal properties. It should be noted that a particular score may have errors associated with it and it should be better characterized by upper and lower limits. This is an important idea from a practical standpoint and one which should and can be incorporated into MCDA–DSS within the framework of tests for sensitivity or robustness.

The assignment of an impact score to a particular cell may lead us to believe that we are objective and that our personal biases are removed. To some extent this is true. However, we should acknowledge that while the magnitude of an impact may be assessed with some objectivity, depending upon the instrument, the importance of this impact is directly related to the opinions, perceptions or the expectations of the interest groups. A further complication is added for some impacts because the physical intensity can be perceived differently from the psychological intensity, yet it may be the former that produces damage to our health. For example, a facility at site A may generate 10 decibels more noise on a sound meter than at site B, the physical energy is ten times as great yet subjectively the difference only appears to be twice the amount. A 20 decibel increase produces 100 times more energy but only a fourfold increase in perceived loudness. As ear damage is related to the physical intensity levels we should be wary of using perceived intensities, yet it is these which cause psychological annoyance. Great care is needed to examine the nature of the impacts; simple recording of numbers without supplementary explanations may lead to spurious conclusions. Yet again we stress the need to deal carefully with magnitude and importance as separate, but related issues. A plan to destroy fifty oak trees to construct a facility may be seen as most unacceptable if these are the only trees in the region; on the other hand removal of fifty such trees from a large forest may be of little consequence.

The basic reason for standardizing data rests with the argument that the standardized values will give an indication of the underlying structure in the information. If we wish to combine values for a set of criteria it is necessary that the scales be commensurate and raw data are standardized to achieve this end. There are a variety of ways to standardize raw scores and I will summarize five basic approaches. In a detailed survey of this topic Karski (1985) has referred to fourteen methods initially proposed by Langley (1974) in his work on evaluation techniques for the Department of the Environment in the UK.

Let us consider a set of five plans (A, B, C, D, E) and a single criterion, for example, jobs created. The results of the four standardization procedures are given in Table 3.1. The four procedures used to construct Table 3.1 are summarized below.

1. Raw score/sum of all scores;
2. Raw score/maximum score;
3. (Raw score minus minimum score)/(maximum score minus minimum score);
4. Raw score/√raw scores.

It should be noted that the relative positions of the plans remain unchanged; however the differences between plans depend upon the standardization procedure. This is shown in Fig. 3.3, hence if the classification procedure relies on this information then potentially the final results, which indicate the relative positions of alternative plans, is subject to the particular standardization routine which is adopted.

The maximum values in procedures 2 and 3 can be set by using hypothetical or acceptable levels and it is not obligatory to use the maximum value from the set of raw scores. The fourth procedure tends to put greater emphasis on the larger values and hence extends the scale in comparison to the results using procedure 1. The second procedure always gives a value of 1.0 for the highest level and procedure 3 scales all the observations between zero and unity. It should be noted that for the job creation criterion a high value increases the attractiveness of a plan, whereas if construction costs

Table 3.1 Results of four standardization procedures

		Raw data	1	2	3	4
Plan	A	18	0.12	0.24	0.20	0.21
	B	30	0.21	0.40	0.35	0.35
	C	20	0.14	0.27	0.22	0.24
	D	4	0.03	0.05	0.00	0.04
	E	74	0.50	1.00	1.00	0.87

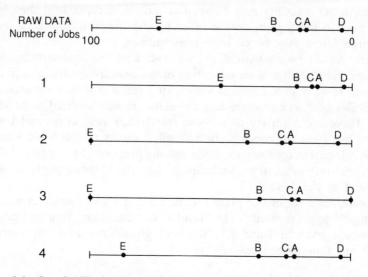

Fig. 3.3 Standardized value scales

were used the reverse would be the case. If this is the situation then the standardized scores have to be adjusted accordingly, for example by subtracting them from 1.0.

The fifth procedure uses a transformation function to convert the raw scores to a scale that ranges from zero to unity. This scale is sometimes called a 'constant worth', a 'subjective' or a 'utility' scale. The transformation function is called a function form in MATS, one of the DSS to be discussed later. An example of two function forms which could be used to derive scores using the job creation data is shown in Fig. 3.4. The linear dotted function shows a constant increase in utility as the number of jobs rises. The solid line indicates the very high utility associated with the initial increases in jobs to a level of twenty, then a decline in slope.

The matrices given in Figs. 3.1 and 3.2 focus attention on the options and begin by identifying M feasible alternatives. This is the set $\{P_1, P_2, P_i, \ldots P_M\}$. The generic planning problem seeks to find a classification of these options in order to identify their relative attractiveness, and one way of doing this is to compare them to a given standard or reference option. It is this standard which can be referred to as a benchmark plan. There are a number of different ways that we can approach the problem by defining this benchmark plan and the four most common ones are:

(a) status quo option plan;
(b) ideal best plan;
(c) hypothetical worst plan;
(d) plan of minimum satisfaction.

One way to generate benchmark plans is to seek input from each interest group, so that similarities and differences can be explored.

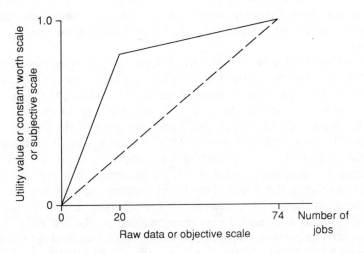

Fig. 3.4 A transformation function

In Hall's (1980) overview of some recent great planning disasters which was mentioned in Chapter 1, he pays particular attention to the fact that underestimation of costs and overestimation of benefits are the major factors which have contributed enormously to the disasters. Explicit recognition of possible errors associated with the values in the matrices may help to reduce the incidence of planning mistakes. Having said this we must try to face up to the problem of determining the errors, and perhaps the most satisfactory approach is by using a series of sensitivity tests each assuming a different amount of error. For example, we might produce a classification of the plans using information in a matrix of the style shown in Fig. 3.1 under the assumption that the estimates for the impact scores $(_jS_i)$ were perfectly accurate. Next we could modify these estimates by a given amount and examine the new classification. Estimates for the errors could be offered by technical analysis or examination of past experiences, another approach is to make arbitrary adjustments in order to identify the maximum amount of error which would be needed in order to change a classification radically. This type of sensitivity test looks at the robustness of the classification of the options. It might be the case that a small change in the score for a particular criterion could alter the relative attractiveness of the plans quite dramatically. In other cases it could be that considerable variations in the scores consistently produce the same classification.

Whenever an MCDA–DSS is used to analyse a set of data it is important to conduct a series of analyses to take account of possible errors in the impact scores. Two of the DSS that are used in the case studies discussed in Chapter 4 (MATS and PG%) contain explicit routines to undertake this kind of work. Specifically, they compare pairs of options with respect to a given criterion and examine the changes to the scores necessary to make the options equally attractive; PG% also determines the changes that must be made to a set of weights for the criteria in order to make two alternatives equally attractive. Consideration is also given to determining the effects on the attractiveness of options that result from changing the weights for the criteria.

Having made a case for sensitivity tests to deal with possible errors associated with impact scores I can continue the argument by suggesting that we should also undertake sensitivity tests for the criteria. At the outset of a facility siting exercise we may be able to define a long list of criteria which will encompass all the possible goals and objectives of the various interest groups. However, before a specific MCDA–DSS is used it is necessary to organize the criteria in a particular way. Typically there are three basic strategies for handling criteria. First, by assuming they are all of equal importance, hence the length of the list determines those criteria that will be considered in the analysis. Second, by ordering the criteria from most to least important, and third, by assigning weights to the criteria to indicate their relative importance. A variation on the second method is to divide the complete set of criteria into groups and possibly order these groups according to their importance.

In summary, before we apply a MCDA–DSS it is appropriate that we have a basic understanding of the three major components of the specific facility siting problem, and also a clear definition of the purpose of the exercise. The construction of matrices of the style shown in Figs 3.1 and 3.2 may contribute in this regard. The next step is to examine the scores in the matrices and characteristics of the constraints regarding the options as well as alternative ways of dealing with the evaluation criteria. Perhaps the most satisfactory approach to handle most of the issues relating to these is within the framework of a set of sensitivity tests. I would argue that no single MCDA–DSS should be proposed to generate the right answer, rather that the techniques should be selected to help in the classification of the three components, the generation and evaluation of the options and consideration of the implementation aspects.

3.4 Survey of MCDA–DSS techniques

In this section I will focus attention on a selection of MCDA–DSS which can be used to analyse the information in the matrices discussed in the previous section. The overall purpose of the analysis will be to deal with the generic problem that has already been posed in section 3.2. Essentially this requires that the alternative facility siting plans be classified and that this classification should be based upon the opinions of interest groups regarding the evaluation criteria and the impact scores. Obviously these criteria must be developed from and directly related to the goals and objectives of the planning exercise. Selected MCDA–DSS will be described in general terms, while recognizing that these techniques and systems can only help to organize information which must be included within a broader planning process as was discussed in section 3.1, and taking into account the concepts that will be presented in Chapters 5–7.

The MCDA–DSS that I will consider can be arranged into seven types as follows:

1. Lexicographic ordering methods;
2. Graphical approaches;
3. Consensus maximization approaches;
4. Additive models;
5. Concordance methods;
6. Mathematical programming;
7. Composite.

Each of these will be treated separately.

3.4.1 Lexicographic ordering methods

An introduction to lexicographic ordering is given in Massam (1980) and basically it assumes that the criteria can be ordered from most to least important. The site plans which satisfy the first criterion are then judged with respect to the second criterion, and if more than two options satisfy this criterion a third one is used and so on down the list until just one option is identified, and it is this one which is offered as the most satisfactory. It should be noted that a unique solution is not guaranteed. In its basic form this procedure does not allow any trade-off among criteria; in technical terms this is referred to as a non-compensatory approach. If a single site scores highly and above all others on the most important criterion, then it would be identified as the best no matter how well other sites performed for the other criteria or how badly this first one performed for the other criteria, and there could be no modification. The method seeks to identify a single best site. At first glance we might believe that a non-compensatory approach is generally an unacceptable one in site planning as compromises and trade-offs appear to characterize many facility siting choice problems. However, for some planning problems precise explicit constraints or threshold levels for criteria do exist and options which do not satisfy these have to be excluded. It might be the case that such an approach determines that no feasible planning solution exists given a particular constraint level for a specific criterion and this means that the search exercise stops, or the level has to be changed.

The cartographic sieve-mapping and overlay approaches of McHarg (1969) often involve constraint mapping and as such are a type of lexicographic ordering method. A number of geographic information systems (GIS) have been developed to undertake this sieving process. Regions or districts may be excluded from consideration as possible locations for a facility if they contain archaeological remains for example, or if they do not satisfy specific hydro-geological threshold levels no matter how attractive they are with respect to other criteria. Other similar approaches are provided by conjunctive and disjunctive models. While the former uses the principle that an alternative is rejected if the score for a particular criterion does not reach a minimum standard, the latter selects an alternative on the achievement of the highest score for a selected criterion. Details of these models are given in Hwang and Yoon (1981), Massam (1980) and Solomon and Haynes (1984). In general, in order to pose a siting problem in lexicographic terms it is necessary to have a clear strong consensus on the importance of a small number of criteria which must be satisfied, prior to the consideration of other criteria which may be traded one against another. An alternative way of posing the lexicographic problem may be to try to order the interest groups rather than the criteria, and to see if particular siting plans emerge which satisfy the highly ranked target groups. For many facility planning problems target groups can be defined as those which specifically should be helped by a plan, and these groups could head the list.

3.4.2   Graphical approaches

Information on alternative sites for a set of criteria can be summarized in graphical form in a variety of ways. Perhaps the simplest is to draw a set of graphs for pairs of criteria and to plot the alternative plans together with benchmark options. This graph can be used to identify those plans which are among the best. An example of this is shown in Fig. 3.5 in which the set of plans $\{P_1, P_5, P_3\}$ is superior to $\{P_2, P_4\}$ and can be referred to as 'efficient' plans using the language of economics. The possibility frontier joins such alternatives. In order to compare the three efficient solutions we need to know

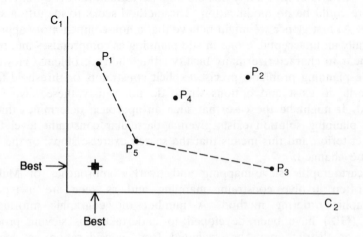

Fig. 3.5 Graphical presentation of five plans using two criteria (raw scores)

the way in which the decision-maker trades off C_1 against C_2. If we can identify the shape of the indifference curve for these two criteria, then we may be able to determine the best alternative. This approach is theoretically elegant and potentially able to handle many criteria and as such it has considerable intellectual appeal, however problems relating to the determination of the shape of indifference curves for practical choice problems militate against its widespread adoption in site plan evaluation and selection. Also there are difficulties of incorporating several interest groups and uncertainties regarding the selection of criteria and the determination of the predicted impacts.

In Fig. 3.5 the benchmark is defined by minimizing the values for the two criteria; however, potentially three other combinations may be feasible for an ideal benchmark and a set of four benchmarks is listed as follows:

Benchmark	C_1	C_2
1	Minimum	Minimum
2	Minimum	Maximum
3	Maximum	Minimum
4	Maximum	Maximum

The selection of the efficient alternatives obviously depends upon the definition of the benchmark and its position on the graph and the particular problem will dictate the appropriate definition. One further point should be stressed, namely that prior to constructing a graph it is mandatory to have interval or ratio data. As mentioned in section 3.3, ordinal data should not be used.

Casual perusal of Fig. 3.5 might suggest that P_5 is the preferred plan as it appears closest to the best benchmark. However, we cannot support this unless we know that the criteria are measured on commensurate scales. If we wish to adopt this approach then we could standardize the criteria scores and the benchmark scores, then measure the distance between each plan and the benchmark and use these distance measures to classify the alternatives. This approach has been called the technique for ordered preference by similarity to ideal solution (TOPSIS). It is discussed in some detail in Hwang and Yoon (1981) and it is incorporated into one of the DSS to be discussed later.

Recently Halfon (1989) has developed and applied a graphical procedure which depends upon use of a Hasse diagram for classifying a set of thirty-eight waste disposal sites using information on a set of thirty criteria which relate to geological and pollution characteristics. He refers to the procedure as a vectorial approach method (VAM). A Hasse diagram is commonly used in lattice theory to show connectivity and Halfon argues that this 'useful graphical tool . . . displays the ranking results and allows users to visually compare . . . sites based on thousands of test results, which might otherwise be very confusing when displayed in table form' (Halfon 1989: 600). It should be noted that VAM uses ordinal data and hence the final classification of alternatives is a ranked scale without specific information on the magnitude of the differences among the alternatives. The waste problem cited above can be envisaged as a priority problem, namely rank the sites from most to least contaminated with a view to determining the sequence for the allocation of resources to decommission them and make them safe. As a site selection issue this is the problem of finding the worst site and the one most in need of attention. Computer software to undertake VAM is available from Dr E. Halfon at the National Water Research Institute, Burlington, Ontario, Canada. Basically VAM comprises a series of steps:

Step 1. Set up a basic data matrix in the form of an options table which describes the impact scores for a set of alternate sites on a set of evaluation criteria.

Step 2. Draw a regular polygon in which each vertex represents an alternative. It is this polygon which will be manipulated to reflect the data in the options table. Figure 3.6 shows a polygon for a set of six sites.

Step 3. Compare all pairs of sites with respect to the criteria, treating the latter one at a time. Four possibilities exist for the comparisons of site i and j:

    Case A: $i = j$ for all criteria;
    Case B: i is worse than or equal to j for all criteria;
    Case C: i is better than or equal to j for all criteria;

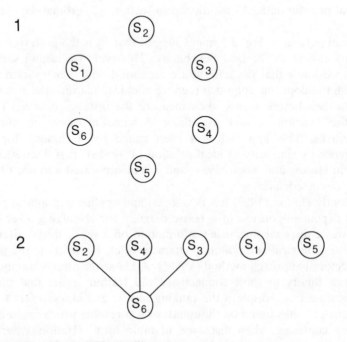

Fig. 3.6 Hypothetical Hasse diagrams

Case D: all other possibilities; the alternatives are considered incomparable.

Step 4. Draw directional arrows on the polygon between all pairs from the worse alternative to the better one.

Step 5. Delete redundant arrows that is those which contain information which is completely included by other paths.

Step 6. Reorient the polygon to place the best alternative at the bottom of the diagram. This is the Hasse diagram.

Step 7. Consider the issue of incomparability, noting that alternatives may fall into this category if the scores for the evaluation criteria are in conflict. Such alternatives stand apart from the linked polygon and as such the final figure can take the form of a hierarchy. A hypothetical example is shown in Fig. 3.6, with four sites in a hierarchy and two sites outside. Sites S_2, S_4 and S_3 are equally attractive and inferior to S_6, while S_5 and S_1 cannot be compared to the others.

Step 8. Interpret the final graphical output in the context of the initial siting problem. This a critical step and one that the software is not capable of making.

An empirical facility siting problem which was tackled using Halfon's VAM is given in Chapter 4.

3.4.3 Consensus maximization approaches

Over 200 years ago Borda (1781) and Condorcet (1785) began the formal search for a procedure to aggregate individual preferences for a set of alternatives into a group consensus. While their concern was to consider a set of alternative candidates in an electoral process the generality of their problem is immediately apparent for it lies at the heart of collective choice. There have been a number of useful reviews of this literature, for example Fishburn (1971, 1974), Richelson (1978) and Cook and Kress (1984). In order to provide some organization to this literature in this chapter I will arrange the material under three headings which will allow us to move from the earliest simplistic approaches to more recent analytical work which is based on an axiomatic approach. I will also examine one of the basic algorithms and indicate some problem areas. The three headings are:

1 Borda–Kendall method;
2 Cook and Seiford distance method;
3 Some problem areas.

In Chapters 6 and 7 the topics of collective choice and consensus will be addressed more completely as complementary to the material presented in this section.

3.4.3.1 Borda–Kendall method

If we have information on a set of alternative sites presented as an ordered set of preferences for interest groups as shown on matrix 1 in Fig. 3.1, then one way of deriving the consensus ranking of the plans is to sum the 'ranks' assigned to each plan by each interest group. It is implicit in this procedure that the ordering of the preferences is an interval scale of integers from 1 to M, if there are M plans. The term 'rank' is often used though strictly speaking we should not use it as we are conducting arithmetic operations with the numbers and assuming that the scale in fact has cardinal properties. This approach has been referred to as *average ranking* by Hwang and Yoon (1981).

Cook and Seiford (1982) claim that Kendall (1962) was the first to study this ordering problem within a statistical framework using the notion of an estimation for the true ordering on the basis of the individual estimates provided by the separate interest groups. Intuitively this is not too satisfactory as each group is in fact concerned only with its own view and hence the idea that all groups have a common goal lacks credibility. Kendall's solution to the ordering problem is to use the sum of the 'ranks'. This is the same approach offered by Borda and hence this procedure now bears the title the Borda–Kendall (B–K) method. It is widely used because of its basic simplicity yet because it appeared to be *ad hoc* and lacking a solid theoretical foundation it has not enjoyed great respect among analysts. Critics have suggested that the preferred approach for deriving a consensus should satisfy the basic axioms of collective choice theory as enunciated by Arrow (1951). One of Arrow's axioms deals with pairwise determination and this requires that society's ranking of any pair of alternative plans depends only on the individuals' rankings of these two alternatives. The way an individual rates another alternative should not bias the comparison of the two under consideration. This axiom is sometimes referred to as the irrelevant alternative axiom. Further details of this axiom are provided by Massam (1988a).

3.4.3.2 Cook and Seiford distance method

Let me now consider the consensus problem more explicitly by examining the Cook and Seiford distance measure and the sample data they used. They examine a matrix of the style shown in Table 3.2. The data in Table 3.2 can be converted into a square (5×5) distance matrix in the following way. The distance, d_{11}, is given by

$$d_{11} = |\ 1-1\ | + |\ 4-1\ | + |\ 3-1\ | + \ldots + |\ 3-1\ | = 13$$
$$d_{21} = |\ 4-1\ | + |\ 3-1\ | + |\ 2-1\ | + \ldots + |\ 4-1\ | = 21$$
$$d_{55} = |\ 2-5\ | + |\ 2-5\ | + |\ 1-5\ | + \ldots + |\ 5-5\ | = 20$$

to give the following matrix as shown in Table 3.3. Table 3.3 can be used in

Table 3.2 Ordered preference matrix: 10 interest groups: 5 plans

	I_1	I_2	I_3	I_4	I_5	I_6	I_7	I_8	I_9	I_10
P_1	1	4	3	1	2	1	4	1	3	3
P_2	4	3	2	4	5	4	1	3	1	4
P_3	3	1	5	2	4	3	5	4	5	2
P_4	5	5	4	5	1	2	3	2	4	1
P_5	2	2	1	3	3	5	2	5	2	5

I_1–I_{10}: interest groups; P_1–P_5: alternative plans;
1, 2, . . . 5: ordered preferences, 1 is best.

Source: Cook and Seiford (1984).

Table 3.3 Distance matrix

13	11	11	17	27
21	15	11	11	19
24	16	12	12	16
22	16	14	14	18
20	12	12	16	20

Source: Cook and Seiford (1984).

Table 3.4 Assignment matrix

	Priorities				
	1	**2**	**3**	**4**	**5**
P_1	*(13)				
P_2			*(11)		
P_3				*(12)	
P_4					*(18)
P_5		*(12)			

* indicates the priority or position of each plan; the values in parentheses are taken from Table 3.3.

Source: Cook and Seiford (1984).

an assignment algorithm to find the total distance associated with any ordering of the five sites, and hence we can try to find the ordering which gives the smallest distance. The distance matrix can be viewed as an assignment matrix as shown in Table 3.4.

The order of the sites shown in Table 3.4 from most to least preferred is P_1, P_5, P_2, P_3, P_4 and the total distance, expressed as a dimensionless number, for this order is 66. This is the minimum value, however it is not a unique order. The following order P_1, P_5, P_3, P_2, P_4 is also given by Cook and Seiford as having a distance value of 66. The order P_1, P_5, P_2, P_4, P_3 is given using concordance analysis (this approach is discussed later in this section) and this too has a value of 66. Any other order has a larger value;

therefore Cook and Seiford conclude that the consensus or compromise ordering is given by the minimum distance assignment. This is conventionally referred to as the median ranking.

3.4.3.3 Some problem areas

There are two problems associated with the material just discussed. First, while the median ranking gives an optimum solution to the distance-minimizing type of consensus problem it is less satisfactory if we examine the results in terms of the opinions of the interest groups. This is an important practical matter if we are concerned with finding the site which is acceptable to a majority of the interest groups. Second, the results of using a distance measure are likely to be treated sceptically as the consensus measure is a dimensionless number and the distance techniques appear to be at arm's length to a planning process which typically involves estimation of preferences as merely starting points in a framework of bargaining and negotiation.

3.4.4 Additive models

Perhaps the largest single collection of MCDA–DSS are subsumed within this category of models. In general the additive models (often referred to as compensatory models), seek to reduce the site evaluation and selection problem to one in which each of the alternatives is classified using a single score which represents the attractiveness or utility of a site. The selection of a preferred one is based upon these scores. Hwang and Yoon (1981: 99) suggest that the 'simple additive weighting (SAW) method is probably the best known and very widely used method of MCDM'. While we might contest the legitimacy of using a simple additive function for combining impacts in order to obtain a single value for each alternative plan it has been argued by Hwang and Yoon (1981: 103) that 'theory, simulation, computations, and experience all suggest that the SAW method yields extremely close approximations to very much more complicated non-linear forms, while remaining far easier to use and understand'.

For those who rely on the use of SAW to tackle a site selection problem it is most important that clear recognition of the potential errors be incorporated into the study, and specifically that sensitivity tests be run as part of the analysis. Solomon and Haynes (1984: 74) also conclude that while there are a variety of models for accumulating impacts into a final score, 'the use of the simple weighting summation model is probably justified'. It is the use of a formal single dimensionless number which causes some problems for anyone who wishes to use the results and participate in a debate which involves compromises, trade-offs and a discussion of impacts in terms of jobs, houses, costs, environmental damage and the like. The aggregation of impacts across a wide range of variables is worrying to practising planners. Some argue that the worth of a particular site is not a simple additive function of the worth of the various components or even a readily identifiable multiplicative function, for that matter. This is stressed in a paper by Roy and Bouyssou (1986). In philosophical terms we are reminded of the debate propounded by Moore in *Principia Ethica* when he argued that 'the worth of what he termed an organic whole bears no regular proportion to the sum of the values of its parts'. In particular, 'the value of the whole must not be assumed to be the same as the sum of the values of its parts' (Rosenbaum 1975: 127). Yet this concern does not seem to hinder the development of the additive models. However, we can observe that there appears to be limited dialogue between theoreticians and practitioners in this area. Perhaps this will change as more co-operative work is undertaken as suggested earlier in this chapter.

In order to strengthen our position if we wish to defend the use of a simple additive model the following two conditions should be satisfied. These conditions were introduced in Chapter 2. First, that preferences for, or the trade-off, for pairs of criteria, for example C_1 and C_2, should be *preferentially independent* of fixed levels for any other criteria, for example C_3. Second, that C_1, for example, should be *utility independent* of the other criteria. Intuitively these conditions are appealing, however very rarely are they verified prior to the application of an additive model. One case of verification is given by Keeney and Nair (1977) in their study on the use of a set of six criteria for evaluating nine alternative sites for a nuclear power plant in the Pacific north-west of the USA. They use a multi-attribute utility model.

The utility model uses an expected value criterion (EVC) for judging the worth of a particular site and this approach can be criticized on the grounds that the alternatives are presented just once for evaluation. Radford (1980) puts the point succinctly as follows:

[EVC is] Generally agreed to be appropriate in decision problems that are repeated many times in exactly the same form. Choice of the course of action that gives the greatest average benefit is intuitively accepted under these circumstances. However, the use of EVC is less readily acceptable in a single occurrence of a decision situation involving uncertainty.

The basic procedure for most types of additive model can be summarized as a set of six steps as follows:

Step 1. Define the set of sites $S_1 \ldots S_M$. Define the set of interest groups $I_1 \ldots I_L$. Define the set of criteria $C_1 \ldots C_N$.

Step 2. Obtain impact values for the criteria, for each site and convert the raw data into standardized values using function forms or other normalization procedures. The opinions of the interest groups can be used to obtain the function forms.

Step 3. Determine the precise way in which the standardized values are aggregated to give a final utility value for each site. The opinions of the interest groups can be used to obtain the relative weights for the criteria.

Step 4. Determine the utility value for each site.

Step 5. Undertake a series of sensitivity tests to examine the effects on the utility values of altering in a systematic way:

  (i) the alternative sites to be considered;

  (ii) the set of criteria to be considered;

  (iii) the accuracy of the raw data;;

  (iv) the function forms for each criterion;

  (v) the weights for the criteria, and the function which is used to accumulate the scores for the criteria into a final score for each site.

Step 6. Justify the sensitivity tests in the context of the planning exercise and the negotiation framework and the legal processes, write reports and summarize results in terms of the distribution of costs and benefits and present the perspectives of each of the interest groups. Avoid using dimensionless numbers. Incorporate the results into the larger planning process and repeat steps if necessary.

It should be remembered that this sequence is cyclical and while it appears rigid in its formal presentation, in fact practical applications demand that it be rather loosely defined so that the exercise might in fact begin at step 2 when a particular interest group, acting as a proponent, brings forward a specific site for a particular type of public facility. While all steps are important, it is step 6 which needs great care in order to establish the legitimacy and credibility of the whole exercise. Without this step the earlier ones tend to operate *in vacuo*, and it will not contribute to a debate which considers accountability and consensus as two of the important elements in effective collective choice which yields acceptable sites for public facilities.

Formal additive procedures that have recently been developed include:

1. Simple multi-attribute rating technique (SMART);
2. Multi-attribute trade off system (MATS);
3. Planning assistance through technical evaluation of relevance numbers (PATTERN);
4. Probabilistic linear vector analysis (PROLIVAN);
5. Saaty's analytical hierarchy procedure (AHP);
6. Nagel's policy/goal percentaging (PG%).

Edwards (1971) formally presented SMART and it is closely related to the multi-attribute utility approach that has been applied by Keeney (1972) and the earlier work of Raiffa (1968). Gardiner and Edwards (1975: 13) suggest that SMART 'is oriented not towards mathematical sophistication or intimacy of relation between underlying formal structures and the practical procedures that implement them but rather towards easy communication and use in environments in which time is short and decision makers are multiple and busy'. These are indeed commendable realistic goals, but the optimism is tempered by their recognition that 'at present, we know of no public context in which even limited experimentation with the methods we advocate is occurring. But we have hopes.' (Gardiner and Edwards 1975: 36) Two years later Edwards (1977) reported a small set of planning problems that could be treated using SMART. This slow diffusion of a methodology has been recognized and an initiative of a US public agency to develop and promote a computerized system called MATS is under way to enhance planning practices.

Brown and Valenti (1983) developed MATS in the Environmental and Social Branch of the Division of Planning Technical Services Engineering and Research Center at the Bureau of Reclamation in the US Department of the Interior. Attempts are under way to disseminate the procedure to US agencies to encourage its widespread incorporation into public planning exercises. Other jurisdictions, for example Ontario are now beginning to use MATS to help inform the debate on facility siting.

With respect to PATTERN, the impacts are scored from 0 to 1, as are the weights. A final score for each plan is determined by summing the weighted impact values. A critique of PATTERN as applied to a site planning problem for a marina at Dow's Lake, Ottawa is provided in Massam (1986). This paper clearly makes the case for incorporating sensitivity tests into the analysis. The procedure PROLIVAN relies on the calculation of scores for each alternative plan using a simple weighted model, but errors for the scores are also included so that in the final presentation of the utility scores for each plan confidence limits are defined. A typical example in given in Fig. 3.7.

If we compare the four plans in Fig. 3.7 using the mean scores it would

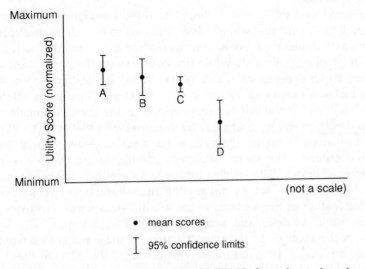

Fig. 3.7 Typical examples of results of PROLIVAN: four alternative plans (A, B, C, D)

appear that A is the best, followed by C, B and D. However, when we consider that measurement errors for the impacts could have occurred, then the overlaps among plans A, B and C suggest they are all very similar in terms of overall utility. Plan D appears to be the least preferred.

Details of AHP are given in Saaty (1980) and basically for a single decision-maker a pairwise comparison matrix of the criteria is set up and the weights for the criteria are determined by using the normalized principal eigenvector. An example of a pairwise comparison matrix was given in Fig. 2.2. Next, for each criterion a pairwise matrix of the alternate plans is established and for each plan a score is calculated, again using the normalized principal eigenvector. A final score for each plan is calculated by summing the weighted values for the set of criteria. The plans can then be ordered using these scores. Typically a nine-point scale for the pairwise comparisons is used, a score of 1 indicates the two alternatives or criteria are equally important while a score of 9 indicates that the first alternative or criterion is clearly and strongly, in fact, exceedingly, preferred to the second. Debate continues about the use of this scale to represent comparisons among pairs of alternatives and criteria, as well as the validity of the underlying axioms of Saaty's method. In 1990 the editor of *Management Science* noted in a comment on Saaty's procedure that 'both sides [proponents and opponents] have taken great pains, to explain their respective positions to each other, and, as the reader can see, the result has not been consensus . . . now it is up to readers to form their own judgements'. The positions of the two sides are represented by the proponents, Saaty (1990) and Harker and Vargas (1990) in answer to the criticisms of Dyer (1990). The views of Vargas contradict the opinion of Shim (1989) which was referred to in Chapter 2 in his enthusiastic appraisal of Saaty's method.

Nagel developed PG% in an attempt to offer a straightforward piece of user-friendly software that would allow decisions to be made more easily by demanding that planning goals and scores for a set of alternatives and weights be explicitly defined. While his focus was on the application of the procedure to legal decisions it clearly has broad application and could be used to tackle a facility siting problem. A brief introduction is offered in Nagel (1986) and elaborations are provided in the user's manual: *Teach Yourself Decision-Aiding Software*, by Nagel (1989, 1990). With PG%, a user can evaluate a set of alternatives on a set of goals – these are the evaluation criteria. The scores are made commensurate by converting all values to percentages. The weights for the goals are included in the additive model to generate a set of values for the alternatives. A particularly interesting feature of PG% concerns the use of two types of sensitivity tests. First, threshold analysis and second, convergence analysis. The former determines the changes to the impact scores or the weights that would be necessary to make two alternatives equivalent. In MATS there is a sensitivity test that will conduct the first part of this, namely the determination of impact scores. Convergence analysis 'shows the level at which the weight assigned to a goal becomes sufficiently high to produce results that are close [the definition is given by the user, 5% for example] to those which would occur if that goal were the only one considered' (Nagel, 1986: 91). This inclusion of sensitivity tests is very important, as has been mentioned earlier.

3.4.5 Concordance methods

In July 1966, Roy, Sussman and Benayoun presented a highly significant paper in Rome at a study session on Methods of Calculation in the Social Sciences. At the time this research team was associated with SEMA-METRA in Paris, France and they were seeking to use their formal training in mathematics to develop tools that could be used to tackle practical multi-criteria choice problems. Their work was based upon a systematic analysis of the relationship between all pairs of a finite set of options using information about the impact scores for each option on a set of criteria. Data on the relative importance of the criteria were needed in the formal procedure they developed. The procedure sought to measure the dominance of one option over another with a view to identifying the option which outranked the others. The terms 'outranking' or 'concordance methods' are now generally used to refer to many of the techniques which have grown from this seminal work. The method they offered was christened ELECTRE and Roy, Sussman and Benayoun (1966) referred to it as elimination and choice translating reality. It was based upon the derivation and manipulation of two indices, first, a concordance index and second, a discordance index. Details are given in Massam (1988a).

The diffusion of ELECTRE to other parts of the world has been slow despite the fact that Hwang and Yoon (1981: 127) consider 'the ELECTRE method to be one of the best methods because of its simple logic, full utilization of information contained in the decision matrix, and refined computational procedure'. However, this optimistic view is tempered by the opinions of Cook *et al.* (1988: 910) who conclude that 'while concordance methods do provide a valuable framework within which to examine multi-criteria problems, the subjective nature of project ratings, weights and thresholds represent serious concerns from a reliability standpoint'.

Roy and Bouyssou (1986: 212) admit that ELECTRE 'has no axiomatic basis, and consequently it is often difficult to interpret certain parameters used in it', however they add that 'only considerations based on common sense allow the decision-maker and the analyst to give them a numerical value'. The role of intuition and professional judgement is clearly recognized, but we are left with some difficulties when faced with the task of improving accountability if we rely solely on judgement. Vincke (1986: 164) notes that 'there is no doubt that there is a lack of basic theory for this approach and, in our opinion, this is one of the reasons for the reservations expressed by some theoreticians (in the United States and Europe)'. The method appears to be something of a black box with too many arbitrary decisions.

An evaluation of the relative merits of concordance analysis compared to Hill's (1968) goals achievement matrix and a compromise solution method developed by Zeleny (1982) has been made by Won (1990) with respect to comparing urban transportation projects. He concludes that all three approaches have merit to assist decision-makers, as a wide range of impacts can be included and qualitative data are incorporated. Interestingly the final comment of Won reminds us of the vital necessity to link the MCDA–DSS to the goals and objectives of the planning exercise and the need to incorporate the formal analysis into the existing planning process. Won considers that: 'The linkage to overall planning process is weak in the Concordance Analysis and the Compromise Solution while the philosophical basis of the Goals Achievement Matrix is more suitable for the overall planning process.' (Won 1990: 137)

3.4.6 Mathematical programming

In the 1980s a family of DSS called dynamic interactive decision analysis and support (DIDAS) based on mathematical programming was developed at the International Institute for Applied Systems Analysis in Laxenburg, Austria. The objective of these systems is to support the generation and evaluation of a set of alternatives using interactions with one or more decision-makers who can systematically examine a substantive model of the decision situation and who might change their preferences and priorities during the decision-making process. The DIDAS systems are designed to tackle a variety of multi-objective decision-making problems, including facility siting ones. In general, the problem is solved by a feedback exchange of information between an analyst and a decision-maker. Many methods are available for interactive solution of the multi-objective decision-making problem and a useful review of these methods is provided by Seo and Sakawa (1988). The DIDAS systems are based on a mathematical programming structure and the reference point approach developed by Wierzbicki (1982), which combines the well-known goal programming methodology and the method of the displaced ideal after the work of Zeleny (1976). The basic idea behind the reference point method can be described as follows:

1. The decision-maker is expected to specify reference values for each objective function under consideration;
2. Modifications to the values can be made interactively as a result of learning and a better understanding of the problem during the solution process;

3. This interactive process is continued until an ultimate compromise or satisficing solution is determined as acceptable.

One of the most suitable DSS for the solution of a location problem is the dynamic interactive and network analysis system (DINAS). Full mathematical details of the algorithms used in DINAS are provided in the paper by Ogryczak *et al.* (1988). Originally DINAS was designed to solve a class of transhipment problems among demand and supply points structured on a network of nodes and arcs. Coefficients are assigned to the arcs and nodes and they can be treated as objective functions which are to be minimized.

Taking into account the general structure of the network model, the decision-making problem can be defined as follows: determine the number, the location and the sizes of facilities (nodes) to be selected from a set of given potential nodes, and find the flows from the fixed nodes to the facilities so as to optimize a set of objective functions given a set of constraints. This problem is usually expressed in a mathematical form as a substantive model of the decision-making situation and then it is used in an interactive procedure.

Depending on the decision-making context the general structure of the model can be modified and the problem can be solved using DINAS. A discussion on the application of DINAS to tackle public facility location problems is given by Malczewski (1991) who focuses on an empirical problem concerning the location of paediatric hospitals in Warsaw while taking into account accessibility factors and environmental effects especially those concerning air pollution. Further work on the use of DINAS for tackling a hospital location problem in Warsaw is reported in Malczewski (1990) and Malczewski and Ogryczak (1990).

The multi-objective solution of a decision-making problem is obtained in two stages:

1. In the first stage the decision-maker is provided with some initial information in the form of an options table. This gives an overview of the problem. These data are converted to a pay-off matrix or a decision matrix which is generated by minimization or maximization of each of the objective functions (criteria) separately. This matrix provides the basis for the identification of the reference points or vectors. On the basis of the pay-off matrix the user (analyst) can define the ideal or Utopia vector (f_i) and the nadir vector (f_n). The vector f_i is usually not attainable in reality, but it is presented to the decision-maker as a lower limit to the numerical values of the objectives, which are minimized or is presented as an upper limit if the objective functions are maximized. Thus, after the first stage of the analysis, the decision-maker is provided with information on the solution space for each objective function.

2. In the second stage of the multi-objective analysis an interactive selection of a compromise or satisficing solution is made. The decision-maker controls the selection by two vectors: an aspiration level (f_a) and

a reservation level (f_r); in the case of minimization $f_i < f_a < f_r < f_n$ and if an objective function is maximized $f_i > f_a > f_r > f_n$.

Thus DINAS searches for the satisficing solution, while using a linear normalized function as the criterion in a single objective optimization; or to be more precise, the system minimizes the maximum deviation of the results from the decision-maker's expectations with respect to the objectives under consideration. The values of this function depend upon the aspiration (f_a) and reservation (f_r) levels previously specified by the decision-maker. The obtained value is an efficient, that is a Pareto-optimal, solution to the original multi-objective model, i.e. the substantive model of the decision-maker as a current solution. Then, the decision-maker can judge the solution as acceptable or unacceptable. If it is found to be unsatisfactory then new aspiration and/or reservation levels can be entered for all or some of the objectives. Depending on this new information supplied by the decision-maker a new efficient solution is computed and presented as a current solution. This process is repeated until a final compromise solution is deemed acceptable to the decision-maker.

Another attempt to use mathematical programming is provided by the work of Bernardo and Blin (1977) who have developed an approach for classifying a set of options using ordinal information on a set of evaluation criteria. They have structured the problem as a linear assignment problem which can be written in the form of a classic linear program. Details of the algorithm are given in Hwang and Yoon (1981: 98), where it is referred to as a linear assignment method (LAM). They argue that LAM 'eliminate[s] the tedious requirements of the existing compensatory models; e.g. the rather lengthy procedures of 'tradeoff' analysis are not required'. But they go on to say, almost in a contradictory fashion, that 'Even though lengthy data gathering effort is eliminated, the method does satisfy the compensatory hypothesis . . .'. In the light of such assertions it is likely that LAM is not an especially credible MCDA–DSS.

In general terms the mathematical programming approaches, while technically highly sophisticated, are less likely to be accepted by decision-makers than other approaches which have simple algorithms. Further the computer software, for DINAS for example, is not readily comprehensible to a user compared, for example, to DAS or AIM, as discussed in the next section, or MATS.

3.4.7 Composite

A number of attempts have been made to combine a selection of techniques and systems to produce composite models or integrated approaches. I will refer to two recent efforts. First, an eclectic approach which has been developed by Lofti, Stewart and Zionts (1989) under the title of an aspiration-level interactive model (AIM). A brief review is given in Lofti (1989). Basically,

> It [AIM] assumes that the user has a set of alternatives with each alternative having a score on each of a number of objectives or measures of performance. The user determines his levels of aspirations for different objectives [criteria] in an interactive computer environment in which he is given considerable feedback as to the degree of feasibility of each level of aspiration as well as the degree of feasibility with respect to all levels of aspiration as a whole. (Lofti, Stewart and Zionts, 1989: 1)

One consequence of using the concept of aspiration levels for objectives (or criteria) after the ideas of Wierzbicki (1982) is that it is not necessary to stipulate specific weights for the criteria to indicate their relative importance. The user is provided by the system with ideal and nadir levels for the impact scores for each criterion. In this way we know the upper and lower limits within which we should define the aspiration levels. If the aspiration level is very close to the ideal value, for a particular criterion, then this can be interpreted to mean that the user assigns a high level of importance to this criterion. Specifically an operational definition of weight is derived from this assumption, namely

$$W_i = (A_i - N_i)/(I_i - N_i)$$
where, W_i is the weight for criterion i ($i = 1,2,3, \ldots, n$), A_i the aspiration level for criterion i, I_i the ideal level for criterion i and N_i the nadir level for criterion i.

Given the weight for each criterion, AIM provides the user with the nearest non-dominated solution to the specified aspiration levels. This solution is generated on the basis of an achievement scalarizing function that minimizes the maximum deviation between the specified aspiration goals and the outcome. This procedure is discussed by Wierzbicki (1982) and it is used in DINAS.

As a starting point in the analysis using AIM the aspiration levels can be set to the ideal levels, and this ensures that all the criteria are considered as equally important. Modification of the aspiration levels can be made in a systematic fashion so that for each set of values the alternative location which is closest to the aspired goals is identified.

The software that Lofti (1989) describes is easy to use, and even though only a set of ten evaluation criteria can be accommodated the use of such software in training sessions and workshops with facility planners can help to organize the debate on the development of a traceable process.

Hwang and Yoon (1981) have reviewed a large number of multi-criteria decision-making techniques and they have offered a unified approach that begins with an options table and then an analysis based on dominance and threshold levels. The former identifies the sub-set of options which are equal or inferior to other options, and the latter searches for options that fall below threshold levels for each criterion. These levels are defined by the user. Following these two preliminary steps the data in the matrix are analysed using the following four different approaches.

1. Linear assignment method (LAM);
2. Simple additive weighting method (SAW);
3. Elimination and choice translating reality (ELECTRE);
4. Technique for ordered preference by similarity to ideal solution (TOPSIS).

Four classifications of the options are provided and then three methods are used to seek the consensus ordering of the options. First, mean ranks are calculated. Comments on the weakness of this approach have been made earlier in this chapter. Second, the Borda method is used to determine the number of times one option is superior to another, and third the Copeland (1951) method which subtracts from the Borda value the number of times an option is inferior. The three consensus orderings are then analysed to determine the partially ordered set (POSET) following the ideas of Dushnik and Miller (1941) and this yields a final ordering of the options from the most to least attractive. A computer program that undertakes all this analysis is available from Armada Systems, Toronto, Canada. This piece of software is marketed under the title decision analysis system (DAS). Both of these composite approaches will be applied to the empirical data in Chapter 4.

3.5 How useful is a particular MCDA–DSS?

In order to try to provide some guidelines for anyone who is concerned with trying to answer this question it is worth beginning with a brief statement of the fundamental aims of MCDA–DSS. I have organized them into a set of six categories as follows; namely the main aims are to help:

1. Identify and organize data on alternative sites and the set of criteria (which relate to the goals and objectives of the planning exercise) which will be used to evaluate, assess and compare alternatives.
2. Identify the characteristics of an ideal, acceptable or benchmark alternative against which the set of feasible alternatives can be judged.
3. Classify in a systematic fashion the set of alternatives using information about the estimated impacts on the evaluation criteria and preference data regarding the relative importance of the criteria.
4. Undertake sensitivity tests to accommodate alternative preferences and opinions of interest groups concerning the definitions of the set of alternatives, the evaluation criteria and the estimation of the impact scores.

5. Improve accountability of the planning process by ensuring that the assumptions about the facility siting problem are clearly defined, the methodology is logically consistent and that the technical processes can be traced, thus guaranteeing that the whole exercise can be replicated and that it can be scrutinized publicly.

6. Assist in the systematic determination of mitigation devices and compensation levels as part of a legitimate planning milieu which seeks to build co-operation among those who enjoy benefits or suffer costs by virtue of their proximity to the particular facility, whether it be of the noxious or salutary variety.

Moving from this set of general purposes I offer a list of ten questions which, if answered positively, when applied to a specific MCDA–DSS, could serve to identify its degree of utility.

1. Can the MCDA–DSS be incorporated into the existing planning process?
2. Are the data readily available?
3. Can new data be added easily?
4. Can sensitivity tests be conducted expeditiously?
5. Is the internal logic acceptable?
6. Do users understand the technique or system?
7. Can the results be displayed to non-experts?
8. Is sophisticated technology needed to make the technique or system operational?
9. Is it expensive?
10. Is the technique or system credible and can it be used to teach, complement and improve professional experience, judgement and intuition?

However, it should be made clear that no matter how many positive responses may be given, ultimately the credibility of MCDA–DSS for helping to tackle specific facility siting problems rests with their acceptability by individuals in key positions, and their demonstrated worth in assisting to avoid making siting mistakes, while at the same time ensuring that their use does not disturb too drastically existing practices and procedures which have evolved in a specific jurisdiction. Nobody in a key position likes to hear of a new technique or system which will make them redundant. No such claim should be made about MCDA–DSS, and it is therefore appropriate that case studies be made available and that workshops with key personnel be organized to help build up credibility.

Finally, we should remember that in its broadest sense every computer-based system which processes a set of information can be classified as a DSS. The purpose of such a system is to help managers to achieve better decisions. By better it is suggested that decisions could be reached faster, probably using extensive data sets and within a framework which allows sensitivity tests, and most particularly so that results can be scrutinized and replicated. The essence is to avoid the black box style of plan evaluation and selection. It should be emphasized that MCDA–DSS does not replace the judgements of decision-makers, rather it provides a computer-based planning tool which seeks to achieve a higher effectiveness of decision-making. This point is discussed in Keen and Scott-Morton (1978). To improve the effectiveness of decision-making we should incorporate into the planning process two elements: first, a substantive model of the decision situation or a decision-making model which is formulated by a team of analysts or a single analyst, and second, the participation of the decision-makers, which I have already referred to as the interest groups or publics, who are directly concerned with implementing the solution to a planning problem; they provide the judgemental information, in the form of preferences, about the significance of impacts, which cannot be expressed *a priori* in a formal language and are therefore excluded from the analyst's initial model. It is argued that these two elements are the integral parts of any facility site planning process. In this context, it is important to be aware that it is often argued that the concept of rationality underlies all decision-making or optimization model-building. This is elaborated in Chapter 6 on choice.

It is often assumed that there is a decision-maker or a group of decision-makers who behave according to coherent and optimal rules. Consequently, an optimization model could be used for the solution of well-structured planning problems. In reality, however, society almost always faces a semi-structured or ill-structured problem and the analyst's model is only a first approximation of the real-world facility siting problem. In particular, the less tangible aspects of the problem are often neglected in the formal approach and it seems that the best way to incorporate these aspects is to involve in the planning process the decision-makers who are ultimately responsible for implementation and those who are accountable to a defined constituency. A suitable MCDA–DSS incorporates both the model formalized by the analysts and the judgemental aspects of the problem that can be supplied to the system by the decision-makers.

A summary of the variety of MCDA–DSS which have been used to tackle siting problems is given in Table 3.5, and in Chapter 4 I offer two detailed case studies. Overall it is argued that MCDA–DSS have a useful role to play in tackling collective choice public facility siting problems, not least of all because they force stakeholders to try to classify goals, objectives, impacts and trade-offs in ways that can be scrutinized. This should contribute towards improved accountability.

Table 3.5 Applications of MCDA–DSS: selected examples

Author/date	Problem/data	MCDA–DSS
Rivett (1977); Massam and Askew (1982)	Given 24 policies and 5 criteria, find the best policy for the hypothetical town of Brove	1. Structural mapping – a multi-dimension scaling approach 2. Utility scores – additive approach using standardized scores 3. Lexicographic ordering 4. Factor analysis leading to a graphical presentation
Marchet and Siskos (1979); Massam (1982)	Given a set of 58 zones find the best alignment for a highway using impact scores for 4 criteria for each zone which links 2 towns at each end of the set of zones	1. Additive utility approaches using function forms to standardize the impacts and determine the criteria weights 2. ELECTRE
Odum *et al.* (1976); Massam and Skelton (1986)	Find the best route for interstate highway I–75 through part of Georgia, USA, given 8 possible alignments and 56 criteria, also long and short-term weights for the criteria.	1. MATS, using three different types of function form 2. PROLIVAN, using random errors for the estimates of the impact scores for the criteria
Jaakson (1984); Massam (1986)	Find the best plan for a marina development given 3 alternatives (including the status quo), 3 interest groups and 5 criteria. Impact scores were provided	1. PATTERN: an additive approach using standardized values for the criteria
Keeney and Nair (1977); Roy and Bouyssou (1986)	Classify 9 locations using 6 criteria for a nuclear power plant	1. MAUT 2. ELECTRE III
Brans, Vincke and Mareschal (1986)	Classify 6 locations using 6 criteria for a hydroelectric power station	1. PROMETHEE (preference ranking organization for enrichment evaluations) 2. ELECTRE III
Roy, Present and Silhol (1986)	Given 7 criteria and 224 options (Metro stations), order the options to prepare a repair schedule	1. ELECTRE III

4

Two case studies: health care facilities in Zambia, waste sites in Ashdod, Israel

4.1 A perspective on case studies

The last chapter offered a review and a critique of MCDA–DSS, stressing their relevance in helping to define options, goals and objectives and relate these systematically to impacts and opinions of stakeholders as part of a process of collective choice which seeks to find acceptable locations for public facilities. In this chapter I will consider two specific facility siting problems and for each a selection of MCDA–DSS will be applied to small sets of data. The first problem deals with the search for locations for primary health care facilities in a large rural region in Zambia. The second study focuses on waste management, and specifically it is concerned with the problem of selecting sites for waste transfer stations in the city of Ashdod, Israel. Whereas the first problem can be considered as one that deals with a salutary facility, the second provides an example of a noxious facility. Each problem is characterized by a set of feasible alternative sites and a set of criteria which will be used to evaluate the options. These two studies are examples of site selection problems which can be viewed as just one type of public facility siting problem. In more general terms a fuller range of generic problems would include:

1. Site selection problems (SSP);
2. Route alignment problems (RAP);
3. Priority rating problems (PRP).

Details of these are discussed in Massam (1988a).

I suggest that these problems cover a full range of public facility site planning issues which are currently being addressed in urban and rural areas of both the developed and developing world, in states with a wide variety of styles of regulations and practices. A centralized strong political system is unlikely to engage in a protracted public debate on the merits of a number of different options in order to provide an environment for consensus. This point has been made very strongly by Ambrose (1986) in his appraisal of the situation in the UK which he argues is highly centralized and has moved some way from a consensual system. The changes in the UK towards a Regulatory State have been discussed in Chapter 1 and the Preface, and in Chapter 7 specific comments on consensus will be presented. Another jurisdiction may place emphasis on the role of public hearings, participation by interest groups, as well as the encouragement of a full range of technical studies in order to move toward a consensual solution to a controversial planning problem. For example, in Ontario, Canada, the Ontario Waste Management Corporation (OWMC) was created in 1981 with 'a primary responsibility to design, construct and operate a province-wide system for the treatment and disposal of liquid industrial and hazardous waste, and to develop a long-term program to assist in the reduction and recycling of such wastes' (OWMC 1985: 1). While the Act creating the OWMC does not explicitly mention consensus, observation of the planning process engaged in by this Crown corporation, especially with respect to its search for an appropriate site or sites for a major waste treatment facility, suggests that participation of interest groups and incorporation of their views into the decision-making process is a key element of the process.

Let me now turn to the three generic problems mentioned earlier. The first two are usually fairly well defined and explicit; for example, the task may be to find a new location for a public facility such as a fire station, a clinic, a school or a waste disposal plant. The route alignment problem can cover a number of transportation and communication examples, including highways, railways, and other mass transit systems, pipelines and power-line corridors. Seen within a narrow context each of these problems can potentially be defined as an evaluation exercise of a set of feasible alternatives compared to the status quo. However, within a broader context we must include the generation of the options, the actions of interest groups over time, the influence of the bureaucracy or agency that is handling the planning exercise and the social, political and economic climate of the jurisdiction within which the problem is being addressed. Hence the need for detailed case studies as we argued earlier. However, at this time I suggest that MCDA–DSS can be usefully applied to these problems as long as they are incorporated into the planning process. As I have stressed earlier, they should not be seen as technical devices to give the right answer, rather as tools to assist in the organization of a meaningful debate among stakeholders regarding the definition of options, the assessment and evaluation of alternative actions and the selection, implementation and monitoring of a preferred option. The overall aim is to improve the quality of collective choice so that responsibility is shared appropriately.

The third type of generic problem seeks to extend the debate on plan evaluation to include the situation in which the purpose of the exercise is to define a set of different projects and to generate a priority listing. This listing could be used to guide expenditure decisions over a given period of time. In Chapter 3 reference was made to the work of Halfon (1989) which sought to classify waste disposal sites in Ontario. This work provides an example of a facility siting problem which focuses on determining the appropriate sequence to clean up sites which are no longer being used. In 1988 the Ministry of the Environment in Ontario, Canada prepared an inventory of all known active and inactive waste disposal sites in the province. Approximately 1500 active sites and 2500 inactive sites were identified. This inventory was the first step in the development of a classification exercise to identify the level of risk to health and the environment of sites, and a clean-up programme. The Federal government has joined with Ontario in the development of an agreement to share the clean-up costs. This initiative was taken in April 1991 and a Five-Year Remediation Program is being developed at a cost of some \$250m. A critical step in the programme involves the classification of sites to determine which ones should be cleaned first and MCDA–DSS can play a useful role in this task.

In Massam (1988a) details of the following case studies for each of the three generic problems are given; two are provided for each of the three types identified earlier:

SSP: 1. The location of health centres in Zambia.
 2. The location of fire stations in North York, Canada.
RAP: 1. The location of a motorway between Bourges and Montluçon, France.
 2. The location of a section of I-75 north of Atlanta, USA.
PRP: 1. Renovations schedule for Paris subway stations.
 2. Ordering of transportation projects in the Ministry of Transportation, Ontario, Canada.

It is important to note that the application of MCDA–DSS to data for each problem, while it yields results which can be viewed as recommendations as to a preferred course of action, should be viewed within a broader context regarding implementation. To this end the formal results must be included in discussions among the interest groups who have specific concerns they wish to see addressed. The case studies in Massam (1988a) elaborate on some of these concerns and comments on these contextual matters will be included in section 4.4.

Turning now to the specific MCDA–DSS procedures that will be used for the Zambia and Israel studies, a summary is provided in Table 4.1.

4.2 The location of primary health care centres in Zambia

The focus of this section is on the complex location problem of selecting villages for primary health care centres (PHCs) for the Sesheke District in the Western Province of Zambia. The provision of rural health care centres

Table 4.1 MCDA–DSS used in the case studies

1.	Analytical hierarchy process	AHP
2.	Aspiration interaction method	AIM
3.	Average ranks	AR
4.	Borda's method	BM
5.	Copeland's method	CP
6.	Dynamic interactive network	DINAS
7.	Elimination and choice translating relativity	ELECTRE
8.	Linear assignment method	LAM
9.	Multi-attribute trade-off system	MATS
10.	Nagel's percentage method	PG%
11.	Positive set method	POSET
12.	Simple additive weighting method	SAW
13.	Technique for ordered preference by similarity to ideal solution	TOPSIS
14.	Vectorial analysis method	VAM

Note: Details of these have been given in Chapter 3.

as a key element to improve the quality of life in Third World countries is well accepted as a guiding principle. The Declaration of Alma-Ata (1978) provided the springboard for a number of countries to begin planning PHCs, and in the case of Zambia by January 1980 a programme to implement such centres had been carefully formulated in a widely discussed document: *Health by the People: proposals for achieving health for all in Zambia.* The development and evolution of this important report are discussed by Kasonde and Martin (1983). The high optimism associated with such a programme in the early days has been tempered by the exigencies of fierce economic constraints in recent years so that the pace of implementation and the allocation of resources, especially trained personnel and suitable equipment, for example basic medicines and refrigerators, have been severely limited. These points have been elaborated by Freund (1986), and by several authors in the book edited by Kasonde and Martin (in press).

One of the critical elements in the development of a PHC programme concerns the selection of appropriate locations for centres. The search for locations which provide maximum accessibility to potential clients has occupied the attention of a number of geographers and planners as was mentioned in Chapter 2, for example Ayeni *et al.* (1987), Bennett *et al.* (1982), Hodgson (1988), Joseph and Phillips (1984), Massam *et al.* (1984), Massam and Askew (1984), and Rushton (1989). The view espoused by these workers is that a systematic evaluation of alternative location patterns is a necessary component of responsible planning, and that the evaluation should focus on the effectiveness, efficiency and equity of alternate schemes. Specifically attempts should be made to provide clear unambiguous measurements of the evaluations and a statement of the goals and objectives of the planning exercise, as well as a systematic monitoring of the performance of the system once implementation has begun. Not infrequently different interest groups have different priorities for the goals and objectives, also typically there is conflict between the pattern of PHCs which maximizes equity and the one that maximizes effectiveness. Trade-offs among objectives relating to effectiveness, efficiency and equity are notoriously difficult to measure in such a way that all the competing interest groups can co-operate in the search for a consensual outcome. Examples of typical interest groups include rural dwellers with their set of attitudes, values and opinions about the worth of PHCs and the services provided, central government bureaucrats and politicians who struggle to deal *inter alia* with economic questions of budgets, training of personnel and interregional tensions.

Also, we must not exclude health care personnel – doctors, nurses and lay staff working in hospitals, clinics and mission stations which are funded by government subventions, charities or international agencies. Residents of the larger settlements, including the major cities, might well prefer investments in major health care infrastructure and sophisticated diagnostic equipment while those in isolated rural regions probably prefer, at this stage, improved access to qualified health care personnel with a suitable supply of medication and preventative services. Central planners have to resolve such conflicting preferences. Further, planners have to take into account variations among regions with respect to seasonal agricultural activities, transportation links which are subject to seasonal closures as well as regional development plans. It is vital to integrate the planning of health care facilities with other infrastructure, and social development and agricultural projects.

In general I support the views presented by Rushton (1989) on the overall utility of spatial analytical tools, in his reply to a critique by Davies (1988, 1989) concerning the use of such approaches in development planning, especially in Africa. I suggest that judicious use of some types of analytical tools may assist to improve the quality of debate regarding the search for, and selection of, locations for health centres and the monitoring of their utility. As has been suggested in Chapter 3 and 4, this is not to suggest that a particular tool such as MCDA–DSS will give the right answer, rather that by using this approach the assumptions about the criteria used to measure effectiveness, efficiency and equity, and the relative importance of the criteria, are available for public scrutiny so that accountability will be improved. Further, that the alternative location patterns are clearly defined and the evaluation of the alternatives and the identification of a preferred pattern can be replicated and the methodology is traceable. One of the merits of using a formal methodology rests on the notion that such an approach will help decision-makers justify their decisions, and as part of an *ex post facto* monitoring exercise information about achievement levels and outcomes can be systematically organized and incorporated into future planning initiatives.

For the purposes of this example it is assumed that the study region, Sesheke District, can be treated as a closed system with negligible movement of patients into or out of the district, further that the task is to select a single location for a PHC rather than several centres for a set of PHCs possibly as part of an hierarchical health care delivery system. The former issue has been discussed in the context of Sierra Leone by Logan (1985) and an example of the latter is provided by the study in Salcetta, Goa, India as reported in Massam, Askew and Singh (1987).

The data used in the Zambia case study were collected by Rais Akhtar in 1985–86. Figure 4.1 shows the base map for the Sesheke District with the set of ten possible locations (A,B, . . .) for a new PHC. These places currently offer some health care services, hence the problem can be defined as one in which we are searching for the most appropriate location for further investments, in the form of a PHC. The population of the district (47 500) was allocated to a set of 84 points distributed throughout the unit. This basic data set of demand was used to calculate a series of accessibility measures to each of the ten possible locations. The accessibility measures are described as follows:

1. Average distance travelled to the nearest centre $d\bar{p}$ (km)
2. Standard deviation of the average distances d/m (km);

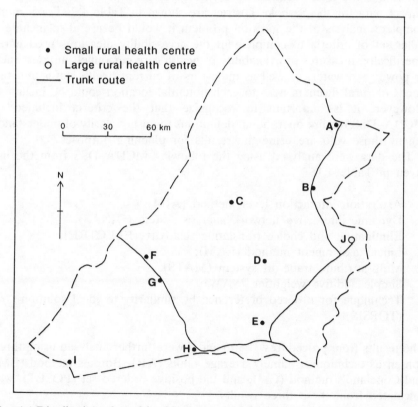

Fig. 4.1 Distribution of rural health centres in Sesheke District, Western Province, Zambia, 1985

3. Maximum distance that has to be travelled to reach a centre dm (km);
4. Population within 12 km of a centre, p_{12};
5. Population within 30 km of a centre, p_{30};
6. Distance to the next nearest centre, d_n.

The first three focus on the essential spatial characteristics relating to effectiveness and equity, and specifically $d\bar{p}$ measures overall accessibility whereas d_m concentrates on the distance only a minority will have to travel. These two criteria which will be discussed further in Chapter 6 have been referred to as Weber and Rawls conditions by Hansen and Thisse (1981a) and it is suggested that the ideal location for a PHC would be one which has minimum values for $d\bar{p}$, d_m. The sizes of the catchment areas served by a centre, given two specific threshold values, are defined by criteria 4 and 5. The larger the values the more attractive the location, hence the ideal centre has maximum values for these criteria. Finally, criterion 6 attempts to measure the distribution of centres throughout the district by considering their proximity to existing health care facilities. In the interests of equity it is important to ensure that health care services are dispersed, and hence for criterion 6 the ideal location should have the maximum value. The basic impact data for the Sesheke District are shown in Table 4.2. For a more complete analysis of the location problem it would be useful to include a fuller set of criteria to complement the accessibility measures used here. Specifically, measures of availability of health care personnel, utilities, such as power and water, as well as indicators of current health status and the needs of rural dwellers near to each potential location could be included. However, it is important to recognize that the criteria included in MCDA–DSS require operational definitions to ensure clarity of understanding by those who are using the results for planning purposes.

The data were analysed using the following MCDA–DSS from the list given in Table 4.1:

1. Aspiration interaction level method (AIM);
2. Dynamic interactive network analysis system (DINAS);
3. Eliminating and choice translating relativity (ELECTRE);
4. Linear assignment method (LAM);
5. Multi-attribute trade-off system (MATS);
6. Simple additive weighting (SAW);
7. Technique for ordered preference by similarity to ideal solution (TOPSIS).

The results from procedures 3, 4, 6 and 7 were further analysed using three consensus techniques, namely average ranks (AR), Borda's method (BM) and Copeland's method (CM), and the positive ordered set (POSET), was calculated from these three results.

A summary of the results is shown in Table 4.3. It is clear that the most preferred locations for new health care centres are places E and H, using the

Table 4.2 Basic data: Sesheke District

Alternative sites	Indicators					
	$d\bar{p}$	d/m	dm	p_{12}	p_{30}	dn
A	133	13	272	0	1500	52
B	81	53	224	2000	5000	45
C	81	29	176	500	3000	45
D	59	26	168	500	4000	43
E	61	34	160	3000	8500	48
F	98	31	168	0	3500	33
G	91	32	176	500	3000	22
H	84	41	192	6000	6500	48
I	152	9	264	1000	1500	90
J	79	47	231	1500	6000	45

$d\bar{p}$ = the average distance travelled to the nearest centre (km).
d/m = the standard deviation of the average distances (km).
dm = the maximum distance that has to be travelled to reach a centre (km).
p_{12} = the population within 12 km of a centre.
p_{30} = the population within 30 km of a centre.
dn = the distance to the next nearest centre (km).

Table 4.3 Summary of results

Alternative	MATS	AIM	DAS (POSET)	DINAS
Sesheke				
Best	E	E	H	E
	H	H	E	H
	D	J	I	J
	C	D	J	D
	J	C	D	C
	F	F	B	B
	B	B	C	G
	G	G	A	I
	I	I	F	F
Worst	A	A	G	A

data shown in Table 4.2, and the assumption that all the criteria are equally important. If a third or fourth site has to be selected then places D and J seem to be attractive. The DAS column in Table 4.3 provides the final ranking of locations which is derived from the full set of analyses shown in Table 4.4. If one location is to be selected then place H is the clear choice from this analysis; it is close to a major highway and it is characterized by a relatively high concentration of population within its service area.

As mentioned in Chapter 3, MATS provides the option of comparing pairs of alternative locations with respect to an individual criterion. Consider locations E and H: we can ask MATS to determine if it is possible to modify

Table 4.4 Results for DAS

Aternative	LAM	SAW	ELEC-TRE	TOPSIS	Av.	No. of Wins	No. of wins-loss	POSET
Sesheke								
Best	I	H	H	H	E	H	H	H
	E	E	E	E	H	E	E	E
	J	D	D	I	I	I	I	I
	B ⎱	J	C ⎱	J	J	J	J ⎱	J
	C ⎰	I	I ⎱	B	D	B ⎱	D ⎰	D
	D	B	J ⎰	D	B	D ⎰	B	B
	H	C	B ⎰	C	C	C	C	C
	A ⎱	F	A	A	F ⎱	A	A	A
	F ⎰	G	F ⎱	F	A ⎰	F	F	F
Worst	G ⎰	A	G ⎰	G	G	G	G	G

the score for a particular criterion in order to make the overall attractiveness of H is equivalent to E. The results of this type of analysis are given in Table 4.5 and it shows that the only ways to make H as attractive as E are to change the impacts on criteria 2 and 6. Those who make the final decision on a preferred site may find this type of information of use.

Let me now turn to the task of assessing the acceptability and credibility of using a formal procedure for tackling this type of facility siting problem. This section draws on work reported in a detailed study of attitudes undertaken in 1987 and 1988 at the Institute of Population Studies (IPS), University of Exeter, UK and York University, Canada (Massam 1988c). Two groups of students participated in this exercise: twelve fourth-year undergraduates at York University who were versed in the basic theoretical aspects of MCDA–DSS, but without any experience of using the software, as it could be applied to a health care facility location problem, and twelve students at the IPS Exeter from a variety of Third World countries who had a range of practical experiences of health care planning in the context of a Third World country.

As part of the project each group compiled a list of statements which they felt were important to judge the worth of an MCDA–DSS. After two iterations and the sharing of lists among the two groups a set of nineteen statements was agreed upon. They are given in Table 4.6. The list is not in order of importance. Each student was required to indicate the degree to which a particular type of DSS agreed with each statement. The frequency of responses is also shown in Table 4.6 and a summary is given in Table 4.7.

A systematic examination of the distribution of frequencies in Tables 4.6 and 4.7 reveals that out of the 456 preferences, 307 are identical for the two groups; this gives a percentage agreement of 67. If we examine the patterns of responses for individual statements we notice that only in two cases (statements 2 and 15) are there very strong disagreements and less than half the opinions for the groups are similar. In two cases (statements 4 and 5) there are tied values.

On the basis of the statements, students were asked to identify the five

Table 4.5 Comparison of selected alternatives using MATS

	Criteria					
	C_1	C_2	C_3	C_4	C_5	C_6
Sesheke (E:H)	NO	YES1	NO	*	NO	YES2

NO = plan H cannot be made equal to E by improving a criterion C_i ($i = 1,2,3,4,5,6$).

YES1 = improving H from 41.0 to 20 for C_2 will give it an overall score equal to E.

YES2 = improving H from 48.0 to 80.5 for C_6 will give it an overall score equal to E.

* = no improvement in the plan score can be gained by changing the impact of C_4 for H.

most important ones for judging the worth of an MCDA–DSS. A modified Delphi procedure was used to arrive at the general consensus for the following set:

S2: 1. Necessary data can be obtained without too much difficulty.
S3: 2. New data can be included quite easily.
S7: 3. The results can be displayed to non-experts.
S5: 4. The procedure does not need sophisticated technology.
S15: 5. The procedure can help to organize discussion regarding placing options.
(S2 refers to statement 2 on Table 4.6)

On the basis of the five criteria and the responses in Table 4.6 it appears that MCDA–DSS are only moderately acceptable to students, certainly for S2 and S3. For S7 and S16 they are very acceptable, and for S5 they do quite well. Further, during group discussions it was suggested that there was a strong consensus that out of the five criteria S2 and S3 are the most important. On the basis of this information and in the light of lengthy discussions with the students, it appeared that probably because this was their first contact with MCDA–DSS they remained only partly convinced that it could help tackle a health care facility location problem. However, they suggested that if information on the following six criteria could be included in the analysis then the utility of MCDA–DSS would be enhanced:

1. Pattern of health of citizens;
2. Seasonal agricultural patterns;
3. Local political elements;
4. Availability of utilities, especially water and electricity;
5. Local social customs and cultures;
6. State of transportation facilities.

During the summer of 1990 a similar exercise was undertaken with a

Table 4.6 Statements about MCDA–DSS

	Strongly Agree	Agree	Unsure	Disagree	Strongly Disagree
1. The method can be incorporated into the planning process	(1)3	(10)8	(1)1		
2. The necessary data can be obtained without too much difficulty	1	(10)1	(1)6	(1)4	
3. New data can be included quite easily	(2)	(6)5	(2)6	(2)1	
4. Formal sensitivity tests can be conducted	(4)1	(6)5	(1)6	(1)	
5. The internal logic of the procedure is acceptable	2	(3)8	(9)2		
6. The procedure is comprehensible to planners	(2)4	(8)7	(1)1		(1)
7. The results can be displayed to non-experts	3	(11)9	(1)		
8. The procedure does not demand sophisticated technology	2	(7)8	(1)	(3)2	(1)
9. The procedure is not expensive to implement	3	(5)3	(5)5	(2)1	
10. The procedure can help improve intuitive evaluations of plans	(2)6	(10)5		1	
11. The procedure requires users to attend training sessions	(1)	(6)8	(2)2	(3)2	
12. The training sessions should use real data	(1)2	(9)5	(2)1	4	
13. The training sessions should use hypothetical data	(1)1	(8)4	(3)2	4	1
14. The procedure cannot improve upon practical experience		(1)1	(3)6	(8)5	

Table 4.6 continued

	Strongly Agree	Agree	Unsure	Disagree	Strongly Disagree
15. Planning problems are solved essentially through informal discussions	2	2	(2)4	(10)4	
16. The procedure can help to organize informal discussions regarding planning options	(2)4	(9)8	(1)		
17. The most successful plans are the result of strong leadership	1	(4)4	(5)4	(2)3	(1)
18. The most successful plans are the result of local involvement of users	3	(6)6	(4)1	(1)2	(2)
19. The most successful plans are those that are implemented properly	2	(7)7	(5)1	2	

Key: (1) refers to the responses of YRK students;
   1 refers to the responses of IPS student.

group of fifteen students at York University within a discussion format. Almost without exception, members of this group had good familiarity with MCDA–DSS and especially those referred to in Table 4.1, and the consensus was that such tools have a useful role to play in location planning. These students were critical of the six vaguely worded conditions identified in the original study. In conclusion it appears that as familiarity with MCDA–DSS increases then the credibility of their evaluation capacity improves. Clearly there is a need for workshops and training sessions to demonstrate the potential of MCDA–DSS and to improve credibility.

Finally it is important to recognize that the solution to the PHC location problem is just one part of the overall strategy that is necessary to improve health care. Within any defined geographical region such as a district like Sesheke, the status of health of individuals is related to a number of factors and as Gilles (1976: 49) notes:

Most tropical countries are faced with many problems of community-wide endemic and sometimes epidemic diseases which may have disastrous physical and economic effects on the population. As a background to these diseases there are nutritional, environmental, socioeconomic and genetic factors which affect the people directly or influence the progress of the disease patterns themselves.

Table 4.7 Summary statistics from Table 4.6

Statement	Number of agreement	Disagreement	Strongly agree (frequencies)	Agree
1	20	4	4	18
2	6	18	1	11
3	16	8	2	11
4	12	12	5	11
5	10	14	3	11
6	20	4	6	15
7	18	6	3	20
8	18	6	2	15
9	19	5	3	8
10	14	10	8	15
11	20	4	1	14
12	14	10	3	14
13	14	10	2	12
14	18	6	0	2
15	12	12	2	2
16	20	4	6	17
17	20	4	1	8
18	16	8	3	12
19	16	8	2	14
Total	307	149	57	230

The procedure was organized in the following steps:
1. (At York) examine Table 4.6 and determine 5 statements with the largest frequency responses in the Strongly Agree and Agree categories (see Table 4.6). This yields the following 5 statements: S1, S5, S7, S10, S15.
2. Distribute these to YRK students and Table 4.6 and seek majority votes for this or a modified list. Results were: S1, S2, S7, S10, S15.
3. (At Exeter). Discuss problem with students and distribute two lists: S1, S5, S7, S10, S15 and S1, S2, S7, S10, S15 and Table 4.6. Seek a majority vote for a list. Results were: S1, S2, S7, S5, S15.
4. (At York). Distribute list S1, S2, S7, S5, S15 and Table 4.6. Seek a majority vote. Results were: S2, S3, S7, S8, S15.
5. (At Exeter). Distribute list S2, S3, S7, S5, S15 and Table 4.6. Seek a majority vote: no change.

Maegrith (1973: 1) opines that: 'The prevention and control of diseases are inextricably involved with all the other factors involved in the way men live, with agriculture, education, planning and economies.'

Also, we must acknowledge that MCDA–DSS, while they have considerable sophistication to analyse data, can only complement intuition and professional judgement and they rely on the data provided. Political expediency, uncertainty about outcomes and intangible costs and benefits are typically part of the milieu within which planning occurs.

It is with all these points in mind that I conclude that there is a clear need for health care planners to learn more about MCDA–DSS, and that those who develop software need to work closely with practitioners to build the necessary consensus which is a prerequisite to effective accountable responsible collective choice and the identification of acceptable locations for facilities. Given that a number of MCDA–DSS can run on small portable computers and are very user-friendly, thus not requiring sophisticated technical expertise it is not unreasonable to argue that they could readily be employed in Third World countries such as Zambia by health care planners as tools that could assist in determining the most appropriate locations for PHCs.

4.3   The location of waste transfer stations in Ashdod, Israel

The search for appropriate methods for the safe and acceptable management of urban waste is a pressing problem facing many governments. The city of Ashdod in Israel recently decided that in order to improve the efficiency of their waste management programme it was advisable to use solid waste transfer stations as intermediary collection depots between the many individual households that generated waste and the disposal facilities located outside the city. Gil and Kellerman (1989) have suggested three reasons why transfer stations are useful improvements for small cities in general and Ashdod in particular. First, because small or medium-sized communities may not generate sufficient waste to support a disposal facility. Second, if the distance to the disposal plant is long the use of small collection trucks may be unnecessarily high and third, the location of a single facility in a remote location to serve several communities will remove the negative environmental impacts from residential areas.

The specific location problem to be addressed here concerns the selection of two sites from a set of eight for the city of Ashdod, Israel. The options are shown in Fig. 4.2, and the decision-makers have stipulated that one site has to be in the north and one in the south of the city. Ashdod is located about 34 km south of Tel Aviv on the Mediterranean coast and has a population of approximately 70 000. Household waste is stored in some 400 containers of about 4–8 m^3 which are located throughout the city. Prior to the study a fleet of trucks served the containers and one at a time they were transferred to the disposal site. The total distance travelled to collect and transport the containers was about 6500 km. However, according to Gil (1987) it was suggested that if two transfer stations are used there could be a significant reduction in transportation costs and in fact the total distance could be reduced to about 1000 km. The prospect of savings provided clear motivation to search for appropriate sites for transfer stations, and at this stage it was recognized that the problem involved much more than a consideration of transportation costs and accessibility.

Gil and Kellerman (1989) have identified five major categories of impacts that had to be taken into account in the course of the evaluation of the eight optional sites. The categories included ecological, political, transportation, economic and spatial impacts, and for each one a small set of criteria were

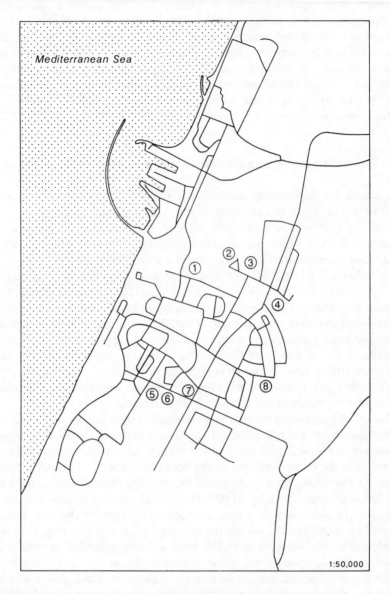

Fig. 4.2 Ashdod, Israel (*Source:* Gil and Kellerman 1989)

designed to yield a set of seventeen types of impacts. For each of the eight sites Gil and Kellerman (1989) provide standardized scores to describe the impacts for each criterion, and they also offer a set of weights for each criterion to indicate its relative importance. The rationale for these scores and weights is not provided in their paper, though it appears likely that they were produced through a consultative process among the analysts and the decision-makers if the latter are prepared to accept the findings of the analysis. It can be assumed that the set of eight sites represents a feasible and generally acceptable set of options. These steps which involve defining options, criteria and weights are critical ones as they represent a sharing of responsibility as part of effective collective choice. The basic set of data falls into the category of an options table of the style described in Chapter 3 and shown in Fig. 3.1, with the additional information on a set of explicit weights for the criteria.

In the original study by Gil and Kellerman (1989) a simple additive weighting model was used to calculate a dimensionless score for each site and a classification of the options from best to worst was derived. Their results can be compared to those produced by the application of other MCDA–DSS and specifically the following ones drawn from the list in Table 4.1 have been used to analyse the same set of data:

1. Analytical hierarchy Process (AHP);
2. Average ranks (AR);
3. Borda method (BM);
4. Copeland method (BC);
5. Elimination and choice translating relativity (ELECTRE);
6. Linear assignment method (LAM);
7. Positive set method (POSET);
8. Simple additive weighting method (SAW);
9. Technique for ordered preference by similarity to ideal solution (TOPSIS).

As in the previous study DAS was used to combine procedures 5, 6, 8, 9, using 2, 3, 4 to yield the POSET ordering (7). The AHP was used to generate a set of weights for the five categories of impacts.

Two waste management planners were interviewed separately and they were asked to provide pairwise comparison scores for each combination of criteria. Their results are shown in Fig. 4.3. Planner A is a government official in the Ontario Ministry of the Environment and Planner B is an academic, and both have considerable experience in waste management in Canada and elsewhere. The results indicate the high importance attached to ecological impacts and the low importance attached to political and economic ones. Transportation impacts occupy an intermediate position, though for A they rate highly while for B they assume less importance.

If we assume all the impacts are equally important then an initial set of results is produced as shown in Table 4.8. We can conduct a series of sensitivity tests, first by using the original set of weights provided by Gil and Kellerman (1989), and then by using the two sets provided by the two planners. In Table 4.9 a comparison of the results is given and specifically I include only the POSET rankings.

If we consider a smaller set of data than the 8 × 17 matrix it can be instructive to compare the results. For this part of the analysis the basic

PLANNER A

	A	B	C	D	E			Weights	
A	8	3	6	3		A	ecol	47.0	[▭]
B		-5	-3	-5		B	pol	3.9	[□]
C			5	1		C	tran	21.2	[▭]
D				-5		D	econ	6.6	[□]
E						E	spat	21.2	[▭]

PLANNER B

	A	B	C	D	E			Weights	
A	9	7	7	3		A	ecol	53.0	[▭]
B		-5	-2	-5		B	pol	3.9	[□]
C			1	-5		C	tran	9.1	[□]
D				-5		D	econ	6.9	[□]
E						E	spat	27.2	[▭]

Pairwise Comparison Data for level 1, with respect to : GOAL

1: Equal   3: Moderate   5: Strong   7: Very Strong   9: Extreme

Fig. 4.3 Preferences of two planners

Table 4.8 Results using DAS: decision matrix method

		1	2	3	4	5	6	7	8
		LAM	NAW	ELECTRE	TOPSIS	Avg. rank	No. of Wins	No. of Wins-Loss	Final rank
Alternatives									
1	S_1	4.0	698.1	1.0	80.7	1.8	9.0	9.0	1.0
2	S_2	1.0	664.0	2.0	72.8	1.8	8.0	7.0	2.0
3	S_3	7.0	586.6	2.0	67.4	4.3	6.0	3.0	4.0
4	S_4	5.0	545.3	2.0	62.3	4.3	5.0	1.0	5.0
5	S_5	2.0	635.4	2.0	70.4	2.5	7.0	5.0	3.0
6	S_6	8.0	411.3	4.0	49.3	7.0	2.0	-5.0	8.0
7	S_7	7.0	524.7	2.0	60.0	5.3	4.0	-1.0	6.0
8	S_8	5.0	489.3	6.0	55.4	6.3	3.0	-3.0	7.0

options table is defined as an 8 × 5 matrix, and the scores for each category are the average values from the initial matrix. For example for the ecological category, six criteria are used originally, hence the smaller set takes the average value based on these six sets of scores. In the case of the transportation category only three criteria were used originally.

The modified data set is analysed using the following MCDA-DSS: AIM,

Table 4.9 Summary of results: attractiveness of eight sites $(S_1 \ldots S_8)$

| | Gil and Kellerman | Initial weights | All equal weights | Planners' opinions | |
				A	B
Best	S_1	S_1	S_1	S_1	S_1
	S_2	S_5	S_2	S_2	S_2
	S_5	S_2	S_5	S_5	S_5
	S_7	S_7	S_3	S_4	S_4
	S_3	S_3	S_4	S_8	S_8
	S_4	S_4	S_7	S_7	S_3
	S_6	S_6	S_8	S_3	S_7
Worst	S_8	S_8	S_6	S_6	S_6

MATS, PG% and VAM. The application of MATS to this set of data yields the graphical output shown in Fig. 4.4 and a summary of the comparisons of the best pair of sites, namely 1 and 5, is given in Table 4.10.

The results for AIM using the assumption that the aspiration level is set as high as possible, that is, to the level of the ideal value for each impact category, are almost identical to those for MATS. The basic results using PG% suggest that the best sites are 1, 5 and 2 and the worst sites are 6, 7 and 8. Two types of sensitivity analysis as discussed in Chapter 3 can be

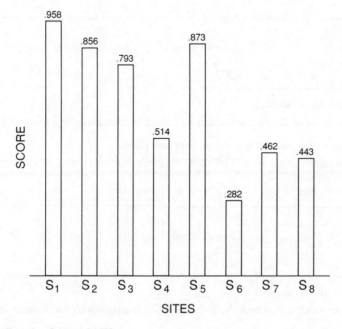

Fig. 4.4 Results from MATS

Table 4.10 Comparison of options 1 and 5 using five criteria ($c_1 \ldots c_5$)

C_1		
	Overall score	Current level of C_1
S_1	0.958	5.2
S_5	0.873	4.8

Making the plans equal:

S_5 cannot be made equal to S_1 by improving C_1. Improving C_1 for S_5 from its current value of 4.80 to the best value of 5.20 would make up only 29% of the overall difference between plans.

Significance of the overall difference between plans:

An improvement in C_1 from 2.00 to 3.36 is equal in value to 100% of the overall difference between S_5 and S_1.

C_2		
	Overall score	Current level of C_2
S_1	0.958	6.0
S_5	0.873	6.0

Making the plans equal:

No improvement in the plan score can be gained by changing the impact of C_2 for S_5.

Significance of the overall difference between plans:

An improvement in C_2 from 3.00 to 4.28 is equal in value to 100% of the overall difference between S_5 and S_1.

C_3		
	Overall score	Current level of C_3
S_1	0.958	6.0
S_5	0.873	6.0

Making the plans equal:

No improvement in the plan score can be gained by changing the impact of C_3 for S_5.

Significance of the overall difference between plans:

An improvement in C_3 from 3.00 to 4.28 is equal in value to 100% of the overall difference between S_5 and S_1.

C_4		
	Overall score	Current level of C_4
S_1	0.958	5.6
S_2	0.873	5.6

Making the plans equal:

S_5 cannot be made equal to S_1 by improving C_4. Improving C_4 for S_5 from its current

Table 4.10 Continued

value of 5.60 to the best value of 6.30 would make up only 50% of the overall different between plans.

Significance of the overall difference between plans:

An improvement in C_4 from 3.00 to 4.40 is equal in value to 100% of the overall difference between S_5 and S_1.

C_5		
	Overall score	Current level of C_5
S_1	0.958	5.8
S_5	0.873	5.0

Making the plans equal:

S_5 cannot be made equal to S_1 by improving C_5. Improving C_5 for S_5 from its current value of 5.00 to the best value of 5.75 would make up only 71% of the overall difference between plans.

Significance of the overall difference between plans:

An improvement in C_5 from 3.25 to 4.31 is equal in value to 100% of the overall difference between S_5 and S_1.

conducted using PG%: convergence and threshold analysis. The former calculates the weight for a criterion necessary to ensure that the final scores for the options on this criterion are similar to those using the initial set of given weights. Application of this analysis indicated that to achieve this result it would be necessary to double the weight for any particular criterion. This suggests that the ordering of sites is robust and slight changes, in percentage terms, to the given weights are unlikely to shift radically the relative positions of the options on the attractiveness scale. With respect to threshold analysis, if it is assumed that site 1 is the clearly preferred site the next task may be to try to differentiate among sites 5 and 2. The threshold analysis seeks to find the set of weights necessary to make the two sites equally attractive and the results indicate that it would require large changes in the weights to ensure that sites 5 and 2 were equally attractive.

The final MCDA–DSS that has been applied to the Ashdod data is VAM. As mentioned in Chapter 3, this method requires as initial input a set of comparisons among all pairs of options. In Table 4.11 the results of the pairwise comparisons are given using the following codes: 'b' means better than, 'w' means worse than, '=' implies a tie. This information is used to identify the two basic cases, namely C and D. For example, it can be seen that if site 1 is compared to site 2 then it is better or equal for all criteria, hence it is assigned case C, whereas when compared to site 3 it is assigned a D as it is inferior for the economic category of impacts.

In Figure 4.5 the basic polygon is shown with the set of arrows indicating the dominance relationships; the hierarchical Hasse diagram also indicates

Table 4.11 Comparisons and categories for Ashdod data

S_1 with S:	2	3	4	5	6	7	8
Ecological	b	b	b	b	b	b	b
Political	=	=	b	=	b	b	=
Transport	=	b	b	=	b	b	b
Economic	b	w	b	=	w	w	b
Land use	b	b	b	b	b	b	b
Case	C	D	C	C	D	D	C

S_2 with S:		3	4	5	6	7	8
Ecological		b	b	w	b	b	=
Political		=	b	=	b	b	=
Transport		b	b	=	b	b	b
Economic		w	b	w	w	w	b
Land use		b	b	b	b	w	b
Case		D	C	D	D	D	C

S_3 with S:			4	5	6	7	8
Ecological			w	w	b	=	w
Political			b	=	b	b	=
Transport			b	w	b	b	b
Economic			b	b	b	b	b
Land use			=	w	b	w	b
Case			D	D	C	D	D

S^4 with S:				5	6	7	8
Ecological				w	b	b	w
Political				w	b	b	w
Transport				w	b	b	=
Economic				w	w	w	b
Land use				w	b	w	b
Case				B	D	D	D

S_5 with S:					6	7	8
Ecological					b	b	b
Political					b	b	=
Transport					b	b	b
Economic					w	w	b
Land use					b	w	b
Case					D	D	C

S_6 with S:						7	8
Ecological						w	w
Political						=	w
Transport						b	w
Economic						=	b
Land use						w	b
Case						D	D

Table 4.11 Continued

S_7 with S:	8
Ecological	w
Political	w
Transport	w
Economic	b
Land use	b
Case	D

Notes: 'b' better than, 'w' worse than, '=' implies a tie.

that 1 is the superior option with sites 5 and 2 tied at the second level. Of the eight sites only five appear on this hierarchy, sites 7, 6 and 3 are separate and unconnected as is shown on the original polygon with the connecting arrows. The decision-maker is left to interpret these results by referring to the original impact matrix.

Non-redundant arrows

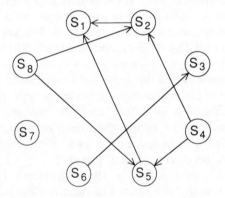

Hierarchy 1

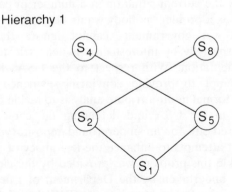

Fig. 4.5 Hasse diagrams: Ashdod data

The analysis of the Ashdod data using a wide variety of MCDA–DSS provides strong support for the selection of sites 1, 2 and 5 as the superior ones, and more specifically given the initial constraint that two sites have to be selected, one from the set (1, 2, 3, 4) and one from the remaining four, it is clear that sites 1 and 5 are the preferred options. It is particularly striking that those two sites are consistently the most attractive ones under the three different weighting schemes for the evaluation criteria. In conclusion it should be noted that these two sites have been approved by the decision-makers in Israel and the transfer station plans have been implemented.

4.4   Some contextual issues

Several times in Chapter 3, and in this chapter I have stressed the necessity to integrate MCDA–DSS into planning procedures if they are to serve to inform the debate on facility siting issues by contributing to the sharing of accountable responsibility with a view to achieving effective collective choice. To this end workshops using hypothetical or actual data sets which allow decision-makers to work with analysts using MCDA–DSS can help to build credibility. Further, at such sessions it is important to allow a wide-ranging discussion to occur so as not to prevent comments on criteria, goals, objectives, impressions, attitudes, etc. which at first appear to make the application of formal MCDA–DSS cumbersome and difficult to operational-ize. Decision-conferencing is developing as a means to achieve meaningful outcomes from discussions and this topic will be discussed in Chapters 6 and 7. In essence as part of collective choice it is clearly appropriate to adopt the negotiating style promoted by Fisher and his colleagues as reported in Chapter 2, while seeking to define the requisite model environment as promoted by Phillips and noted in Chapter 3 as a means of building consensus. This will be discussed in Chapter 7.

One of the most pressing facility siting problems facing societies is concerned with the search for locations to store nuclear waste. Blowers and Lowry (1991: 15) review the current situation in a number of countries and begin by noting that, 'It is a problem nobody wants because it is a problem that has no solution', yet governments cannot ignore the problem. Concerted opposition especially by interest groups near selected sites has served to delay implementation. With respect to the USA, Keeney and Winterfeldt (1988) attempt to provide convincing evidence about the technical worth of using formal multi-attribute analysis to tackle the problem of evaluating five sites in the USA and defending the choice of Yucca Mountain as the preferred site for an underground repository for nuclear waste. They suggest that attempts to enhance the legitimacy of using multi-attribute analysis to tackle this problem was provided by the close scrutiny of the method that was undertaken by the Department of Energy (DOE) and the Board on Radioactive Waste Management (BRWM) of the National Academy of Sciences. Keeney and Winterfeldt (1988: 697) point out that,

After adopting MUA [multi-attribute analysis], the BRWM in reviewing the implementation of the 'new' methodology stated 'the multi attribute-utility method used by DOE is a satisfactory and an appropriate decision-aiding tool. The multi-attribute utility method is a useful approach for stating clearly and systematically the assumptions, judgements, preferences, and tradeoffs that must go into a siting decision.

Indeed members of Congress and other politicians were supporting the approach, 'the analysis proved to be very useful in appraising the logic and consistency of the decision making process'. However, a different perspective is provided by Wald (1989: 1) in the *New York Times*; he claims that the US Department of Energy 'has been harshly criticized by the Nuclear Regulatory Commission, the Environmental Protection Agency and scientists from the U.S. Geological Survey as well as experts outside the Government for its efforts to demonstrate the Yucca Mountain, 100 miles northwest of Las Vegas, is a suitable site'. He goes on to report that the Under Secretary of Energy made it clear on 28 November 1989 that the Energy Secretary had decided to start again because of 'dissatisfaction with earlier assessments' of the site. Further, he claimed that 'the department never had a good, scientifically sound plan' (Wald 1989: 1). While recognizing that the problem of disposing of radioactive waste will not go away, Wald goes on to argue that high officials in the department have revised the date of opening until 2010 and a department representative claimed that with a fresh start, 'For the first time the department now has in place an integrated, responsible game plan.' (Wald 1989: 1) Implicit in this claim is the notion that technical multi-criteria analysis must complement accountability and be publicly scrutinized in such a way as to identify an acceptable consensual outcome. The building of consensus is imperative as is the development of a planning process which encourages a sharing of responsibility among accountable stakeholders.

Clearly, while the use of MCDA–DSS has a measure of credibility its use does not guarantee acceptance of a specific site by all stakeholders. In order to try to deal with potential implementation difficulties Blowers and Lowry (1991) suggest a set of six principles which they suggest should help to build public support for unpopular and unwelcome siting of facilities for the deep disposal of nuclear waste. The principles are summarized as follows:

1. The wastes should be retrievable to take advantage of new technologies, as yet undefined, to treat them.
2. Compaction and incineration should be applied prior to storage to reduce the volume as much as possible.
3. Detailed comparative study of alternative sites is needed to demonstrate that the preferred site is technically and geologically satisfactory.
4. Public debate on energy policies and consequent waste problems must be encouraged.

5. Appropriate compensation should be provided to the host community.
6. The host community should have a role in the management and monitoring of the waste.

While the principles stated above appear reasonable they offer no guarantee of a trouble-free site selection process as is clear from examination of the situations in a number of countries. An attempt in the USA to develop a credo to tackle siting problems which incorporates some of these principles will be discussed in Chapter 7 when attention focuses on consensus.

An attempt to modify this set of principles in Canada was discussed in Chapter 1 through the addition of the call for volunteer host communities. We should also note that even though technical advice is sought and professionally determined safety standards are involved, under principle 3, there is no shortage of controversy about the credibility of such so-called objective standards. Welsh (1991) provides a careful review of recent books by Berkhout (1991) and Mounfield (1991) on nuclear energy and waste, he focuses on the concept of 'boundaries of control', and recognizes the absence of some absolute deterministic standards. For example, one of the problems of demonstrating the technical and geological feasibility of a site rests on 'the absence of any expert consensus on the most suitable geological formations or the optimum technical features of a waste repository. There are thus numerous "boundaries of control" requiring definition and resolution.' (Welsh 1991: 18)

Involvement of stakeholders in the site selection process involving MCDA–DSS while necessary is not sufficient to guarantee untroubled implementation of a preferred option. Perhaps one important extra piece of information is needed, namely details of the consequences of not reaching a consensus or agreeing on particular 'boundaries of control' or delaying a decision. Such information has to be brought forward and incorporated into the political debate.

Turning now to the siting of a salutary health care facility in Zambia, to illustrate the kinds of comments that could be raised by health care officials and others dealing with the PHC location problem I suggest a list of obvious ones. They have not been ordered by importance.

1. Who will provide the capital and the operating funds?
2. How important is it to take advantage of economies of scale and concentrate investments in large places?
3. How important is it to ensure an equitable pattern?
4 What are the likely effects of a choice of centre on utilization patterns, supplies of goods and materials and availability of personnel?
5. Are there seasonal variations in migration, agriculture etc. which may influence utilization patterns?
6. What are the long- and middle-term plans for the development of an hierarchical referral health care system?

7. What plans exist for rural development, marketing, and the general provision of services to rural dwellers?
8. How important is it to involve local groups in the selection process and the implementation of a programme of upgrading?
9. In what ways are the use of the centres influenced by the practices involving traditional medicines, and in what ways can the centres complement existing values regarding sickness and health care?

I argue that discussion on these issues must be allowed and encouraged while keeping in mind the final objectives of a satisfactory negotiated outcome, namely a solution which is perceived to be fair, efficient, wise and stable. In this case the solution is the planning process that involves the various interest groups and embraces technical analysis using MCDA–DSS. An important element of a satisfactory planning process is a democratic political system in which accountability is highlighted. The next chapter will focus on this topic.

5

The importance of accountability

To make public services answer better to the wishes of their users, and raise their quality, have been ambitions of mine for 20 years.

> John Major, UK Prime Minister in a foreword to his Citizen's Charter, 1991.

5.1 Views of accountability

The last two chapters emphasized the use of formal techniques to organize information about the advantages and disadvantages of alternative locations for public facilities. Among the benefits of using such techniques it is argued that because the information has to be presented clearly it can be scrutinized by stakeholders, and further the method for classifying the alternative locations is traceable to give results which can be replicated. Both of these important characteristics potentially improve accountability and should assist in the identification of acceptable locations for facilities. The concept of accountability will be examined in this chapter and at the outset it is argued that the effective management of a Regulatory State demands a high level of accountability.

According to Day and Klein (1987b: 1) 'accountability is one of the fashionable words of our time', but more trenchantly it must be acknowledged that accountability is one of the hallmarks of a properly functioning democracy and an important means which might help ensure that resources are used as effectively as possible. Hutchinson, a professor of law at Osgoode Law School in Toronto, writing in Canada's national newspaper, *The Globe and Mail* (17 October 1991), reminds us that: 'In a democracy, power comes only on condition of accountability.' Given that the provision of goods and services from publicly financed facilities is a critical element in the modern Regulatory State as argued in Chapter 1, it is hardly surprising that those who provide the funds (via taxes and user fees) and enjoy the benefits or suffer the consequences of the facilities demand that those who plan and manage such facilities do so effectively; hence the need for good systems to monitor inputs and outputs, and to identify those who have specific responsibilities and can, in the last resort, be held liable.

This task of identifying responsibility has become increasingly difficult as the complexity of modern bureaucracies for public goods and services has grown.

Nesbitt (1984) argues that among the tools that are being developed to accommodate the growing desire of citizens for greater accountability we must include 'initiatives' and 'referenda'. In the USA the popularity of the former expanded in the 1970s when 175 state-level initiatives were ruled on; this is almost twice as many as in the 1960s. In 1970 there were ten state 'initiatives' and this had grown to fifty-five by 1982. There were hundreds of local 'initiatives'. This tool for promoting action by citizens is now legal in almost half the states and in 100 cities. Basically 'initiatives' appear on a ballot through direct citizen action while a referendum provides a means for citizens to approve of legislative action. Nesbitt (1984: 181) suggests that: 'The rise of the initiative, along with the referendum and the recall (which permits voters to recall an elected official and is legal in twelve states), represents an uncompromising demand on the part of the voters for accountability from government.'

Judgements by individuals lie at the heart of accountability, though it is often argued that information provided by rigorous so-called objective analyses using MCDA–DSS, for example, inform the debate, and trade-offs are made as political decisions with the consequences of attracting support or possible opposition from voters, or generating opposition from disgruntled citizens. On the other hand, managerial accountability suggests a more technical process conducted by experts and professionals according to accepted standards or criteria of performance. A distinction can be drawn between fiscal, process and programme accountability or between regulatory, efficiency and effectiveness auditing. Ensuring that monies are spent as intended is typically referred to as fiscal or regulatory accountability, while the exercise of testing compliance and examining to see that value is achieved is covered by process or efficiency accountability. Finally, and perhaps most difficult, is the task of ensuring that the expected results have been achieved as an exercise in programme or effectiveness accountability. Obviously in all these cases careful explicit monitoring is required as well as specific statements of goals, objectives and targets.

This first section will offer a series of overviews on the concept of accountability, beginning with some basic definitions and leading towards broader remarks on responsibility as related to the location of salutary and noxious facilities. Section 5.2 will examine selected empirical studies which have sought to link public participation with the delivery of public services. The studies will embrace work undertaken in a number of Third World countries in urban and rural regions as well as comparative studies of planning in the UK and the USA.

In section 5.3 emphasis will be placed on three empirical studies which focus squarely on accountability. The first deals with management and accountability within the context of the government of Ontario. The second focuses on a detailed survey undertaken by Day and Klein (1987b) with 114 members of different authorities in a region in the UK who have various degrees of responsibility and are accountable in different measures for five critical public services. The services include health and water, for which officials are non-elected, education and social services which use elected management committees and the police which relies on a hybrid arrangement. The third case deals with a series of interviews undertaken in Toronto in 1990 with selected individuals, and the focus is on waste management planning in the Greater Toronto Area (GTA), and specifically the pressing problem of identifying appropriate locations for new landfill sites. Section 5.4 seeks to provide some suggestions for improving accountability by raising awareness among officials and citizens yet maintaining realistic goals for expectations of improvements to performance levels. On a more practical front, comments on compensation packages and sanctions will be made as devices to help with the implementation of facility plans. Compensation provides clear recognition of legitimate claims by disgruntled interested parties who seek to ensure that the process of accountability allows them to enjoy alleviation from unwanted impacts. Sanctions can be imposed as fines, for example if liability is determined.

The *Oxford English Dictionary* (1978) defines accountability as including 'liability to give account of, and answer for, discharge of duties or conduct', and accountable as, 'liable to be called to account, or to answer for responsibilities and conduct; answerable, responsible. Chiefly of persons.' *Webster's New World Dictionary* (1986) adds the notion of obligation to the definition of accountable: 'obliged to account for one's acts'. It is implicit that such acts may be of omission as well as commission. The legal profession offers definitions of accountable. *Black's Law Dictionary* (1968): 'subject to pay; responsible; liable', and *Ballentine's Law Dictionary* (1969): 'responsible: liable to be called to account'. It is clear that a key element in the definitions of accountability revolves around the notions of responsibility and liability. The former suggests a strong element of obligation while the latter indicates that a sanction can be imposed, if the responsibility is not honoured, on the person or persons who are accountable. It is interesting to note that while dictionaries of social science, for example, Shills and Lipsitz (1968) and Gould and Kolb (1964) provide lengthy definitions and elaborations of the concept of responsibility they do not offer explicit definitions of accountability.

There is an impressive array of claims from politicians, academics and the public that accountability is an important concept, and fundamental if public monies are to be used effectively in support of initiatives to promote welfare. Newman and Turem (1974: 5) discuss the crisis of accountability and they claim that 'accountability comprises a series of elements ranging from problem identification to goal formulation, and it raises the central questions of efficiency and effectiveness in reducing social problems'.

Accountability captures a wide variety of notions concerning relationships between individuals and institutions which can involve ethical statements of good behaviour and norms as well as careful documentation and specification regarding the discharge of services. However, it is important to recognize that unless lines of responsibility for actions by individuals are clearly demarcated and recognized as legitimate it is not possible to identify whether or not an individual is acting in a proper accountable fashion. Hence as a starting point it is a necessary conditions of accountability that responsibilities be established. One of the more perceptive and clearly organized reviews of the concept of accountability is provided by Day and Klein (1987b) in their chapter titled: 'The career of a concept'. They draw on both secular and religious references, and place the concept into the broader context of social organizations which embrace political systems and bureaucracies. Starting with the simplistic Athenian model in which the people are linked directly to delegates via an auditing system, they show how linkages among monarchies, deities, ministers, political parties and bureaucrats, as components of an auditing system, have evolved through feudal systems to simple modern centralized governments and so to the highly complex decentralized styles of government we now see in place. Some of the most recent additions to the set of components identified above must include professional bodies, service deliverers and ombudspersons. The importance of public facilities that provide goods and services is implicit in the work of Day and Klein (1987b) as they claim that the Welfare State is in fact the service-delivery state, and most services are delivered from facilities. Further, as has been noted in Chapter 1, they argue that the emerging state which is developing from the Welfare State, or the state which emphasizes private initiatives, or the collapsing command economy state can be characterized as the Regulatory State. It is within such a state that private initiatives to produce collectively consumed goods are closely regulated by government actions and here accountability has a key role to play.

York (1988: 3, 7, 3) devotes a detailed chapter to accountability in his study of the planning of human services. He recognizes that 'although an elusive concept to define, accountability normally refers to the ability to furnish a justifying analysis or explanation', and more specifically 'the human services have entered the so-called "age of accountability"'. This recent turn followed events in the 1960s and 1970s during which programme administrators simply cited 'success stories as the sole basis for the justification of an agency's budget request'. More specifically, altered relationships among legislatures, politicians, bureaucrats, administrators, clients and the general public have given rise to growing concerns about the use of public funds to promote welfare, and occasionally highly publicized mistakes have been singled out as representative of the generally sloppy way in which some agencies conduct their business.

Challenges to the human service agencies have come from all political quarters, and studies by Fischer (1973, 1978: 10) include assertions that 'lack of evidence of the effectiveness of professional case work is the rule rather than the exception' and 'at best, professionals are operating with little or no empirical evidence validating their efforts, since lack of effectiveness was the rule rather than the exception'. Romzek and Dubnick (1987: 223) support this contention and note that 'accountability is a fundamental but underdeveloped concept in American public administration . . . beyond . . . basic notion of answerability, there has been little refinement of the term'. Their article on the role of accountability in the *Challenger* disaster of 1986 offers suggestions for incorporating what they call an institutional analysis to supplement the concentration on the technical and managerial causes of this tragedy. In essence they define four types of accountability as commonly used by a public agency to manage expectations. These include legal, political, bureaucratic and professional; each stems almost directly from the three levels of organizational responsibility and control, namely technical, managerial and institutional.

With respect to the technical level of organizational responsibility and control, an agency tends to concentrate on the effective performance of specialized and detailed functions. The purpose of the managerial level is to mediate among the technical sections, and also to mediate between these technical sections and the individuals involved in solving the organization's duties. Basically, this level co-ordinates the actions of the various segments of an organization. The institutional level of the organization focuses on the need to be involved in the wider social system. By doing so an organization obtains legitimation and backing, and this is usually represented by financial support, which is a necessary condition to realize its goals and objectives.

The four types of public administration accountability that are used to manage the expectations of an agency are based on variations of two critical factors offered by Romzek and Dubnick (1987: 228), namely: '(1) whether the ability to define and control expectations is held by some specified entity inside or outside the agency; and (2) the degree of control that entity is given over defining that agency's expectations'. The relationship between these two factors determines the four types of accountability systems.

It is clear that for the first factor, expectations must be controlled by some authoritative source, and such internal control emanates from either hierarchical relationships or informal social relationships. External sources of control consist of formal laws or legal contracts or informal power held by interests which are outside the agency. In consideration of the second factor, when the sources of control exert a high level of control over an agency, the controller has a large influence on the actions that the agency takes. The lower the level of control that the controller has, the more autonomous is an agency.

One of the four types of public accountability systems, that is the bureaucratic accountability system, manages the expectations of public agencies by concentrating on the priorities expressed by senior administrators in the bureaucratic hierarchy. In addition, many of the agency's activities are closely monitored by supervisors. Romzek and Dubnick (1987: 228) identify two components that operationalize a bureaucratic accountability system: first, 'an organized and legitimate relationship between a superior and a subordinate in which the need to follow 'orders' is unquestioned; and close supervision or a surrogate system of standard operating procedures or clearly stated rules and regulations'. A second type of public accountability system is a legal accountability one, and the source of control in this type of accountability is external to the agency that is being controlled. A high degree of control is exerted on the agency since the controller, whether an individual or a group, can impose legal sanctions or enforce formal contractual agreements. Under this system the external controllers devise laws and policies which by law the organization must execute.

Third, there is professional accountability. Central to the functioning of a professional accountability system is the fact that public administrators must defer problem-solving in the organization to expert employees. Certain skilled employees with specific expertise are responsible for agency activities and since these experts are employees of the agency, the source of control is internal. Even though these experts may be strongly influenced by external forces such as professional standards it remains that the source of control lies within the agency.

Political accountability is a fourth type of public accountability system and in this system there are two main participants. One is the representative (public administrator) and the other comprises the constituents and includes not only the general public, but elected officials and agency officials. In general, public administrators must respond to the policies and programmes these constituencies demand. Although political accountability may facilitate the unequal representation of one group's interests over another, its major benefit is that it provides for more open and representative government by utilizing devices such as freedom of information Acts. Such Acts will surely help to inform constituents and thus help improve the quality of debate, not only on strategic issues of public policy but more particularly on facility siting matters. This point has been mentioned in Chapter 1 with respect to public inquiries into the siting of radioactive waste dumps in the UK.

It should be noted that there is no single public accountability system that is the preferred option for every public agency. An appropriate accountability system is determined by the technical, managerial and institutional levels of organizational responsibility and control previously discussed in this chapter. Any legitimate public accountability system should incorporate all three levels of organizational responsibility and control.

The case for monitoring, assessing, evaluating and auditing is persuasive as has already been mentioned in Chapter 2; however, it is necessary to go further and include such evaluation exercises into a managerial system which clearly identifies lines of responsibility and hence accountability. There are three major reasons for this. First, to take into account questions of liability and legal responsibility. Those who make decisions which result in damage, mistakes and errors, may have to bear specific consequences under liability, and such individuals may be subject to penalties, fines or prohibitions from practising. Further, they may have to offer compensation to those who suffer the consequences of ill-conceived projects. Second, in order that

collective responsibility be exercised effectively it is desirable that constituents, as voters, be aware of the decisions and consequences taken by
their representatives, so that if such decisions and consequences are seen as
inappropriate or unacceptable, then those who are responsible can be
replaced. This concept of representative government is a fundamental
element of a democratic system, yet it is constantly being tested, specifically
with respect to relationships between those who are elected, namely the
politicians, and those who carry out their policy decisions, that is the civil
servants and bureaucrats.

The determination of the nature and degree of public accountability of
civil servants is far from easy to define and implement. For example,
promised benefits resulting from a new public facility as promoted by a
politician may not yield the high levels suggested and budget overruns may
occur. Should the politician resign because of this or should the bureaucrats
who generated the estimates of costs and benefits be removed? Also, we
should not overlook the fact that often private consultants are employed to
provide estimates of costs and benefits. Should they be held accountable if
their estimates prove to be erroneous? Third, as has been widely
recognized, it is vitally important for bureaucrats, politicians and the public
to seek ways to reduce the chances of facility siting mistakes, and to this end
by drawing attention to the concept of accountability, by putting in place
auditing and monitoring systems to assess costs and outcomes it is argued
that the chances of continuously making mistakes could be reduced.

In a recent article by Tausig (1991: 3) in the Canadian publication
University Affairs under the title 'Accountability takes on new meaning' the
author notes that proponents of auditing exercises should recognize that 'in
fact . . . it's not about auditing at all. It's about accountability and
management reporting of effectiveness.' Tausig (1991: 3) notes that
according to the Canadian Comprehensive Auditing Foundation the concept
of auditing includes more than traditional financial accounting 'by measuring
the extent to which organizations manage financial, human and physical
resources . . . with economy, efficiency and effectiveness'. Comprehensive
auditing in Canada was begun by James Macdonell, the Auditor-General of
Canada from 1973 to 1980, and it was developed primarily for public sector
agencies. While it is recognized that accountability is a key concept which
underlies comprehensive auditing there is a lack of consensus regarding
precisely what kinds of outcomes and outputs should be measured, and
particularly how to implement operational definitions which enjoy legitimacy
and credibility from both the consumer's (as taxpayer and user) perspective,
and with respect to the manager's (as bureaucrat or politician) responsibilities.

According to Pinch (1985) public-choice theories which can be used to
explain the allocation of resources and hence facility siting issues are the
contemporary interpretation of the long-standing liberal–democratic view of
representative, responsible government which stems back to the ideas of
John Stuart Mill. He made the case for the delegation of power and

authority to representatives to take executive decisions, and to allow individuals to hold such representatives accountable for their actions or inactivity. Elections provided the opportunity to express opinions about representatives whose behaviour supposedly is motivated to reflect the interests of the voters. This general view of accountability, while it enjoys widespread credibility and acceptance, has been criticized as bureaucracies have expanded and lines of authority have become blurred and governmental activities have increased in scope, impact and complexity. All too often it is hard to identify precisely who took which particular decision within the site planning process and what part each decision played in the final implementation of a plan. Hence, it is exceedingly difficult to know who is responsible for a siting mistake and conversely who deserves praise for a well-located facility.

It is clear that political accountability provides a critical category and specifically it deals with individuals who have delegated authority and are answerable to constituents via an electoral process. Given the mix of often conflicting information, perceptions and expectations of constituents it is hardly surprising that it is almost unheard of that a facility siting problem is of direct political concern within the context of a national election where the emphasis tends to be on general strategic questions as well as personalities of candidates. However, the major exception is perhaps provided by debates on the strategic questions of electricity production, nuclear power and hence facility siting of power stations and dumps for radioactive waste. Many governments are having to face these issues squarely and of course the growing public concern with environmental degradation of the planet.

Between elections it is not unusual for governments, opposition parties and special interest groups to focus on specific facility location problems, and at such times arguments for action typically take on political overtones. Consider, for example, the current debate between the British government and the government of the People's Republic of China (PRC) regarding the siting of a new airport in Hong Kong. This debate has to be seen within the context of the negotiations pertaining to the transfer of Hong Kong to the PRC in 1997 and more specifically the determination of answers to questions regarding the payment for and control of the facility. Clearly, the siting of this massive investment and the related infrastructure has a strong geopolitical dimension. The British Prime Minister, John Major, and his Chinese counterpart Li Peng, signed (September 1991) a memorandum of understanding to develop the new Chek Lap Lok Airport on Lantau Island. This is one of the world's largest infrastructure projects estimated at almost $7.5bn and critical for Hong Kong's future growth as a global business centre. The project will involve massive land reclamation, the siting of a new town, a six-lane expressway, a 32 km high-speed rail link, a double-decker suspension bridge and a third tunnel link to Hong Kong Island. It is planned that by 1997 the first runway of the new airport will be operative.

Turning to some facility siting issues in Canada, I will outline just four which have been reported in the media during the early part of August 1991 as examples of location problems which are presented as political issues of allocating resources, and making collective choice trade-offs as well as purely technological problems. The first two examples include proposals by the federal government and the government of Ontario to site new facilities. The former refers to the selection of four communities across Canada (Halifax, Montreal, Toronto and either Calgary or Edmonton as well as a special jail in the Prairie Provinces for aboriginal women) for prisons for women (*The Globe and Mail*, 1 August 1991), and the latter deals with the selection of sites in the Toronto area for landfill dumps (*The Globe and Mail*, 9 August 1991). Both are described as responsible actions by government which respond to public needs, and clearly the actions are geared to enhance the image of government. With respect to the prisons, 'The announcement was greeted with joy in Halifax after a year of speculation and intense lobbying by women's groups, and municipalities and provinces eager to have the facilities and the jobs they will provide' (*The Globe and Mail*, 1 August 1991).

The second two examples refer to a proposed health centre in North Toronto, and the need for new courts in Ontario. The delays in providing resources to build the new health centre in North Toronto and funds to select additional court facilities to alleviate the pressure on courts in Ontario have been cited by advocates as actions which deserve political attention. In the case of the health centre the opposition member of the provincial parliament (D. Poole) is attempting to build public support for her efforts to persuade the government to release funds through the Ontario Ministry of Social Services for the facility. Among other arguments Ms Poole is suggesting that senior citizens are suffering because the facility has not been built (*The Upper Town Crier*, August 1991). The Toronto lawyer Clayton Ruby draws attention (*The Globe and Mail*, 2 August 1991) to the need to use 'imaginative solutions' to deal with the enormous backlog of criminal cases in Ontario and included among the solutions is the idea, as proposed by the Supreme Court of Canada, that courts be set up 'in other nearby government buildings. Or perhaps an interim solution could be achieved by the installation of portable structures similar to those used in the school system. Another temporary solution might be to encourage changes of venue.' By presenting the case in *The Globe and Mail*, Canada's national newspaper, Clayton Ruby presumably wishes to encourage public reaction to politicize the problem whose solution could, in part, be construed as a facility siting issue. In October 1991 the Attorney-General of Ontario announced that the provincial government was examining the possibility of siting new courthouse complexes in five cities: Brampton, Cornwall, Hamilton, Toronto and Windsor. A $6m. study is currently under way and he suggested that the new facilities are needed to reduce the cost of holding and transporting accused persons.

Political accountability also involves the process by which officials are appointed to serve on boards and commissions to hear proposals from proponents to build facilities. The linkages between political parties, elected officials and appointed officials are not easily traced. In the case of Ontario, members of the Environmental Assessment Board (EAB) or the Ontario Municipal Board (OMB) are appointed by the Lieutenant-Governor of the province on the advice of the Minister and have responsibility for interpreting and administering the planning legislation, especially the Planning Act, the Environmental Assessment Act, the Environmental Protection Act, the Expropriations Act and the Ontario Heritage Act. Proponents of facilities have to put their cases before these boards to seek permission to proceed, though it should be noted that the Minister has the authority to exempt a project from such scrutiny, and not all projects have to be presented before the OMB or with environmental impact assessments. Also, disgruntled individuals can appeal to the courts to seek compensation and redress for perceived grievances. The public credibility of the EAB and the OMB is established and maintained by the independence which members show when dealing with cases. It is clear that these boards stand at arm's length to the political process, though their actions can be scrutinized publicly and the members could be removed if they acted in a grossly negligent fashion. However, their decisions are not driven by the direct need to cater to constituents.

5.2 Accountability, community participation and facility planning

The first part of this section will offer some general remarks on participation, planning and accountability. This will be followed by comments drawn from selected empirical studies in urban and rural contexts. Specifically I will look at planning in rural areas as related to primary health care and especially family planning in five Third World countries, drawing on the extensive work by Askew and his colleagues. Also I will summarize the detailed critique by Moser (1989) in which she examines a selection of urban projects in eight Third World countries. Finally Johnson's (1984) comparative work on citizen participation in local planning in the UK and USA will be reviewed.

The cry for more participation by individuals especially those advocates of minorities, is usually cast within a political framework in which it is argued that power resides in the hands of a few and a wider sharing will yield results which more closely reflect the aspirations of consumers. Richardson's (1983: 2) book focuses on the idea of participation as an abstract and analytical concept and she claims that: 'The idea of consumer participation is a relative newcomer to the agenda of social policy.' Drawing on a variety of examples from the UK which include social service departments, community health care and housing she draws attention to the much-quoted Skeffington Report (1969: 5) on *People and Planning: public participation in planning*, among other reviews and normative documents and concludes that 'amid the reams of rhetoric which have been produced on this subject, there has been a dearth of serious analysis'. Richardson's book is an attempt to rectify this situation. For a spirited review of participation in the context of advocacy planning in the USA the monograph by Kasperson and Breitbart (1974) is an excellent overview. They remind us of the dilemmas, described by Ibsen in his play *Enemy of the People*, faced by a society when an enlightened scientifically minded selfless individual takes it upon himself to advise citizens of the need to spend public funds to relocate a facility which, while generating local wealth, is damaging their health. Specifically, the local doctor wishes to use the media to point out the health risks of the local bath installations which are a key tourist attraction.

Throughout Richardson's study the term 'participation' is taken to imply some action; it entails more than taking individual responsibility – it also involves sharing in an activity with others. As a normative statement participation at the formative stage of planning must be complemented by actions at the time of execution and monitoring. The mandate for the Skeffington Report focused on the search for the best methods to secure participation of the public at the formative stage. Skeffington made it clear at the outset that the responsibility for the preparation of plans should rest squarely on the local planning authority which has the necessary technical and professional skills to set into statutory form proposals and decisions. The high hopes and expectations in the 1960s of those who felt that immediate benefits would flow from increased public participation have not, according to Richardson, yielded positive results. However, in spite of the lack of empirical evidence on the effects of participation and the difficulties in devising indicators of the changes which participation is supposed to effect, there is a continued thrust to maintain the pressure on those who take decisions to be increasingly responsible and accountable for their actions, and to keep members of the public informed as policies are formulated, implemented and monitored. If nothing else, participation and an open sharing of information may increase consumer influence and reduce arbitrary decisions. Richardson (1983) concludes that while there is no single 'correct' view on participation, the hope that a consensus will emerge as to why it is or is not desirable is likely to be unfulfilled. Perhaps the current emphasis on accountability will provide a useful context for participation which both consumers and suppliers of public services can relate to.

Attempts to improve the quality of life of those living in Third World countries focused initially on improving economic conditions to allow them to 'catch up' to so-called developed countries. Birth control programmes supported by national governments and international agencies, administered through centralized government health systems were aimed to curb rapid population growth and help ensure economic advancements. Askew and Snowden (1985) have examined this simplistic philosophy in the context of the changing role of community participation with respect to reproduction and the diffusion of innovations to achieve control over birth rates. While early supporters of community participation tended to stress that it would assist in the diffusion of technological devices for birth control, the more enlightened view of late focuses on the principles enunciated in the Jakarta conference statement on community-based projects by family planning associations around the world:

family planning services are most effective when they are initiated, managed, evaluated and controlled by people of the community and when they are sensitive to the values, needs and problems of people. Mobilising community resources and generating local leadership will increase programme orientation towards people and self-reliance, therefore community participation in the planning and provision of family planning services must be ensured (UNFPA, IPPF and Population Council 1981 quoted in Askew and Snowden 1985).

Clearly, this statement has to be read with the Alma-Ata Declaration on the critical role of primary health care delivery systems which was referred to in Chapter 4 in the context of the search for locations for health centres in Zambia.

In a word, the contemporary view of the role of community participation in planning in the Third World is closely linked to a humanistic view of development in terms of human capabilities for improvement and change rather than the goal of modernization *per se*. Implicit in this view is the notion that accountability is an important element which links consumers and service providers. Askew and Snowden (1985: 7) note however that:

Primary statements abound with the sentiments of self-reliance, grass-roots activities, involving the people at all stages of a project, encouraging people to manage projects themselves etc. The reality is quite different and has to be because of the way in which the large agencies and government departments operate.

Hence the dilemma: perhaps a clearer focus with explicit attention on accountability would provide a way out of the apparent impasse. While funding agencies have tended to consider accountability in terms of financial responsibility, a broader view could embrace the legitimizing of activities through more thorough analyses of what precisely is meant by accountability and responsible participation by potential clients. Askew and Snowden (1985) go on to argue that by looking at the interactions among the four major groups involved in family planning (the community, the implementing agency, the funding agency and the policy-makers), and by following the genesis and evolution of projects a conceptual diagnostic tool can be developed to judge and assess the place and the impact of community participation. This imaginative tool is discussed in a report of the Institute of Population Studies, University of Exeter under the title: *Research into Community Participation in Family Planning Projects: summary of progress 1981–1985* (Askew 1985).

The diagnostic tool has been developed and tested in a wide variety of Third World contexts by Askew and his colleagues at the IPS and International Planned Parenthood Association (IPPF). Seven case studies of community participation projects which have been implemented by the non-governmental family planning associations (FPAs) of India, Bangladesh, Pakistan, Sri Lanka and Nepal have been examined by Askew (1989: 185) and he concludes, somewhat encouragingly that:

> The results suggest that, despite the policy rhetoric seeking greater community involvement and self-reliance in program implementation, FPA's must commonly use participation as a means to generate new demand for services by presenting family planning in a manner that is acceptable and appropriate to the communities involved.

A more recent elaboration of this work is provided by Askew *et al.* (1989) in which more explicit links are made with the Alma-Ata Declaration, stressing the roles of evaluating and monitoring community participation especially focusing on the roles of women in maternal and child health and family planning programmes. Given that the essential purposes of community participation are to improve service delivery, and to have meaningful control over the provision which reflects values of citizens while recognizing the inherent practical difficulties in evaluation, it is not surprising that opinions differ as to the means to achieve effective participation. As Askew and Snowden (1985) note: 'The term community participation will thus remain so much rhetoric to be replaced by some other approved term in the fullness of time.' Perhaps accountability will be the preferred term.

Moser (1989) offers a review of community participation in urban projects funded by a variety of agencies such as the World Bank and UNICEF (in India, Kenya, Pakistan and Zambia), as well as projects supported by national governments (in Nicaragua and Peru), and those implemented by non-government organizations (in El Salvador and Pakistan). Not only are the four fundamentally important questions examined as to why, when, who and how is participation practised, but contradictions are identified. The aim is to offer policy-makers assistance to recognize the strengths and weaknesses of participation in different scale projects. Community participation as an individual and group activity can be viewed both as an end in itself as a manifestation of liberty and freedom of expression at all stages of a planning process, and also as a means to secure more efficient and effective use of resources to cater to expressed needs within a dynamic evolving planning system. With respect to who participates, it is worth noting the critical roles of women in Third World societies who may be excluded from important facility siting decisions which are taken over by community leaders who typically are men. Housing, health care, family planning and education facilities must serve all members of society and this means that the views of men and women must be sought. This point is crucial in the work of family planning, as has been recognized by the

Institute for Planned Parenthood Federation as it seeks to work with women to find acceptable measures to control the reproductive cycle and pregnancy. It is not sufficient to seek accessible locations for family clinics and assume that the services offered will be accepted by all potential clients. Hence participation is a key element in the siting of such facilities to ensure the acceptability and suitability of the services that are offered.

One of the best known Third World urban projects is the vast Lusaka Project which was implemented by the Lusaka City Council over the period 1974–81. It comprised the provision of physical and social infrastructure to approximately 17 000 dwellings as well as the servicing of 7600 plots in adjacent overspill areas. Other plots were also serviced, and a diversity of community facilities was provided. While there was a lack of opportunities for residents to participate directly in the project due in part to the view that social discontent might result if citizens' expectations were not met, time was also of the essence and participation is a time-consuming business; also participation tends to focus on narrowly defined needs, whereas co-ordination and broad technical plans were needed to integrate the whole project. However, in the siting of roads and social facilities community participation in the squatter settlements was encouraged at the planning phase and this was seen as the major exception in the whole exercise. Striking the right balance between expediency and participation is difficult. However, it is worth noting that the highly successful programme in El Salvador saw facilities, such as housing, as a means and part of a process of social change.

Moser (1989) has identified some troublesome contradictions which are inherent when community participation is incorporated into urban projects in Third World settings. First, it must be recognized that for large-scale projects national government support is a *sine qua non* yet empowerment of minorities can cause central governments to fear the consequences, hence the preference to encourage participation for relatively small-scale projects though there are exceptions. A further point turns on the phasing of the participation. Generally national governments prefer to maintain close control at the implementation phases while offering financial encouragement for participation at the earlier project design phase. Some agencies, for example the World Bank, avoid the problem by transferring responsibilities to each country to seek definitions of wider social objectives without stipulation of the means by which these are to be achieved. Further, Moser claims that agencies like UNICEF avoid the problem by concentrating on so-called politically non-threatening segments of the population, namely women and children.

Johnson (1984) has undertaken an important comparative study of citizen participation in local planning in the UK and the USA. He looks at six general categories of planning decisions, rather than specific facility siting projects. His categories include:

1. Small-scale development control decisions;
2. Larger-scale development control decisions;

3. Joint public–private sector development decisions;
4. Public enterprise development decisions;
5. External influence decisions;
6. Comprehensive plan and policy decisions.

Johnson notes that the local authorities in these two countries are constrained by what he calls vertical accountability as they are charged with carrying out national policies in such areas as health, education, transportation and environmental protection. Important cross-national differences do exist. US local jurisdictions are legally under state governments which make the laws under which they operate, yet there appears to be 'no consistent means by which state agencies review local decisions and actions' (Johnson 1984). The courts, either state or federal, therefore perform this function. In contrast on planning issues British county and district councils are supposedly more directly accountable to central government, specifically to the Secretary of State for the Environment in England and Wales or the Secretary of State for Scotland. Thus officials have the option to examine a proposed plan or decision for reconsideration even without an appeal and they can reverse the decision. Administrative rules heavily influence British planning law as do Acts of Parliament and to a much lower degree is there reliance on the courts as in the USA.

The public survey is a special kind of open participation which is widely practised in American communities and it can be used to obtain views, from those who do attend public meetings or voice their opinions otherwise. However, as Johnson (1984) notes, such surveys are not without problems as, *inter alia*, they can be expensive and the results can be biased depending on the style of the questions and the sampling procedure. In the UK opportunities are often generally more formally prescribed than in the USA. Johnson (1984) shares the view of Richardson (1983), regarding the paucity of research on the effects of participation, yet he does argue that it can enhance responsiveness and he goes on to claim this is the twin to accountability which moves beyond responsibility and liability to embrace efforts to build confidence in citizens by legitimizing planning processes. However, it is clear as Johnson (1984: 210) argues that once facilities and infrastructure are in place they cannot readily be removed and while

> accountability implies that officials be called to answer for their acts after the fact. But even if citizens were to evaluate a project negatively and remove the officials responsible, the non-reversibility of planning and its effects on a community negate that power. Obviously, citizen participation must play a vital role in a continuous accountability relationship during the planning process if it is to have any value.

Thus the case is made that for urban planning projects in the UK and the USA even a modest level of citizen participation has helped to ensure a measure of accountability to the populace by formal representatives and professionals. This in turn has led to more responsible and competent representation and arguably the quality of collective choice has improved.

5.3 Case studies

Three case studies that focus explicitly on accountability will be discussed in this section. The first, produced by a group of management consultants (Price Waterhouse and the Canada Consulting Group 1985: 1), follows the enunciation in 1982 by the Management Board of Cabinet of the government of Ontario that:

> It is a requirement of responsible government that public service managers be held accountable for their management of public resources. . . . Accountability is identified as one of three basic characteristics of the management process. It is also closely related to the other two components, achieving results and decentralisation of decision making.

The second study deals with a set of public services in a region in the UK. This work by Day and Klein (1987b) explores the different ways in which accountability has been understood and its place in the provision of five services: education, health, police, social services and water. The final case will deal explicitly with a facility location problem in the GTA, Ontario, and the perceptions concerning the role of accountability in the siting process of new landfill waste facilities.

The succinct 1982 document *Accountability*, produced by the Management Board of Cabinet in Ontario, highlights the basic principles and features of the concept in the organization and management of the province's government. It is noted that: 'All public service managers assume with their jobs and assigned tasks a contract of accountability. They may not always be certain, however, of what they are accountable for, to whom they are accountable, and the need for accountability in the public service sector.' (1982: 1) In order to rectify this situation the document was written and widely distributed. Accountability is recognized as meaning answerable for fulfilling assigned, delegated and authorized responsibilities and decisions, actions and their consequences have to be explained. Internal accountability should ensure that line superiors hold their managers responsible. This is to be achieved most effectively by clear reporting structures, and it is argued that the complementary external accountability holds government bureaucrats answerable to the public. This is typically undertaken via ministerial responsibility with the involvement of a number of officials and bodies, for example, the Provincial Auditor, the Legislature and its committees, perhaps most notably the Public Accounts Committee, as well as the media and public interest groups.

In Ontario it is argued that the accepted managerial philosophy of the public service is captured by the notion of managing by results (MBR), and this relies heavily on using accountability as a motivating force. While the claim is made that MBR requires that responsibilities be thoroughly and unambiguously defined, in practice this is far from easy and discretion, expedience as well as professional judgements all come into play. Performance measures are, in theory, necessary elements but it must be recognized that they often escape formal elaboration. Finally, in summary form a set of five necessary conditions is offered for the maintenance of accountability in the public service as a vital driving force for effective democratic government. The principles are as follows:

1. The need to delegate authority and responsibility;
2. The need to define unambiguously plans, objectives and guidelines;
3. The need for clear reporting of information;
4. The need to define the results that managers are working to achieve, and the need for consensus regarding such results;
5. The need to implement performance measurement and evaluation.

The mandate presented to the management consultants who were asked to examine accountability in the Ontario government asked them to make recommendations to improve *inter alia* first, the government's accountability structure, by clarifying the responsibilities of and relationships between ministries and central agencies; second, management policies to encourage prudence, probity and efficiency; and third, the attitudes and motivations of managers in the civil service by promoting a working climate that fosters adherence to the rules, value for money and innovation. As mentioned in Chapter 1, this study 'was initiated by the government in response to concerns that lines of accountability were unclear, that rules were not always followed and that controls might not be adequate' (Price Waterhouse 1985: 5).

The report concluded that while a reasonably successful accountability structure is in place it could be strengthened and certain links should be clarified and enhanced. This point about the clarification of lines of responsibility has already been stressed in section 5.1 as a necessary condition for a successful accountable arrangement. It is also suggested that the Manual of Administration be made a more effective instrument of policy. The initiative to have a clear documentation of rules and regulations will improve the procedures which ensure that accountability and responsibility are carefully defined. And as a consequence those who act irresponsibly can possibly be identified and called to account. A critical element in this process concerns the elaboration of expectations and performance review. The report makes this clear as an important element. With respect to facility siting the point has already been made in Chapter 2 about the need for evaluation, monitoring and auditing. Without such performance assessments it is hard to envisage an effective system of accountability. In summary three elements can be identified as necessary conditions which should be present for a true accountability system to exist.

1. Responsibility and authority is a delegated relationship from one person or organization to another.
2. For the exercise of responsibility and authority a base of objectives and expectations is needed and performance must be reviewed.
3. A rendering of account must occur which may lead to approval and rewards or disciplinary action.

The Ontario study recognizes that modern governments in many jurisdictions, the UK, Australia and Canada, for example, carry on the affairs of government through numerous and overlapping lines of accountability, but in keeping with the British parliamentary tradition of ministerial responsibility for a ministry's total performance, it is imperative that lines of accountability by a deputy minister, to the Premier, to the Management Board and to the Civil Service Commission complement and support the responsibility of the Minister. This lies at the heart of the British parliamentary system.

The linkages between the public, members of appointed boards, bureaucrats and politicians are only partially examined in this study with the focus on the latter two groups. A more complete study should look at the four groups and the full range of interactions and controls that each has.

Day and Klein (1987b) assert that there is an important distinction between two views of accountability: first, as political responsibility for the ends of administration or second, as an evaluation of performance. This latter view is too narrow in their opinion as it does not recognize the fact that accountability is a social and political process. In their evaluation of services, which was achieved through a series of detailed interviews and examination of minutes and reports, they recognize three basic characteristics of public services. First, the degree of heterogeneity, that is, the extent to which the service is a single clearly identifiable product. Second, the complexity which refers to the nature of the interdependencies of the agents who provide the service, and finally the uncertainty regarding the impact of the service in the achievement of particular ends. The five services they considered (education, health, police, social services and water) cover a wide range for these three characteristics. With the exception of water the other services have high levels of uncertainty. For example, there are a variety of opinions about the relationships between school activities and their contributions to general educational aims, which in themselves cover a range of objectives, hopes and expectations. Health and social services are extremely heterogeneous and necessitate co-operative efforts among many agents. Education and police are judged as relatively low in complexity yet intermediate in heterogeneity. Water stands alone as low in heterogeneity and uncertainty, and intermediate in complexity, given that the product has a high level of definition.

The set of 114 interviews included both elected and appointed members and individuals were asked to describe their perceptions and definitions of their own roles in accountability. The interviews revealed some interesting paradoxes; for example, for education, health and police, the interviewees believed they were accountable yet they felt they had low levels of control, whereas for social services and water, accountability and control were perceived to be in step. Non-elected members of the health and police authorities were worried about their ability to control the services for which they were responsible, and hence they were troubled about their own ability to be accountable. With respect to the directly elected members of the education and social services committees, while the former had considerable doubts about their ability to control the service the latter were more confident, yet both perceived themselves to have high levels of accountability.

The non-elected members of the water authority saw neither the exercise of accountability nor that of control as problematic. Even without the legitimation of an election they shared the same level of confidence as to their role as the elected members. Overall many members tended to define accountability in terms of their responsibility as they internalized the concept rather than following lines of constitutional accountability with appropriate sanctions. In general there was a view that their responsibility was to the 'community' at large. Rarely it appeared did they discuss the services with individual citizens or voters. The notion of performance measurement, while generally alien to most for all services except water, is not hard to understand given its elusive nature. It is the need to improve this element which is clearly critical if alternative policies are to be evaluated and judged. Day and Klein (1987b) speak forcefully in favour of the necessity for public debate on the means and the ends of an administrative system and the need to seek clear assessments of managerial efficiency and performance. A key group, the actual service providers, must be included in the system which accommodates accountability, responsibility and control as well as goal identification and performance assessment.

In this final case study I will discuss an interview survey that was undertaken in 1990 in Toronto which focused on accountability. The substantive facility siting problem that was used for the interviews concerned the search process for sites for landfill dumps in the GTA. This topic has attracted considerable attention in the last three years as it has recently become very clear that the existing sites will be full by about 1992, and as the public has become aware that Canadians produce more household waste per capita than anyone else in the world the situation demands immediate attention. In the GTA approximately 4.3 million tonnes of material is deposited in waste disposal facilities every year. Further that about 30 per cent of the waste sent to landfill sites is packaging. Initiatives to reduce, recycle and reuse have been combined with the imposition of higher dumping charges as of 1 March 1991 ($150.00 per tonne). Source separated recyclable materials can be accepted at the recycling depots for $75.00 per tonne, and all fees are 17 per cent higher at transfer stations. Also, effective from 1 April 1991, loads containing more than 25 per cent of the following materials were banned from waste management sites in metropolitan Toronto:

1. Fine paper (office and computer paper);
2. Recyclable wood waste (some may be accepted if required for landfill purposes);
3. Recyclable scrap metal;
4. Clean fill, concrete and rubble (same proviso as for item 2);
5. Usable manufacturers' rejects and surplus goods.

After 1 July 1991 these were completely banned and join the following list:

1. Drywall material;
2. Tyres;
3. White goods (large appliances);
4. Recyclable corrugated cardboard.

There is considerable public support for these initiatives. In February and March 1990 the Institute for Social Research at York University undertook a survey of opinions of a sample of 800 citizens in metropolitan Toronto regarding the quality of life. The results clearly indicate a high level of concern about the need to address environmental problems, and over 50 per cent of the respondents suggested that 'garbage sites' and 'industrial waste' were 'extremely serious' problems. Also, 52 per cent believe that the quality of life in Toronto has deteriorated in the last five years, and environmental problems are a significant factor in this perception (ISR 1990).

In April 1991 the Environmental Minister, Ruth Grier, indicated that the GTA is responsible for finding new landfill sites within the region and waste cannot be exported to other regions. The Interim Waste Authority Limited (IWAL) was established with a strict timetable and mandate to use appropriate technical surveys and public consultation to find three sites. One site is to serve metropolitan Toronto and the York region, one each for Peel and Durham. A site has already been selected for Halton. Each site will be allowed to take rubbish from elsewhere in the GTA. The study region is shown in Fig. 5.1. For each siting exercise a major planning company has been employed and they are relying on the work of a number of sub-contractors and consultants. A combination of traditional scoping and screening routines, together with more formal trade-off analyses of impacts and weighting exercises within the context of MCDA–DSS involving different types of data are being used. Overall the work has to be accommodated by the practices in Ontario which are contained within the Environmental Assessment Act and related pieces of legislation. These have been discussed in Chapter 2. In many ways this practical siting exercise

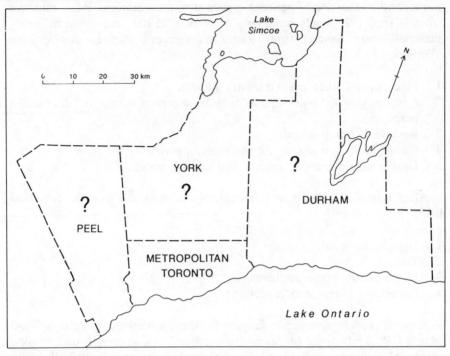

Fig. 5.1 Study areas for three waste sites

provides a clear case study of the type of problem that is central to the rationale behind this book. However, in this section I wish to address just the views of a number of individuals regarding their perceptions of the levels of accountability afforded by the existing procedures, including the legislation, which relate to the general problem of searching for a site for a new landfill dump. The interviews were undertaken prior to the establishment of IWAL. However, at the time another agency (the Solid Waste Interim Steering Committee) existed to consider the problem, so the general issue was widely known.

A group of twenty subjects agreed to spend time with an interviewer and discuss their views on accountability, the existing planning practices in Ontario and the problem of siting a noxious facility such as a landfill dump. The subjects were selected using a referral system, beginning with two government officials in the Ministry of the Environment, two planning consultants and two academics who are all directly concerned with the specific siting problem. Each was asked to provide names of appropriate subjects and after several iterations a group of twenty willing subjects was identified. Confidentiality was preserved. The group comprised:

Academics	2
Consultants	8
Elected official	1

Environmental advocates	2
Government officials in Ministry of the Environment	4
Lawyers	3

The set of interviewees included an individual who through membership of the EAB has considerable experience of siting landfill dumps in Ontario. The elected official was by far the most recalcitrant subject arguing that, 'I really am too busy to be interviewed about accountability: and what would my constituents feel if they knew that I had been spending time on this kind of survey rather than on their problems.' Brief remarks were solicited, however, after considerable delays.

The interviews did not rely on the completion of a formally scored questionnaire, rather, using a prompt sheet, the interviewer encouraged a discussion on a range of matters relating to the concept and definitions of accountability as related to the existing planning and legislative practices in Ontario, and monitoring procedures as well as implementation aspects, all with respect to the search for new landfill sites in the GTA. While twelve individuals responded very positively to the question: 'Is accountability meaningful?' fourteen acknowledged that there were no formal definitions for the term, and only three (an environmental advocate and two consultants) suggested that there should be. With only one exception each respondent was prepared to offer a definition of accountability; only the politicians claimed that 'it had no meaning or relevance to waste management issues' – a view that contrasts sharply with current public opinion in the GTA. A majority felt that the existing Environmental Assessment Act (EAA) and the EAB practices were not working well for the siting of this type of noxious facility. The procedures were often described as too cumbersome, rather slow and lacking clear definitions of responsibility at the preparatory stages and hearings. The focus of attention regarding definitions of accountability directly relates to the need for an open process which is traceable, and which can be replicated, and the bearing of responsibility by individuals, groups or agencies for their actions. Some drew attention to the need for explicit sanctions and the important place for monitoring and evaluation of impacts.

There were a variety of opinions as to who is accountable in the site selection process including the Ministry of the Environment, environmental assessment review teams, consultants and proponents, though the majority identified the Ministry of the Environment and especially the EAB as clearly the most important body, especially the latter, who should be accountable for their actions. Should an accident occur at a site it was felt that the holders of the certificate of approval, together with the engineering consultants and the EAB, should be held directly accountable and liable. Approximately one-third of those interviewed shared this view, five had no specific suggestions and the balance indicated that it was 'hard to pinpoint exactly who is accountable'. Clearly there is a lack of consensus on this important element of site selection, as there is on the existing practices for monitoring performance and relating this to accountability. While the general feeling of the government officials was that the existing process is working quite well, though lack of resources, especially personnel to work with proponents, militates against making significant and needed improvements, others argued that clearer unambiguous guidelines should be provided; some made the strong point that the public is consulted but they bear little or no accountable responsibility for their statements, yet they do exert a measure of control over the process. Opinions split evenly among those who felt the EAA deals adequately with accountability, and those who sharply disagree. Four individuals reserved judgement on this.

Even on the basis of this small survey it is clear that the concept of accountability and responsible action is widely felt to be important in the siting of a noxious facility, such as a landfill dump; however, there is a lack of consensus or clarity as to the ways in which the concept is, or even should be, made operational. Perhaps the lone politician was right when he suggested that the legislation exists, siting decisions are made, the public attend meetings to stop projects and they can always vote for a candidate to change things by collective choice as practised in a democracy. Democracy is messy and could well defy neat technical definitions of concepts like accountability. However, there seems to be an overwhelming view that attempts should be made to provide improved guidelines and practices to heighten public awareness as to who is responsible and accountable when a complex location problem, such as a landfill dump, is undertaken, and more particularly who is liable and to what extent if something goes wrong. Further, how can such accidents be avoided in the future? For all these reasons the search for improved accountability is a legitimate exercise. Remarks on this will be offered in the final section of this chapter.

5.4 Improving accountability

At several places in this chapter I have identified a number of generally accepted necessary conditions to ensure that accountability in public facility planning is effective. For example, there is a need to designate clear lines of responsibility and control and identify explicitly those who bear responsibility for particular actions. Further, precise goal statements and appropriate monitoring procedures are required to compare performance levels against expectations. Ultimately all these features have to be placed within a managerial and political system which allows positive and negative sanctions to be employed, appeals to be heard and dealt with, and legitimate procedures for making changes to be observed. However, it is worth remembering that even if all these conditions are in place it is still necessary to offer concrete advice on specifics so that a facility planning exercise is conducted in a way which is both legitimate and enjoys a high level of public credibility. With this in mind this final section of this chapter will focus on three specific elements which refer directly to accountability and responsibility, namely compensation, negative sanctions and government initiatives to promote public participation.

While it is easy to state in simplistic terms that compensation aims to redress or offset unavoidable or unpredicted negative impacts which do actually result, or are expected to result from a particular siting decision, it is far from easy to provide criteria or managerial procedures to determine the type, levels and distribution of compensation. Armour (1988b) and Skaburskis (1988) offer useful summaries of the problems of dealing with compensation for site location problems. Because of the basically different views of compensation typically offered by proponents of a plan on the one hand, and interest groups on the other, the move towards incorporating compensation into site planning exercises has been slow and difficult. *Ad hocism* tends to be the norm.

Armour (1988b) has identified the two major arguments that have been made against impact compensation. First, proponents may be held up for ransom by exaggerated loss claims and exorbitant demands, she argued that possibly the involvement of interested parties from the outset of the siting exercise may minimize this problem. Second, compensation can be viewed as a form of bribery by unscrupulous proponents who may seek to manipulate the 'weak' community into accepting a noxious facility with the promise of specific benefits, for example tax relief, recreation facilities and the like. It is suggested that by ensuring that the rationale underlying the provision of compensation is clearly spelled out, and that it be reasonable and fair: terms which are hard to define operationally. Zeiss (1991) has examined the attitudes of individuals who live near to waste sites. Specifically he interviewed samples of residents living near to three landfill and two incinerator plants in the Pacific north-western states and the western provinces of Canada. He was particularly interested to determine their preferences for different impact management procedures. He concluded that, 'Residents hold clear preferences for impact reduction through prevention, followed by control and mitigation. They least prefer compensation and often reject compensation measures as bribes.' (Zeiss 1991: 231)

O'Hare, Bacon and Sanderson (1983) have discussed the advantages and disadvantages of using administrative procedures for settling compensation claims, and Skaburskis (1988) makes a strong case for the value of developing criteria within operational compensation guidelines to assist negotiations and help in the understanding of the bases on which to make a claim and defend a specific compensation package. Arbitrators need such help to underpin their credibility and O'Hare, Bacon and Sanderson (1983: 85) suggest that a legitimate process 'requires that community representatives trust the agency to make an award that they consider fair', but we must recognize that such processes 'suffer[s] from all the problems of government attempts to determine taste, values, and costs without a free market to drive it. It is also an invitation to real bribery, or abuse of the developer by agency members seeking political gain.'

Further arguments in favour of providing criteria include the views by Skaburskis (1988: 672) that:

The criteria can be useful in defining where political decisions have to be made. It can help establish the rationale for senior government contributions towards the compensation package. It may also help reduce the expense of relying on quasijudicial tribunals, or the court to settle disputes.

Using Downs's (1970) criteria of attributability, significance, identifiability and the need for a net loss, Skaburskis (1988) defines two groups of compensation types: economic efficiency objectives and equity criteria. Armour (1988b) also uses the equity-related criteria and her other set are referred to as 'impact-related'. Examples of the latter include:

1. In-kind compensation to replace a specific loss;
2. Service subsidies;
3. Property tax abatement;
4. Property value protection;
5. Property buy–out.

Examples of agencies which have employed some of the above are Ontario Hydro which has used buy-out programmes to alleviate public concerns regarding property devaluation close to the Bruce nuclear power installation. Currently the Ontario Waste Management Corporation is employing a Property Value Protection Programme as part of its efforts to assume accountable responsibility for perceived impacts relating to its proposal to site a waste treatment facility in the Niagara peninsula.

Armour's (1988b) list of equity-related criteria include:

1. Local purchasing and hiring policies;
2. Tax subsidies;
3. Tipping fees;
4. Co-use of the facility;
5. Bonus services or service improvements;
6. Bonus facilities;
7. Environmental management protection;
8. Funding of special research studies;
9. One-time cash payments.

At first glance it is not easy to understand how such criteria deal with distributional matters which surely lie at the heart of equity. Skaburskis (1988: 679) addresses this squarely by noting that: 'The [equity] criteria can be used to assess the impacts that have different effects on different groups of people living in the affected area and determine whether or not compensation should be paid by the developer or the provincial government.' His reference to the provincial government occurs because the case he examines refers to compensation for a hydroelectric dam on the Columbia River in the province of British Columbia; he offers a set of six equity principles:

1. Compensate relevant groups or individuals;
2. Compensate for relevant redistributional consequences;
3. Avoid double counting the costs;
4. Attempt local correction of redistributional consequences;
5. Compensate individuals;
6. Compensate where practically possible.

These complement six efficiency-related principles:

1. Newcomer fees should not be applicable.
2. Real costs should be identifiable.
3. Impacts should be attributable.
4. Only net costs should be compensated.
5. Impacts should be significant in magnitude.
6. Impacts should not be double counted.

Within the context of accountability it is necessary to identify as precisely as possible the causes of unwelcome impacts and a mechanism to deal with them. To this end it seems most appropriate to use a set of efficiency and equity principles as proposed by Skaburskis (1988), as an agreed basis for negotiations among the parties as they move towards a consensus on specific details of compensation packages. The province of British Columbia has produced a set of *Environment and Social Impact Compensation/Mitigation Guidelines* (1980). However, these guidelines do not provide operational criteria, hence the call by Skaburskis (1988). In conclusion it is worth noting that the development of an appropriate compensation package is just part of a broader impact management programme which aims to ensure that principles of responsibility and accountability obtain. Such a programme typically embraces mitigation as well as compensation, together with contingency planning and appropriate information dissemination.

Turning now to the second element, namely negative sanctions, I am referring specifically to the imposition of fines where liability is clearly identified. Siemens, Schalit and Nieuwboer (1985) ask the question: who pays for waste site clean-up costs? They comment on the Comprehensive Environmental Response, Compensation and Liability Act (CERCLA) of the USA which is more commonly known as the Superfund Law. They note that with respect to waste 'strict liability means anyone who has been a waste generator (i.e. has thrown something away or arranged to have it hauled away) is unavoidably linked to anything that happens in the future to that material and, therefore, may be guilty and required to pay whatever may be necessary for cleanup' (Siemens, Schalit and Nieuwboer 1985: 349). It appears that the enforcers and the USA federal courts are assigning responsibility to those companies which in some sense created the problem by disposing of the waste. In summary, however, it is clear that notions of equity need to be involved to sort out the cost-sharing arrangements among the parties, each of whom bears some responsibility and accountability. The whole financial burden should not presumably fall on the initial producer to the exclusion of the transporter, the disposal agency or government and hence taxpayers.

The US engineering and construction firm Bechtel National Inc. has been developing a systematic methodology with the acronym AGREE to facilitate negotiations by expediting the process with resulting financial savings. Bechtel argues that AGREE, like the MCDA–DSS discussed in Chapters 3 and 4, is a logical, traceable and repeatable procedure, and thus will probably enjoy public credibility; so-called facts and data replace blame and guilt. Costs and scores are assigned to each toxic substance and each generator and contribution rates are determined. The costs are accumulated and assigned to each generator. Obviously the successful application of this interactive programme requires a close integration of technical information and a strong consensus as to the credibility of the procedure. Until such credibility is established the assignment of costs will be linked to blame and guilt and addressed in the courts using the principles of the rule of law. In this regard we can note the importance of inspectorates to monitor the performance of facilities to see if they match the approval levels. Should the impacts exceed such levels then a process can be invoked to assign blame, liability and determine clean-up costs and compensation.

In Ontario it is the practice to summarize the details regarding legal cases which involve allegations of environmental damage in a newsletter: *Legal Emissions*, a publication of the Ministry of the Environment. Brief details of the cases, liability and the court's decisions are given. It is clear that greater attention than in the past is being focused on the task of identifying the culprits when environmental damage occurs, and to make fines significant disincentives to inappropriate mitigation and initial compensation packages. Specifically there is a move to make individuals in organizations personally liable rather than the corporation *per se*. Also there are attempts via careful investigative journalism to draw public attention to the payment of surcharge fees by waste generators and so to encourage debate on the legitimacy of such fees and the determination of the levels. For example, in an article in the *The Globe and Mail* (17 August 1991) eighty-four companies in metropolitan Toronto were reported to have projected surcharges of $6.3m. for 1991. Muldoon, counsel for Pollution Probe, a Toronto-based environmental group, argues that, 'Rather than putting money for surcharges . . . we should be putting money into treatment and prevention.' The other side of the coin has been presented by Toronto Councillor T. O'Donohue who suggests that because Toronto has the sewage capacity to treat industrial waste it is appropriate to use it, especially as many small companies cannot afford to install their own abatement equipment.

Unfortunately the debate is far more complex than presented in these two positions. Consider, for example, the litigation against the US company, Union Carbide, whose Bhopal pesticide plant leaked a deadly gas in 1984, causing the world's worst chemical spill in which over 3000 people were killed and 20 000 are suffering permanent injuries. On 3 October 1991 seven years of legal wrangling came to an end when the Indian Supreme Court ruled that the payment of $US470m. to over 500 000 victims was adequate. The Supreme Court ruling overturns an earlier verdict which dropped criminal proceedings against Union Carbide, its Indian subsidiary and eight senior executives, including the multinational's former chairman, Warren Anderson. Union Carbide and its executives may again face charges of criminal negligence.

Dianne Saxe, a Toronto lawyer who practises environmental law, has recently drawn attention to what she calls, 'Taking off the veil' in an article in *The Globe and Mail* (12 August 1999). She argues that the purpose of the corporate veil is to hide the link between a corporation and individuals through whom it works. The veil and the related principle of limited liability allows executive officers to take risks on behalf of a corporation that they would not necessarily take for themselves. Such risk can relate to innovative actions which may enhance productivity and competitive strength; however, they may produce unforeseen or socially unacceptable impacts, such as high levels of toxic waste. To hold individual executive officers totally liable is likely to militate against innovative corporate policies, but risk-taking behaviour has to be curbed by responsible corporate accountability. Saxe concludes, 'The corporate veil has been tried and found wanting. We need something new to take its place.' If the Regulatory State is to work effectively and allow initiatives of private organizations to cater to the needs of citizens for collectively consumed goods and services, then continuing efforts will be needed to monitor performance and bring this information forward so that collective decisions can be made in ways that are accountable. Further, that the facility location decisions are seen as acceptable decisions by stakeholders.

In summary, it seems clear that there is a general move by courts to impose significant fines and to seek to identify executives who bear responsibility and are accountable. The imposition of modest pollution fees to corporations is clearly unsatisfactory. Either such fees must reflect efficiency and equity compensation criteria or fines, and if the latter they should serve as significant disincentives rather than licensing charges.

The final element regarding the improvement of accountability concerns empowerment, and specifically the improved involvement of groups and individuals who believe themselves to be disenfranchised by a siting process. If the purpose of providing certain public goods and services from fixed facilities is to improve the overall quality of life then it is incumbent on those who devise site planning procedures to ensure that the public good is considered, and more particularly it is necessary to give to citizens the opportunity to express opinions and have these incorporated into the final siting decision. The public is demanding more accounting of the proposed actions of proponents, and to this end in Ontario a specific piece of legislation, the Intervenor Funding Project Act, was introduced in 1988 for a trial period until April 1992. This replaced *ad hoc* funding programmes that had been in place since 1985. The Act is designed to support effective participation by bona fide intervenors. An eligibility test is used to determine the bona fides of a claimant by ensuring *inter alia* that they have a clearly ascertainable interest which should be represented and that they lack the necessary funds. Also an established record of concern and commitment to the interest will help their case. An evaluation of the Act by the Canadian Environmental Defence Fund in 1990 indicated that the Act is generally achieving its objectives and it should become a permanent feature of the planning environment in the province. Ontario is the only jurisdiction in Canada to have legislated intervenor funding, although some provinces and the federal government do give grants of this kind.

Recognition that the public is demanding a greater say in the production, consumption and distribution of public services has prompted the British government to produce a Citizen's Charter (HMSO 1991). The Prime Minister argues that such a charter 'is about giving more power to the citizen'. Time will tell if citizens accept this view and accountability is improved so that the quality of services reflects a socially acceptable balance between the availability of resources and perceived outputs. Ultimately accountability is about control and power, and a critical dimension in the way such relationships function must involve questions of choice. This is the topic of the next chapter.

6

Towards an understanding of choice

Choice must have some reason of principle.
  (Leibniz)

6.1 An introduction to choice

Choice can be considered as a decision involving selection among a set of alternatives. For facility siting, within the context of a democratic society and Regulatory State, the notion of choice embraces a number of imperatives which include freedom, responsibility and legitimacy. Dissent and opposition have an important role, and those who argue against a particular siting proposal have rights and obligations which must be protected. To quote Peet (1991: 519) in his critical review of the work of Fukuyama (1989) on the global political events of recent years, especially the demise of highly centralized regimes: 'This prospect of a more democratic future, the making of societies where a wiser people make just decisions, where people collectively control their destinies, places us not at the end of history but at its beginning.' Idealistically we can hope that the emerging Regulatory States will satisfy some of these inspirational objectives.

In the early 1970s Haefele (1973) examined the evolution of political mechanisms in the USA since the seventeenth and eighteenth centuries which have been used to tackle collective choice problems. It is his view that for those problems such as facility siting which generate environmental impacts, modern government is weak, further that as private property rights have not in general been assigned to all the air and water, and this common ownership has led to public disregard. This unfortunate situation has been analysed by Hardin (1968) and commented upon in Chapter 1. We should remind ourselves that, while it might give some comfort to think we are at the beginning of history, practical changes to encourage a sharing of responsibility will require a fundamental shift in collective choice which has persisted, and certainty was recognized explicitly as long ago as in the time of the Greek philosopher Aristotle. In his *Politics* (Chapter 3, Book II) he claimed: 'what is common to the greatest number gets the least amount of care' (Barker 1962: 44). Societies now face the task of finding ways to incorporate common property resources into the current political and bureaucratic mechanisms that exist for tackling collective choice facility location problems.

A perceptive balanced overview of the variety of economic, social, political and environmental perspectives which characterize facility siting problems, and make them into such thorny issues is provided by Cragg (1987) in a collection of essays that uses the concepts of ethics as the focus of attention.

All the positive and negative consequences of alternative sites are rarely known explicitly in advance, and preferences can change over time. Further, expressions of preference for alternatives can be directly influenced by the way that consequences are described. This latter issue which was initially mentioned in Chapter 1 has been referred to as the framing problem, and comments on this will be given later in this chapter. While we might support the reasonable contention of Tversky and Kahneman (1981: 453) that 'explanations and predictions of people's choices . . . are often founded on the assumption of human rationality', it is far from clear, as they and other workers have shown, precisely what is meant by rationality. For example, short-term benefits can lead to long-term highly significant costs, and maximization of benefits to individuals can yield suboptimal choices for the collectivity. Thus rationality is something of a chimera.

One of the reasons why we wish to study some of the literature on choice relates to the concerns of this book which focus on the types of planning mistakes discussed in Chapter 1. Those who participate in a planning process which is involved in the search for locations for public facilities face a number of explicit choice situations. For example, decisions have to be made as to who is involved, when will information be collected, analysed and distributed for comment, what kinds of data will be used to provide information and what types of analysis will be used.

Hobbs (1985: 301) has turned his attention to the problem of choosing a formal method in which 'disparate impacts are combined so that alternatives can be ranked'. He has proposed a set of four criteria to assist in making the choice. They include the purpose to be served, ease of use, validity and results compared to other methods. As might be expected a preferred method cannot be readily identified and this is problematic. However, if an analyst gives close attention to the assumptions of each method, and alternative methods are employed together with sensitivity tests, then Hobbs (1985: 315) suggests tentatively that: 'These steps will help uncover uncertainties and biases and grasp their significance.' An elaboration of criteria which can be used to judge the worth of a particular MCDA–DSS has already been offered in Chapter 3.

Recognizing that there are several methods which have been proposed to determine weights for decision criteria, the problem is to choose and defend a preferred method. Nutt (1979) has examined this choice problem and specifically he compared the weights derived from selected direct and indirect criteria weighting methods and the variance in weights, for each method, among members of a decision group. The direct methods include 'scaling', 'rank-weight', 'point assignment' and 'odds procedure', and the indirect method focused on weights derived from hypothetical projects. In the comparison exercise the preferences of the decision-makers and the time taken to apply each method were considered. Nutt (1979) argues that a rating method is fast, easy to understand, gives consistent results and yields low variance among the members of a decision group. In sum this method is his preferred choice to determine weights for criteria.

In Chapters 1 and 3 reference has been made to those decision models which seek to maximize expected utility as the chosen objective function. Such models might appear at first blush to be the appropriate ones for tackling a siting problem, but if ethical considerations are to be accommodated then Goodin (1987) argues that the following four principles should be adopted.

1. *Irreversible choices:* these should be avoided if possible.
2. *Vulnerable groups:* offer special protection to those who are especially vulnerable to adverse outcomes from collective choices
3. *Sustainable benefits:* favour such choices which yield these benefits.
4. *Causing harm:* make distinctions in favour of foregoing benefits as opposed to causing harm.

Thus as the overall choice of a practical rule for a decision model the ethically appropriate objective could perhaps best be described as the one that maximizes the minimum pay-off.

Choice is intrinsic to facility siting which is characterized as a specific type of planning problem. The classic paper by Davidoff and Reiner (1962) on choice theory of planning argued that planning can best be characterized as a sequence of choices comprising a value-laden process which lead to a so-called appropriate action. Reiner (1990: 69) has reviewed this earlier work in the light of recent developments in plan evaluation and states squarely that 'Choices . . . must be grounded. Choices must be defensible and they must be communicated.' In particular he argues that there are three categories of choice defence, namely rationality, justice and effectiveness. In a word it is important that whenever choices are made as part of a public facility siting process the arguments must be credible, legitimate and traceable, hence they can be publicly scrutinized and lines of accountability should be identified.

Perhaps the most important question that can be asked about choice as it relates to a public facility location problem is: what is a good choice or an ideal choice? Perhaps a straightforward answer is provided by the assertion that such a choice is one that is made which minimizes regret. That is, once a choice has been made the outcomes are accepted, even though they may not be quite as envisioned prior to the selection. But what about the long-term cumulative outcomes, and over what period of time should acceptability be judged? The criterion of 'minimum regret' is not fundamentally different from the criterion of 'stability' which characterizes a good choice following a negotiated agreement, as elaborated in Chapter 2. From the perspective of classical ethics following Aristotle, for example, it is suggested that the appropriate choice is the one that is right, not wrong, and as such contributes towards, '. . . the Good, i.e. the best of all things' (Aristotle, from Warrington 1963: 3). It can be further argued that a good choice should be thought of as one that is based upon certain legitimate principles which are accepted by those who will bear the consequences of the choice. Again the question of time is raised specifically with respect to future generations. Finally, perhaps a good choice is one that in general terms is the result of a legitimate process which enjoys widespread credibility and acceptance. Legitimacy in these cases is provided by the legislative, judicial and executive branches of government.

It is implicit in a good choice for a public facility that the four types of mistakes identified in Chapter 1 will be kept to a minimum. In summary one would hope that for a specific siting problem appropriate data are collected and analysed properly, a good set of optional locations is identified and unacceptable sites are rejected so that a preferred location is identified expeditiously. All this presupposes a first-order choice that a facility is needed, and this is the appropriate response to handle a particular need.

Following these introductory comments on choice section 6.2 will offer brief comments on the variety of approaches that are available to understand and explain choice as a basic element of individual and group action. In section 6.3 I will examine collective choice problems as represented by voting procedures. This will be followed by a review of selected work on decision analysis and especially on questions of framing of alternative outcomes (section 6.4). Section 6.5 offers a discussion on decision conferencing and the use of group decision support systems (GDSS) and section 6.6 draws attention to certain ethical issues of choice.

6.2   Approaches to the study of choice

A wide variety of approaches to the study of choice have been developed by academics from a number of disciplines. For example, Cohen and Ben-Ari (1989) review literature on 'hard choices' using Bloom's (1975) term. They recognize that incommensurability occurs frequently in situations in which individuals are forced to make trade-offs among different values. The individual who is caught between love and duty, for instance, 'is the subject for a novel, but no amount of theoretical analysis can solve their dilemma' (Cohen and Ben-Ari 1989: 1). While it must be recognized that choice problems do not always present themselves in these kinds of existential terms, issues of incommensurability abound even for so-called prosaic facility siting problems. Consider the decision of the UK government in March 1990 to approve the construction of a critical section of the M3 motorway linking London to the ports of Southampton and Portsmouth. The only option which would minimize environmental damage involved the construction of a tunnel at a cost of approximately £90m. The government rejected this option and opted to route the motorway through an area of scenic beauty, implicitly claiming that the views were not worth this extra expenditure. Barde and Pearce (1991) have examined this problem, and while at first glance we might see a clear case of a hard choice which involved incommensurate values and trade-offs between money and aesthetics, they argue that the judicious use of cost–benefit analysis could have been employed to inform the debate, and perhaps such an analysis would have given rise to support for the investment of funds to preserve a unique set of views.

Cohen and Ben-Ari (1989: 2) make it abundantly clear that practical planning problems typically involve hard choices: 'The problem is "baffling" or "terribly difficult", because the agent who faces what in our view is in principle a rationally irreasonable dilemma, is nevertheless forced by the exigencies of social life to resolve it in practice.' They go on to argue that the sociological literature has largely neglected the problem of value incommensurability, and in their paper they seek to show that sociological analysis can be applied. Specifically, they take a different stance from other disciplines who may be interested, for example, as philosophers, in the logic of choice. They opt for an ethno-logic approach which is concerned with the structure of reasoning of the decision-making agents. They are not directly concerned, as are psychologists and decision-making theorists, with the external observation of behaviour, rather they focus on 'the interpretation of human conduct in situations of choice', (Cohen and Ben-Ari 1989: 3) and are thus engaged in what they call a 'phenomenology of choice making'. Great emphasis is placed on the treatment of value incommensurability and especially the kinds of accounts which people use to justify their hard choices. In some circumstances attempts are made to provide legitimacy for the choices and this may be achieved by obscuring the very nature of the problem, perhaps by surrounding it by myth, divine wisdom or assertions based on so-called expert knowledge.

The important comments by the anthropologist Douglas on the social milieu within which outcomes are elaborated and choices defined have been mentioned in Chapter 1. A complementary approach is adopted by Gulliver (1979), also an anthropologist, in his survey of a wide variety of negotiated settlements in which conflicting values are confronted. He seeks to move beyond case studies and specific claims toward some general statements as to how hard choices are made, and he notes that:

The study of negotiations has attracted the attention of a diverse variety of social scientists . . . there has been a gradual accumulation both of material – conceptual, experimental, and empirical – and of general or partial explanations and theory . . . so far, however, the theoretical dimensions and implications have been poorly developed. (Gulliver 1979: xvi)

Comments on negotiations have been presented in Chapter 2, and clearly there is a growing role for agencies, organizations and individuals who specialize in conflict resolution. A useful survey of this burgeoning field is provided in a source book that was produced for the Faculty of Environmental Studies at York University, Canada, under the title: *Information Resources for Conflict Management* (1989). The wide variety of literature reviewed in this report implicitly focuses on choice, though the term is rarely used explicitly.

One of the consequences of choice, as a rationing or allocating procedure, is to deny an individual or group a particular supply and so to leave their needs unfulfilled. It is this type of choice situation which Calabresi and Babbitt (1978) refer to as a tragic choice, for the losers can indeed suffer dire consequences because their specific needs are not met. The main purpose of their book is to review analytical perspectives that are available for allocating scarce resources and making value trade-offs, within a changing set of societal attitudes, without resorting to revolutionary change and radical alteration of traditions. This leads to a complementary purpose of their work that stresses the need 'to allow us, as citizens, to accept responsibility for the tragic choices decided in our names'. Rather than concentrating on the tragic consequences to individuals that result from specific choices, Calabresi and Babbitt (1978: 17) discuss the tragedies of cultures, 'that is the values accepted by a society as fundamental that mark some choices as tragic'. They recognize that the distribution of scarce resources via markets, political allocations and lotteries, for example, can result in some needs not being satisfied and as a consequence there is suffering by certain individuals which gives rise to compassion, outrage and terror. A society might well seek to make allocations in such a way as to preserve the moral foundations of a society in which consensus is the norm.

In an earlier chapter comments were made on the proposed formula developed in Oregon for rationing health care. If this, or any other rationing procedure, enjoys credibility then the society implicitly accepts the tragic consequences suffered by some individuals. It is argued that tragic choices arise as a combination of insufficiency of supply and as a result of a particular distribution. Consider health care in a rural region of a Third World country such as Zambia as described in Chapter 4. The scarcity of medication and the paucity of centres which are accessible to needy patients can result in pain, suffering and death which could potentially be avoided. The two levels of determination involve specific choices, and in tragic choices they are often made separately, according to Calabresi and Babbitt (1978). Perhaps health care provides the most dramatic examples which involves facility siting problems as part of a system for improving welfare. At one level medical interventions to deal with sickness are provided at hospitals and clinics, yet a prior choice has been made to make investments in these facilities rather than in preventative policies to reduce the demand for health care facilities or at least to reduce the incidence of unfulfilled needs.

The recent book, *Medical Choices, Medical Chances*, by Burstajn *et al.* (1990) sees medical decision-making as a shared responsibility between professionals and patients which goes beyond the mechanistic paradigm in which the model is hard science with the specific aim of finding causes. The authors suggest that contemporary scientific arguments encourage the mutual acknowledgement of uncertainty as well as the recognition of values and feelings to be a valid aspect of explanation.

The progression of choices according to Calabresi and Babbitt (1978: 21) can change the perception of a particular tragic dilemma.

By making the result seem necessary, unavoidable, rather than chosen, it attempts to convert what is tragically chosen into what is merely a fatal misfortune. But usually this will be no more than a subterfuge, for although scarcity is a fact, a particular first-order decision is seldom necessary in any strict sense.

Efforts to provide strict analytical approaches to decision-making situations have been developed using the premiss of rationality as a reasonable assumption of behaviour. This has given rise to theories of rational choice which offer a clarity of purpose which is characteristic of a normative approach which may help to explain the way actual choices appear to be made and to assist in suggesting preferred courses of action. The literature on the topic is vast according to Elster (1986), yet while such theories might tell us what to do in order to achieve particular aims we are left without guidance as to what our aims ought to be. Typically choice problems are posed as a set of axioms about preferences, and the aims embrace notions of maximization of explicit definitions of effectiveness, efficiency and equity. The so-called rational choice involves the selection of an outcome that is expected to yield maximum benefits by maximizing the satisfaction of explicit preferences. Basically this is an approach that enjoys favour among economists.

The most celebrated enunciation and analysis of the formal properties of a social choice process as was noted explicitly in Chapter 3 has been made by Arrow (1951). His original set of five reasonable conditions for such a process were stated as axioms, and he proved that they contained a contradiction since they all could not be satisfied simultaneously. Arrow (1967) has restated his five conditions as four basic principles:

1. Collective rationality: the preferences for a group are derived from the individual preferences.
2. Pareto principle: if option A is preferred to B by each individual, then the group or collectivity ranks A over B.
3. Independence of irrelevant alternatives: only those preferences expressed by individuals are used to determine the group choice.
4. Non-dictatorship: no individual occupies a position such that their preferences alone, independent of the preferences of other individuals, will determine the choice for the group.

Haefele (1973: 18) has examined Arrow's work and provides a critical assessment which asserts that a two-party political system can 'provide a means of going from individual choices to social choices in a way that meets all Arrow's conditions. . . . I emphasize that I say representative government *could* operate as an ideal social choice mechanism, not that it does at present.'

The classic example of a choice paradox that has been identified by Arrow (1951) has also been studied by Axelrod (1984) in his review of the prisoner's dilemma problem. In essence the maximization of self-interest can lead to suboptimal choices for the collectivity when the preferences of individuals are aggregated. In the prisoner's dilemma only two parties are involved. The intervention of a third party, for example, the government (or an enlightened dictator) can yield the optimal solution which is not achieved when each prisoner behaves rationally and maximizes the short-term outcome. In the long run the optimum could be achieved through co-operative learned behaviour as is shown by Axelrod (1984). This work is well known and will not be repeated here.

Hindess (1988) argues that rational actors are supposedly moved by a 'portfolio' of beliefs and desires, yet such a 'portfolio' does not apply to all choice situations because of the presence of very significant social agents such as political parties, capitalist enterprises and state agencies. Such agents cannot be readily reduced to individual staff members who decide and act. The positive features of rational choice are recognized by Hindess (1988), but he argues that many of the required assumptions about actors and their rationality are highly questionable.

One of the most important scholars who has studied rational choice theories is March (1978: 58). He states succinctly the two bases of rational choice, which are essentially two guesses 'a guess about uncertain future consequences and a guess about uncertain future preferences'. His review of bounded rationality concludes with the view that, 'the newer confrontation will lead theories of choice to a slightly clearer understanding of the complexities of preference processing and to modest links with the technologies of ethics, criticism, and aesthetics . . . hope for minor progress is a romantic vision, it may not be entirely inappropriate for a theory built on a romantic view of human destiny'. While the development of such a view continues to elude scholars and others, efforts continue to analyse existing approaches to choice and to suggest improvements. One particular thrust of these efforts focuses on the use of explicit voting procedures to determine collective choices as the accumulated expressions of preferences by individuals. A survey of some of this work will be offered in section 6.3.

Prior to the final part of this section I will offer some comments on an approach to collective choice which was developed in the early 1960s by Buchanan and Tullock under the heading 'public choice'. In December 1967 the Public Choice Society was founded and the journal *Public Choice* was launched. This new approach to the study of public administration has been reviewed by Ostrom and Ostrom (1971) and a useful introduction is provided by McLean (1987). An erudite survey of collective choice theories, and the contributions of public choice scholars, which embraces an analytical treatment of voting practices, all with a focus on environmental impacts, has been provided by Haefele (1973).

In essence the focus of *Public Choice* is on the application of the assumptions and approaches of economics, especially utility-maximizing behaviour by individuals within the context of markets, to the problems of politics particularly as concerned with decisions regarding public goods and services as they impinge on welfare. Since it is argued that the individual is the basic unit of analysis in collective choice the assumptions that are made about his or her behaviour are critical in the development of a coherent framework. Four principal assumptions are typically made. First, individuals are self-interested and have specific and perhaps unique preferences. Second, rationality exists, especially as captured by transitivity and by consistent relationships among options. Third, strategies of behaviour to maximize perceived net benefits are the norm. Satisfaction of such benefits may, however, be a substitute for maximization. Finally, explicit assumptions about the information are needed, specifically information is defined as involving certainty, risk and uncertainty. When individuals are confronted with choices regarding the production, distribution and consumption of public goods and services the situation becomes highly complex, this is due in no small measure to the difficulty in determining the distribution of costs and benefits, the trade-offs among apparently incommensurate impacts, and bureaucratic and political structures which characterize a democratic society which enjoys a high level of social coherence and consensual approval of outcomes.

Public choice addresses collective actions problems such as facility siting, and while a normative theory is unlikely to emerge, progress is being made to provide critical approaches to reduce the chances of making wrong choices. Perhaps the two key elements in this regard are first, accountability as provided by a traceable open process which has logical consistency and second, a system for monitoring the consequences of choices to seek to improve predictions of expected outcomes in future choice situations. It has already been stated in Chapters 3 and 4 that MCDA–DSS potentially have a positive role to play in enhancing accountability and monitoring.

6.3 Voting and collective choice

Bates (1981) has examined the use of voting, and specifically the principle of majority rule, as the preferred approach to achieve the authoritative allocation of resources to help achieve social objectives via the provision of public goods. Specifically he looks at a facility siting problem in which a choice of a site has to be made from a set of feasible alternatives. While efforts to increase public participation in siting problems appears to enjoy widespread support, analysts recognize that there are often serious difficulties in providing an acceptable voting procedure which yields what is called an equilibrium outcome. That is a solution which yields a specific and unambiguous recommendation which could be implemented. The difficulty in finding an equilibrium can result from the fact that the selection of the way votes are counted and alternatives are presented can yield varying outcomes.

Hansen and Thisse (1981a, b) have examined this general problem using rigorous theoretical arguments and facility siting examples have been presented by Hansen, Thisse and Wendell (1980: 1), Hodgart (1978) and Rushton *et al.* (1981). Specifically Hansen and his colleagues assert that: 'It is common in public choice theory that decisions regarding collective goods are outcomes of voting and planning procedures.' More particulary they provide explicit operational definitions of the two types of procedure and they note that seldom is there congruence between the results using the separate procedures. An attempt is made to examine a generic salutary facility siting problem and to determine when solutions coincide, also to examine the magnitude of the differences when solutions do not in fact agree. For a voting procedure the Condorcet location is used. This location is the one which is strictly closest to a majority of users and hence it is declared to be the preferred site. This location corresponds to the concept of the equilibrium solution that Plott (1967) used in his voting theory.

A number of jurisdictions, particularly those that follow the Anglo-Saxon political tradition, have adopted a voting procedure in which the candidate that receives most votes is declared to be the winner. This plurality solution does not require that at least a strict majority of all voters is needed to determine a winning outcome. This first-past-the-post plurality procedure can yield outcomes which, from a purely democratic perspective, appear to be perverse. Namely, the 'winning' option may be, and often is, the option that a majority of people do not vote for.

From a social planning perspective two distinct alternative approaches can be identified to characterize optimal choices. First, it can be argued that a utilitarian or efficient choice is the one that minimizes the average distance that a user has to travel, assuming that the nearest facility is patronized and each user has the same frequency of attendance. This solution is usually referred to as the Weber choice, after the theoretical work in location theory by Weber (1909). Another approach, referred to as the equity solution, employs some of the principles enunciated by Rawls (1971) using his concept of the 'veil of ignorance'. If an individual user did not know in advance his or her specific location among a set of users then Rawls argues that the equity solution would be the one that maximizes the benefit to the individual who is most needy. This can be cast into a spatial choice problem for a salutary public facility which offers a service which is consumed by a user who travels to the facility, for example, a library or a day-care centre. A similar result will occur if we consider a service like fire protection which is delivered from the facility to a consumer. The operational definition of the Rawls location is the one that minimizes the maximum distance travelled by a user or by the agency that delivers the service.

In order to compare the results using voting procedures and planning perspectives a hypothetical facility siting problem can be defined. Consider a set of five equidistant possible locations (A, B, C, D, E) for a salutary facility, such as a day-care centre, and assume that the users of the facility are distributed among these places and that per unit travel cost of effort is the same for each client, also that the frequency of demand is the same for each individual. For ease of calculation the places are 1 km apart. Figure 6.1 summarizes the problem. Under a simple voting procedure, using all the sites as feasible candidates, then given that individuals will vote for the closest one, location E is the winner with six out of fourteen votes. This is the plurality, first-past-the-post, solution. However, if a pairwise voting matrix is constructed in which voters are presented with all pairs of locations, then the results can be summarized as in Fig. 6.2. For example,

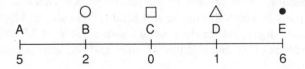

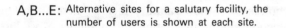

A,B...E: Alternative sites for a salutary facility, the number of users is shown at each site.

○   Condorcet location

□   Rawls location

△   Weber location

●   Plurality location

Fig. 6.1 Hypothetical facility siting problem

	A	B	C	D	E	Row sum
A	X	5	6	7	7	25
B	9	X	7	7	7	30
C	8	7	X	7	7.5	29.5
D	7	7	7	X	8	29
E	7	7	6.5	6	X	26.5

Number
of votes

Fig. 6.2 Pairwise comparison voting matrix

when sites A and B are compared the total set of fourteen voters is divided into five who favour A, as it is closest, and nine who prefer B. When sites C and E are compared, the single voter at D is split equally among the two options, hence the final score in favour of C is $7\frac{1}{2}$ and the score for E is $6\frac{1}{2}$. The row sum values for the matrix give aggregate scores and it is clear that three of the options – B, C and D – all satisfy the condition that a majority of users prefer them in a pairwise comparison contest. Further, site B can be classified as the Condorcet location with thirty out of a maximum possible set of fifty-six votes.

Turning now to planning solutions it is clear that the location that minimizes the maximum distance a user has to travel is C. If, for example, site D or B had been chosen the maximum distance would increase from 2 to 3kms, while sites A or E involve a maximum distance of 4 km. Site C is the Rawls location. With respect to the total distance travelled by all users we find that the site which has the lowest total travel cost, and hence is most accessible at the aggregate level, is site D with a value of 23 units. Sites B and C have values of 25 units, E has 27 units and the least accessible site is A with 29 units.

In summary, for the hypothetical set of data, we see that there are four defensible choices for a new salutary facility, hence the final choice must involve a selection among the voting and planning procedures which could be used. While not all empirical problems yield such diverse results it is clear that the use of a particular voting procedure does not necessarily ease the burden of negotiations with proponents of alternative voting procedures or planning methods which focus on aggregate travel costs or equity considerations.

In the absence of an equilibrium solution we can perhaps use the different sets of results, and especially information on the distribution of costs for suboptimal solutions, in a debate which will lead to a final choice. In Table 6.1 a

Table 6.1 Summary of results: voting and planning procedures

	Voting plurality	Voting pairwise	Rawls	Weber
A	5	25	4	29
B	2	30*	3	25
C	0	29.5	2	25
D	1	29*	3	23
E	6	26.5	4	27

* Satisfy Condorcet conditions.

summary of the results is given for the hypothetical set of data. Such information may be instructive to include in a complex choice debate.

Ultimately, of course, a final choice has to be made, and this is the task of those with legitimate executive authority. Voting results may guide their final choice but the elected officials should bear the responsibility for the decision.

Haefele (1973) reminds us that in the case of the USA the seventeenth and eighteenth centuries witnessed considerable ingenuity in devising representative legislative bodies to address collective choice problems and remove control from Crown-appointed governors and executive councils. However, as time went on and managerial and executive skills were perfected, representative legislative bodies ceased to evolve to deal appropriately with the conflicts of values that currently face society and which must be addressed if meaningful social choices regarding environmental quality are to be made. A systematic review of literature on voting, especially taking into account two-tier legislatures of different sizes, and coalitions, drawing on the work of Shipley and Shubik (1954) as well as the bases of representation, beyond the territorial imperative, and a party system with independent issues being considered leads Haefele (1973: 60) to a set of conclusions which might help handle collective choice problems especially when environmental impacts are of concern.

1. There is a need to redress the balance between the legislative and the executive role in environmental choices at all levels of government. We now face . . . the need for strong legislatures . . . and creation of some twentieth-century research capabilities within the legislatures.
2. There is a need to force environmental issues into partisan politics at every level of government. There is, unfortunately, a trend in the opposite direction, with both parties adopting pious statements but leaving the solution of any controversial issues to administrative agencies that are not subject to citizen pressures.
3. There is a need to focus directly on institutional design. In doing so, we must recognize that making social choices between hard alternatives requires technical expertise and political expertise.

With respect to the design of collective choice mechanisms to tackle facility siting problems these suggestions are most pertinent, and while Haefele had in mind environmental impacts, there is reason to extend them to consider social and economic impacts. In sum it is appropriate that modifications to existing voting procedures need to be linked to party politics to improve the functioning of democratic institutions within Regulatory States.

6.4   Choice and decision analysis

Those who support the use of decision analytical approaches to tackle complex choice problems assert that 'the quality of decisions can be improved by decomposing holistic judgements into more simple ones and integrating the simple ones with the aid of such models as decision trees and multi attribute utility models' (Vari and Vecsenyi, in press). In the 1960s decision analysis emerged from decision theory as a fairly coherent category of approaches that could be used to tackle problems in which choices had to be made. The field is based to a considerable degree on the premiss of rationality in choice, and the corollary that there is agreement about the term 'rationality'. Earlier in this chapter some of the difficulties with this view have been noted. The work on MCDA–DSS that was reported in Chapters 3 and 4 is linked closely to decision analysis.

A clear non-technical review of decision analysis is provided by Phillips (1979) in which he notes that the early work on decision theory was undertaken by the English mathematician, Ramsey, in the 1920s. This work, and subsequent developments, is based on the axiom that people attempt to be consistent when making choice decisions. Specifically Ramsey argued that decisions taken at a particular point in time should corroborate each other and hence be consistent and coherent. Of course, as time moves on it is clear that new options may appear, and assessments of risks, uncertainties, costs and benefits can change. One theoretical structure for handling this type of situation in which continuous shifts in information can give rise to discontinuous changes in choice, that is, for example, from support to oppose, or vice versa, or further, from a state of neutrality or indifference to either support or oppose, is provided by the cusp catastrophe structure following the theoretical work of the French mathematician Thom (1972). An example of such an approach is discussed in Massam (1980) when an airport location decision is examined, over time, and two sets of opposing factors are considered, namely economic benefits and environmental costs. The cusp catastrophe provides a theoretical framework to describe the possible evolution of opinions as conflicting information about costs and benefits becomes available. However, there is no suggestion of a best choice in this positive model. Also, it is very difficult to envisage the calibration of the model. One of the points that does emerge concerns the solicitation of opinions via surveys, and specifically it is suggested that one-time-only surveys of public opinion about a controversial siting issue disguise the evolution of preferences and the shifts.

There are a number of key assumptions about coherence which are common to all versions of decision theory. First, the ordering principle in which preferences are clearly expressed, for example, site A is better than B, or A is equivalent to B. The assertions that 'I do not know' or 'I do not care' are not accommodated. Second, the transitivity principle operates, that is, if A is preferred to B and B to C, then A is preferred to C. Thirdly, the dominance principle which states that if A is as good as B for all criteria, except one, and for this one A is preferred to B, then overall A will be preferred to B. While theoretical arguments using these kinds of axioms as mentioned in earlier chapters can yield coherent choices, it is clearly acknowledged that practical decision problems, such as facility siting, do not readily reduce to neatly defined sets of actors, who can state unambiguously their preferences and who agree on a finite set of options, and the associated positive and negative impacts that embrace economic, social, political and environmental effects.

The process of mental accounting is highly complex, and while significant progress has been made, essentially by psychologists, to understand and explain choices as reflected by stated or revealed preferences there are considerable difficulties in transposing theoretical concepts to practical choice problem-solving. One area of theoretical work which has direct bearing on facility siting concerns the framing or formulation of decision problems. This point has already been made in Chapter 1, and it is important to restate it here because it represents an important aspect of decision analysis. In brief the psychologists Tversky and Kahneman (1981) have shown that the perception of decision problems which involve choice, and the evaluation of probabilities and outcomes can produce shifts of preferences. These shifts can be predicted when a specific problem is framed in different ways. For example, they demonstrate that preferences can be reversed and specifically '. . . the acceptability of an option can depend on whether a negative outcome is evaluated as a cost or as an uncompensated loss' (Kahneman and Tversky 1984). If two alternatives are presented as either a sure gain and a gamble or as a sure loss and a gamble, then people tend to reverse their preferences. Yet analytically both descriptions describe the same outcome, it is only the framing that causes the shift in choices. In summary their work identifies decision problems in which people systemati-cally violate the requirements of consistency and coherence which are felt to be fundamental in decision analysis. Tversky and Kahneman (1981) suggest that the modern theory of so-called rational choice has accepted the axioms of coherence of preferences as the sole criterion of rationality. This avoids the very difficult problem of trying to justify values and the effects of framing of choice questions throw doubt on the adequacy of accepting coherence as traditionally defined.

Kartez (1989) draws on the work of psychologists to elaborate arguments about rationality in planning which involves institutions and public judgements. The substantive context for his work relates to technological choices, for example, as illustrated by the use of nuclear power. He reminds us that:

the influence that institutions can have on public judgements of issues with uncertain consequences, the line between manipulating public judgement and emancipating it from biases and misperceptions is a fine one. Garnering public acceptance often involves a professional dilemma of choosing between the morally questionable shaping of public preferences and the surrendering of complex choices to public biases. (Kartez 1989: 445)

Rosenman, Fort and Budd (1988) comment on a facility siting problem and probably provide the first application of the theoretical concepts of Kahneman and Tversky (1979) on prospect theory. The specific case study concerns the selection by the US Department of Energy of a site in Nevada for the nation's first high-level nuclear waste repository. This problem has been referred to in Chapter 4. The assertion is made that agencies should offer compensation to citizens for the large 'prospect' loss that they perceive when the facility is eventually opened. It is argued that the perceived losses are in fact real ones that have actually occurred in the minds of the public and '. . . that the logic of insuring people against a statistical "risked" loss . . . is inadequate when perceptions, however biased, are given analytical standing'.

In general, decision analysis as incorporated into MCDA–DSS is likely to have a useful role to play in the organization of information to tackle complex location choice problems. The key to its successful application lies with the integration of the tools into the decision-making structure. This can involve both political and bureaucratic aspects especially for public facilities. Recent attempts at integration have been reported in the literature on decision-conferencing and section 6.5 offers comments on selected work.

6.5 Decision-conferencing

With the increased availability of computers, together with a broader understanding by managers and bureaucrats of decision analytical frame-works, as well as the recognition that choice problems are highly complex and typically involve negotiations and compromise, attempts are being made to provide a suitable environment to embrace all these elements. This environment has been characterized as one in which decision-conferencing can play a useful role. Reviews of the field are provided by Fekete-Szues (1991), McCartt and Rohrbaugh (1989), Vari and Vecsenyi (in press) and Wooler (1987).

Schuman and Rohrbaugh (1991: 148) offer a straightforward description of the aims of a decision conference: 'Decision conferences are designed for groups that need to reach consensus about a complex unstructured problem for which there is no "formula" or objective solution, a need increasingly common in the information society.' Facility siting problems clearly fall into this category of problem.

Phillips (1986b) offers a brief review of a selection of decision-conferencing products which have been marketed since Peterson originally formalized the term in 1981. An example of such a product is the priority decision system (PDS) which is available from Work Sciences Associates in London, UK; PDS generates a priority ranking of objectives, given that participants define the objectives and make formal comparisons which are fed to a computer. Options are identified and compared with respect to the objectives, and computer analysis is used to generate an ordering from most to least attractive. Phillips (1986b: 2) comments on PDS and asserts that: 'Since all participants are involved in the weighting and scoring, they are usually committed to the resulting prioritization.'

Another product is called Innovator and it is marketed by Wilson Learning Corporation of Minneapolis. Participants have access to key pads that register their votes, ranking or evaluation of items. This information is aggregated to give displays which allow 'the group to assess the degree of consensus, confidence, or commitment'. Phillips (1986b: 4) identifies another use of the information, that is, to produce 'an opportunity map of items that are important in achieving success'. The items are characterized as four basic elements of an organization namely: gripes, opportunities, overkills and strengths. It is argued that, 'By exploring agreements and disagreements, displayed on a visual picture . . . the group can begin to develop a consensus.'

I suggest that Phillips's general assertions about the commitment to the prioritization produced by PDS and the development of consensus by a group using Innovator are optimistic unless specific conditions can be guaranteed. Specifically I would argue that the participants need to be generally conversant with the specific analysis that is undertaken by the computer, and accept the particular method as legitimate and credible. It is not easy to establish such credibility as has been noted in Chapter 3 in the review of MCDA–DSS. Typically MCDA–DSS are critical components of a decision conference.

Decision-conferencing usually involves an intense session, perhaps over a period of two or more days, in a specially designed room with screen projection devices, computers and printers, and directly involves participants who are key members of the organization that is facing a complex issue. Usually two people, a facilitator and a decision analyst, from outside the organization help the participants to structure the discussion by identifying specific issues which can be incorporated into a formal decision analysis model, then to assist the participants to formalize their preferences and trade-offs, as well as their estimates of impacts. Goals, objectives and targets are discussed with respect to the results of the model, sensitivity tests are conducted, and overall the aim is to explore imaginative solutions to a perceived problem, evaluate the merits of the proposed solutions and seek a consensus as to a preferred option.

Phillips (1986b) has contributed significantly to the field of decision conferencing and he suggests that the purposes of a decision conference are to generate a shared understanding of a problem and commitment to action. Vari and Vecsenyi (in press) define a decision conference as '. . . a computer-assisted, intense group meeting, that uses various technologies (for example, methods for eliciting and modelling human judgements) combined with group facilitation techniques to improve analysis and promote consensus'. Perhaps the critical necessary conditions which must be satisfied by decision conferencing if it is to be applied to a choice problem are first, that a shared understanding, recognition and acceptance of a problem obtains, and second, that those who participate have the necessary executive authority to ensure that a particular commitment to action is actually implemented. Given these two stringent conditions it is not surprising to note that typically examples of decision-conferencing have been restricted to corporate choice problems in the private sector in which key executives have the necessary authority to implement choices.

Proponents of decision conferences express the view that groups of executives working on major issues in their organization can make better decisions in less time using this approach. However, the measure of success used is typically revenue or profit, and while this is probably appropriate for a private sector organization it is clearly inappropriate for a public facility location problem, not least because such data do not exist. The question becomes: can decision-conferencing be incorporated into the collective choice process for a public facility? I tend to support a tentative affirmative response, if the participants represent key stakeholders. Therefore some of the necessary conditions for the successful use of decision-conferencing for tackling public facility siting problems are, first, that such stakeholders can be identified and second, that they are willing to participate, and further, that while they may change their opinions during the conference, at the end of the day they subscribe to a consensual outcome which is felt to be a stable solution. These requirements will not be easy to satisfy.

In recent years there have been attempts to develop GDSS which, according to Lewandowski (1989), have to accommodate four basic characteristics of the environment in which a choice is made:

1. Spatial distance, this refers specifically to the location of participants.
2. Temporal distance, this refers to the sequence in which participants express their responses.
3. Commonality of goals, this refers to the degree of co- operation which is shared by participants.
4. Structure of the process, this refers to the sharing of rights among participants on an equal or other basis.

Perhaps the most widely known GDSS are the Co-op system by Bui

(1988) and the Mediator system which was developed by Jarke, Jelassi and Shakun (1987). Underlying much of the work on GDSS are the general assumptions of rationality which characterize decision analysis as well as the strategy of using an arithmetic operation to aggregate individual preferences and weights to determine a value for the group. Lewandowski (1989) notes the difficulties of applying GDSS to real applications because of the requirement of large resources of personnel and time that are needed, as well as the requirement of a high level of motivation of individuals to participate meaningfully. It should also be stressed that the choice of model to structure the information on options and the estimated impacts is far from straightforward, as has been mentioned earlier in this chapter.

A related approach to decision conferencing and GDSS is the use of a public value forum as a strategy to identify opinions to be included in complex social choice problems. This new approach that has been pioneered by Keeney, Winterfeldt and Eppel (1990) seeks to complement other strategies, such as surveys, indirect and direct value elicitation, focus groups and public involvement which are used to clarify public values.

A public value forum can involve up to about twenty-five participants in a meeting that may continue for a couple of days. Facilities are required prior to the forum to help identify the nature of the problem and the selection of participants. The latter typically involve stakeholders and representatives. The forum is organized into a sequence of six basic steps:

1. Introduction of choice problem and motivation of the group;
2. Refinement of objectives and attributes;
3. Elicitation of single-attribute utility functions from participants;
4. Elicitation of trade-offs among the attributes from participants;
5. Combining of steps 3 and 4 with expert judgements to evaluate options;
6. Reconciliation of the intuitive evaluations and those derived for the utility model of the options.

This general sequence essentially captures a decision analysis structure which is typical of MCDA–DSS of the kind discussed in Chapter 3, with the added dimension of group participation and the specific attempt to reconcile intuition and formal evaluations in the search for a choice that enjoys collective agreement. Keeney, Winterfeldt and Eppel (1990) have tested the public value forum for an energy choice problem in Germany. They offer the conclusion that the public value forum can help elicit values, and discrepancies between intuitive ones and those derived by a formal model or expert, can be resolved. However, the process is expensive and time-consuming. Overall perhaps the best use of a forum is to employ it as an educational device with leaders of stakeholder groups and key representatives to elicit values with the expectation that the information will diffuse through the collectivity. This may be just a pious hope, but with the increased use and availability of computer-based information systems the future is likely to see more reliance on mechanisms for tackling complex collective choice problems which rely on closer integration of decision analytical tools, direct public participation via decision conferencing, possibly from home bases as well as the offices of proponents and government agencies, and indirect participation via party-political activities. While such a system may help to tackle complex facility siting questions there still remains the task of wrestling with first-order choices and related ethical choices. Brief comments on the latter are given in the final section.

6.6 Choice and ethics

This chapter began with the assertion that choice can be considered as a decision involving selection among a set of alternatives. And according to the philosophers Ullman-Margalit and Morgenbesser (1977: 757) it is generally recognized, 'That the notion of reasoned choice is central to most discussions of decision and action.' Further, following the comments by Elster (1986) on rational choice theories, while it is recognized that such theories might tell us what to do in order to achieve particular aims, we are left without guidance as to what our aims might be. In the search for aims it is appropriate that some mention be made of ethics as the central questions of this long-established field focus squarely on trying to distinguish right from wrong, good from bad, and in general appropriate choices from inappropriate ones. The science of ethics had its origin in ancient Greece, especially in the city-state of Athens which at the time was witnessing political and intellectual expansion. Langone (1981: 11) tells us that: 'Thinkers, dissatisfied and restless, were eager to breathe new life into theories that had focused on abstract concepts such as the nature of reality and the structure of the universe – right and wrong, justice and injustice emerged as subjects for critical analysis.'

The study of ethics cannot be expected to yield formal rules which can be applied to derive a correct choice. Rather such study should help to sensitize individuals, raise consciousness and generally heighten awareness of the fact that choices can have consequences which may impinge on what is felt to be right or wrong. Those who are responsible for making choices which affect the collectivity surely have a duty to consider the ethical perspective of their actions or inactions. Aristotle in his *Ethics* (Warrington 1963) argued that as a guiding principle actions should be motivated by the aim of making right choices that lead to an end which is deemed to be desirable and good. The search for a general meaning of 'good' compels philosophers to struggle with language and values in the hope, albeit a vain one perhaps, that clarification of argument and discourse will ensue. A useful review of the structure of arguments as derived from stakeholders' mental constructs and the generation, comparison and synthesis of alternative problem formulations has been offered by Vari (1991). She draws on the theoretical work by Minsky (1975) which introduced the concept of frame for representing the elementary units of the meaning of linguistic expressions. Potentially, the way argumentation is structured can influence the acceptability or rejection of options. These points are elaborated by Vari (1991) with particular reference to environmental conflict problems in Hungary which concentrate specifically on the siting of noxious facilities.

As an absolute, the concept of goodness defies unanimous definition, yet as a statement of comparison among alternatives for a practical choice problem possibly a degree of consensus can be achieved if an agent is faced with the task of choosing X or Y. This situation of selecting X-rather-than-Y has a moral and legal corollary, according to Mackie (1977: 205), 'for even if X is in itself wrong or bad or illegal or dishonourable, it does not follow that X-rather-than-Y is so. It may be foolish . . . but it may be a wise, justifiable, and commendable action. . . .' Mackie also points out that 'the agent may not have done just-X, but X-rather-than-Y, X-for-the-sake-of this bribe, X-in-response-to that provocation, X-in self defence (or in defence of others), X-in the belief that (such and such)'. Thus it is always important to provide a suitable context for a choice problem.

Frankena (1963) reminds us that Socrates provided some very useful guidelines for tackling the sort of choice problems that Langone (1981) characterizes as thorny. Basically we must try to get our facts straight and keep our minds clear, also we should not let our decisions be determined by emotions, rather we must follow best reasoning. And ultimately, 'The only question we need to answer is whether what is proposed is right or wrong' (Frankena, 1963: 2). An important corollary is pointed out by Mackie (1977: 203), namely that 'morality is concerned not only with good and bad . . . right and wrong. Closely linked with these concepts are those of choice, voluntary action, intention, responsibility, regret and remorse', and in a word, especially when accountability is considered, we must acknowledge what Mackie calls the straight rule of responsibility, that is, 'an agent is responsible for all and only his intentional actions'.

Warnock (1988) cautions that the adoption of certain ethical and moral principles can lead to a stance of so-called moral superiority, but as not all moral ideas are compatible with each other there is a need for tolerance and humility. Gummer (1988) goes further and reminds us that: 'Choice lies at the heart of being human. Without the ability or opportunity to choose, there can be no morality.'

In summary, it seems abundantly clear that the study of ethics while essentially a somewhat abstract intellectual pursuit, has as its purpose noble and highly relevant social objectives. It is therefore incumbent on all who are involved in making choices as part of the complex process for selecting locations for public facilities, give some thought to trying to determine if their actions are right or wrong, and how such actions impinge on welfare and the human condition.

7

The struggle for consensus

*The goal of politics should be unanimous and
rational consensus, not an optimal compromise
between irreducibly opposed interests.*
   Elster (1986)

7.1 An overview of consensus

Successful facility site planning relies heavily on the ability to build a
consensus to ensure that the site which is selected is perceived to be
acceptable by the stakeholders. In earlier chapters emphasis has been placed
on the role that MCDA–DSS can play in helping to improve accountability,
and this material has been complemented by a review of the critical issues in
collective choice which lie at the heart of planning public facilities. In this
chapter the concept of consensus will be examined, and in order to provide
a structure I will begin with a broad overview of the term which includes
some formal definitions. Section 7.2 will highlight the consensus–conflict
debate and some views from political science and sociology. Section 7.3
summarizes the results of a survey of newspaper articles which include the
term 'consensus'. The purpose of this exercise is to ascertain how the press
treats the concept as a reflection of public opinion. In section 7.4 I will argue
that practical attempts are now being developed and applied to use some
fairly formal approaches to group decision-making which rely on consensus
within a broadly based political framework that recognizes mediation as
having an important role to play in consensus-building as applied to specific
collective choice problems, such as facility siting.

   The organization of collective action and the selection of sites for facilities
demands that those in authority who are charged with planning responsibility enjoy sufficient support to ensure that plans are implemented. It is clear
that the legitimacy of such planning activities is enhanced if it is built on a
solid basis of consensus. Robertson (1984) claims that planning has always
evoked and depended upon consensus, and more particularly he suggests
that national development planning, which embraces facility siting exercises,
can be viewed as a major 'institution' of the twentieth-century world. He
goes further and notes that: 'One of the contradictions of planning is that it

must presume, and build upon, public consensus about purposes and processes of development.' (Robertson 1984: 4) For a specific area of development, namely health care planning in Third World countries, Bennett *et al.* (1982: 63) have claimed that 'there is an emerging international consensus that extensions of health services to those without access is a short-term and cost-effective way to reduce illness and death . . .'. As mentioned in Chapter 4 on the study in Zambia, primary health care centres are the preferred choice of location strategy which satisfies this emerging consensus. Robertson (1984: 8) reminds us that: 'National planning is surely mankind's most ambitious effort at improving material and social welfare . . .', and Kerr *et al.* (1973) has suggested that such planning and its accompanying industrialization could lead to agreement among different industry groups. He claimed that consensus develops wherever industrialization is successful. While this assertion may have a measure of truth when the global economy is increasing, it is far less certain a claim with downsizing of enterprises, industrial restructuring, the realignment of states and the current climate of global recession.

Further, with specific reference to plan evaluation Hill (1985: 2) recognizes that:

> The assumed existence of a consensus about what is in the public interest is a key variable for the development of an evaluation strategy. In the command planning mode . . . a consensus on the public interest is assumed to exist with the central decision-making body being responsible for articulating the consensus.

This assumption is not always held to be self-evident, and there is a well-articulated debate, in the field of sociology, regarding opposing social theories on consensus and conflict. This debate is reviewed by Bernard (1983) and it will be mentioned in section 7.2.

Maclean (1982) squarely identifies the need for consent when risk-management problems are being addressed, and clearly in a Regulatory State that is non-authoritarian the notions of consent or consensus are prerequisites for effective centralized decision-making.

Toward the end of the Thatcher years in the UK much was made by some political commentators on the so-called breakdown of consensus. Kavanagh, a highly qualified and respected British political scientist, has carefully documented this phenomenon of the breakdown of consensus in British politics in his book, *Thatcherism and British Politics: the end of consensus* (1987). He notes that the post-war political consensus enjoyed the support of the dominant groups in the two major political parties (Conservatives, Labour). As economic problems grew the tacit agreement, the consensus, started to break down as changes in policy and personnel occurred in the main parties and new challenges were mounted by groups on the New

Right. The thrust was towards privatization, but as Day and Klein (1987a) have noted, as reported in Chapter 1, the new consensus was not a radical dismantling of the post-war Welfare State but rather an evolutionary step towards a Regulatory State.

Hugo Young (1989: 408) has reviewed ten years of Thatcherism and draws attention to her quotation: 'I am in favour of agreement but against consensus', as a measure of her views on the detrimental effects on dynamic committed leadership which excessive consensus-building may have. Just two weeks prior to the Conservative electoral triumph in May 1979 Mrs Thatcher made the following statement at a rally in Cardiff: 'The Old Testament prophets didn't say, "Brothers, I want consensus", they said, "This is my faith and my vision. This is what I passionately believe"' Mayer (1979: 12).

In a somewhat frivolous vein we can reflect on the views of the wife of the mythical British Prime Minister, James Hacker, as portrayed in the comedy series, *Yes, Prime Minister*. 'Annie [Hacker's wife] thought – still thinks, for all I know – that the PM is completely in charge. It's a fallacy. A leader can only lead by consent' (Lynn and Jay 1986: 140). A view which is embraced by the aphorism – in order to lead, it is necessary to follow.

In earlier chapters, which have focused specific comments on MCDA–DSS, reference has been made to formal definitions of consensus as provided by measures of agreement among sets of preferences by individuals. In Chapter 3, for example, the methods of Borda and Copeland as well as recent techniques by Cook and Seiford were presented, and in Chapter 4 a method that was developed by Lootsma was applied to study attitudes about MCDA–DSS. The basic arguments for the legitimacy of these narrowly defined numerical assessments of consensus rests on the view that supports an analytical formal axiomatic approach to collective choice problems. However, even though Wagner (1980: 165), for example, argues that, 'The challenge of devising rational methods for achieving group consensus has provided decision theorists with an important class of practical and theoretical problems', it is clear that the emphasis has been on theory rather than practice. Perhaps the balance has begun to tilt slightly towards the practical side now that formal choice tools of the MCDA–DSS variety are beginning to find a place in decision conferencing as reported in Chapter 6.

Within broader political contexts it appears that a number of political leaders favour consensus-building as a positive process to address collective choice problems which are felt to impinge on economic prosperity and sustainable growth. In 1988 the Single European Act came into effect and Jacques Delors, the President of the EC, has made a number of references to the need for, and advantages of, consensus, as the fundamental element to reinforce the *raison d'être* of the emerging federal system of twelve states within a unified trading system. Delors reported in 7 February 1989 (*The Independent*) that 'during the four years of my first term as president I have devoted all of my energies to reaching a consensus among the 12 members of the community'. The article, an interview with Jacques Delors, by Peter Jenkins, concludes with an encapsulated version of Delors's philosophy:

> His [Delors's] own belief was that without ever-increasing co-operation between the members of the Community, not only was their material prosperity in danger but also their independence and influence in the world. However, Britain had to be part of this enterprise, with its special relationships with North America and its Commonwealth associations, brought a great heritage to Europe. That is why, said President Delors, his efforts would always be towards reconciling the points of view of all member countries. His colleagues, would testify to his 'obsession with consensus'.

The proposed Social Charter which was released by Delors in May 1989 argued that: 'There will be no economic growth in the Community without a social consensus' (*The Sunday Times*, 21 May 1989). The sacrifices of some unknown amounts of sovereignty did not sit easily with Mrs Thatcher who consistently denounced the views on consensus of Delors.

Mrs Thatcher continued to resist and this was reflected in the Tory manifesto on Europe, released late in May 1989, that claimed that too much power is being ceded to the bureaucrats in Brussels who are not sufficiently accountable to citizens and particularly constituencies of the member states. The leader of the British Labour Party remarked early in May (*The Independent*, 10 May 1989) that: 'Our partners in the EC have never had the Thatcherite faith in the markets. They know that long-term competition requires that the market is managed, and they know that economic success is built on consensus not on conflict.'

The elections in June 1989 for the European Parliament gave weight to the argument that the majority of countries were supportive of the principles enunciated by President Jacques Delors, and Mrs Thatcher's rhetoric on the dirigism of the Brussels bureaucrats was a minority view.

In 1981 Alexander Haig, the then US Secretary of State asserted that peace and security are closely linked to economic prosperity and the means to achieve these is via a consensus-building style of government and management. Haig argued that it is essential to

> . . . seek actively to shape events, and, in the process, attempt to force a consensus on like-minded people. Such a consensus will enable us to deal with the more fundamental tasks I have outlined; the management of Soviet power, the re-establishment of an orderly international economic climate, and economic and political maturation of developing nations to the benefit of their peoples and the achievement of a reasonable standard of international civility (*New York Times*, 10 January 1981).

As 1988 came to an end the Soviet Union publicly announced their acceptance and global significance of the need to establish a 'new consensus for a new era', to quote the Deputy Minister Anatoli Adamshin (*The Guardian*, 13 December 1988). The events in the Soviet Union in 1991 and the emerging Commonwealth of Republics attests to the search for new political structures to replace the highly centralized state. A new consensus is being sought.

The USA and the old USSR are struggling with the concept of consensus to see how it can fit in with their histories, political practices and future options. China, too, has entered the debate.

Early in January 1988, James Rusk, the correspondent of the Canadian newspaper *The Globe and Mail*, remarked that: 'There is no consensus among Chinese leaders and policy makers on crucial issues such as whether Mr Gorbachev's apparently conciliatory foreign policy is merely a superficial shift in tactics or a more fundamental change.' It is clear that a fundamental change has occurred, but whether the exact nature was envisaged by Gorbachev in 1988 is highly unlikely. The consensus he sought broke down at the end of 1991 and he resigned on 25 December of that year.

A reflection of the lack of consensus manifested itself on the internal affairs in China surrounding the visit of Mr Gorbachev to Beijing in May 1989 and the occupation by the students of Tien An Men Square, the declaration of martial law and the initial refusal of the army to implement this law. Until political solutions to the question of national consensus and legitimacy of power are resolved it is hard to envisage that the practical steps being taken to improve social and economic conditions in China will occur without considerable conflict.

In the autumn of 1988 there was much debate in Australia on the consensus that Prime Minister Hawke had sought to build among the unions, the business community and state interests. All his skills as a negotiator were needed to limit the damage of conflicts among the interest groups. Martin Flanagan reporting in *The Guardian*, on 25 November 1988 clearly presents the argument that Hawke has captured the political centre in Australia and thus

> committed his opponents to a long and, to date, fruitless search for an idea or philosophy which will win them back the middle ground. . . .
> Hawke came to office with a promise of 'consensus' of bringing the nation together after the division of the Fraser years. What has emerged is a species of politics previously unknown in this country, a merger of government, big business and the trade union movement. All this has been achieved by a man of the 'left'.

As 1991 came to a close Hawke was forced out of power as the Prime Minister. He resigned, called for a leadership vote and lost to Paul Keating. In Canada, Prime Minister Mulroney, and his Conservative government have been seeking a consensus following a period of conflict – especially between the federal and provincial governments, which some claim characterized the closing years of the Liberal government of Pierre Trudeau. This view is of course not generally supported by Liberals, and one member of the party, Roy Maclaren, has written a book to deal with the issue. The title is *Consensus: a Liberal looks at his party* (1984). Maclaren (1984: 81) is of the opinion that consensus can be viewed as the practice of compromise and it should not be disparaged. Further, he claims that: 'the Liberal Party has always been the party of consensus . . .', and this has served Canada well in handling the pluralistic demands of its citizens within a large, highly complex federal system with a tiny indigenous population, two major founding nations and a massive inflow of immigrants especially in the post-war period. Gillies, a policy adviser to Canadian Conservative governments in recent years, has already thrown his support behind consensus as a means of achieving economic and social progress (Gillies 1986).

Recent events in Canada are largely focused on dealing with the effects of the economic recession and the search for new constitutional arrangements for the country. The emergence of a new consensus is not being achieved easily, and it is too soon to speculate with accuracy on the political forms that it will take.

From this brief survey it is abundantly clear that while politicians tend to believe in consensus as a necessary condition to tackle collective choice planning problems, effectively they recognize that the existing management and political practices within states need to be modified to find a new *modus operandi*. It is this new consensus which will characterize the so-called Regulatory State. This does not deny that the concept of consensus is problematic. For example, precisely how do we recognize when it exists? How is it achieved? Is it an end in itself or a means to some other end? What strategies and tactics are available which can be used in its promotion?

Let me now turn to some attempts that have been made to define consensus. According to Angell's review of the term 'consensus' in the *Dictionary of Social Sciences*, edited by Gould and Kolb (1964), Park and Burgess claim that the total set of cultural traits can be considered as evidence of consensus, and such notions as folkways, mores, techniques, and ideals 'may be reduced to the one term "consensus"'. This usage stems from Comte who viewed consensus as that which holds a society together. Kallen's (1931) view of consensus embraces the notion that it represents the resolution of conflicts through co-operative effort and is the culmination of a process 'in which public sentiment and public opinion are brought to bear on a problem' (Angell 1964: 128).

In essence consensus implies the sharing of sentiment and this includes rational agreement, all with a view to the production and maintenance of order. The term 'consensus politics' is referred to in the *Dictionary of Modern Thought*, edited by Bullock and Stallybrass (1980) to suggest the use of moderate policies which rely on economic and welfare policies that do not seriously disturb the status quo. Mention has already been made of the fact that such politics are changing and the so-called Regulatory State is emerging as the consensus option.

Elaborations of these definitions which encapsulate the view of sociologists and political scientists are provided by Shils and Lipsitz (1968) in their respective summaries of 'the concept of consensus' and 'the study of consensus' which appears in *The International Encyclopedia of the Social Sciences*.

Three Latin terms, found in *Black's Law Dictionary*, summarize the overarching view of consensus by social scientists as applied to a sovereign unit, such as a state, or a smaller entity. First, *consensus facit legem* (consent makes the law): this clearly indicates that legitimacy of actions taken by an executive demands the acceptance of the power which that executive holds. Second, *consensus voluntas multorum ad quos res pertinet, simul juncta* (consent is the united will of several interested in one subject matter): without suggesting that unanimity exists for each and every action, no matter how large or small. The subject tends *de facto* to be the process by which actions which affect the collectivity, rather than the substantive issues *per se*. For our field of interest is it therefore sufficient for society to feel that the procedures and regulations governing the search for a site for a public facility are generally acceptable, or is it necessary that a particular site be found appropriate by a sufficient number so that the claim of consensual support can be made? While the former is probably the correct answer, in general terms of social science, especially political theory, for practical matters politicians and others, for example citizen groups, might well prefer the latter. In simple terms we might suggest that consensus allows an executive to make the major strategic decisions, while local tactical issues might be hotly debated and resisted especially by a vociferous articulate minority of local opponents. Surely in sum it would be preferable to have consensus clearly supporting both strategic and tactical planning decisions. Finally, the third term, *consensus tollit errorem* (consent removes mistakes), suggests a sharing of blame or responsibility and perhaps general acceptance of the outcomes of a decision-making process.

A systematic search of the literature in the social sciences for references to consensus reveals a rich collection of papers and books. For example, some 1400 articles were identified via a search by the Institute for Social Research at York University using citation indices for the period 1970–86. The range of interests is considerable, from narrow highly technical formal mathematical definitions of the term to broad general descriptive and normative statements that refer to the dynamics of relationships within a group. For example, psychologists may deal with small groups who focus on consent and opinion formation, often within experimental frameworks, while political scientists turn their attention to relationships between government (types, styles, electoral systems and the like), and the cultural milieu in its temporal and spatial context within which a particular governmental style has emerged, functions and maintains legitimacy. Sociologists have written on the fundamental debate as to the nature of society asking the question: is society basically concerned with consensus-building or conflict resolution and are these categories meaningful?

Approximately 100 articles which contain 'consensus' in the title and relate to public decisions have been identified by Casper (1988) in his bibliography on *Consensus in Public Decisions*. Casper (1988: 1) argues that 'consensus has become the preferred method for resolving problems, issues, and policy questions among American decision-making groups, public and private'. However, it would still appear to be the case that the level of consensus in decision-making in the USA, and most other jurisdictions, is below that which some argue characterizes Japanese practices. A systematic cross-cultural comparison is hard to conduct because of the lack of clear credible operational definitions for levels of consensus.

Turning now from general comments on consensus to those relating to siting it seems that if we could all agree on a process for selecting a site for a public facility, and on the first-order choices which preceded the location problem, then perhaps we would all accept the consequences of this process which yielded a so-called preferred site. However, while there is general agreement about the need for a fair, open, traceable, accountable process, unfortunately the implementation and making operational of this process does not always enjoy widespread consensus. Recently an attempt has been made in the USA to develop a facility siting credo drawing on the expertise of siting experts. This draws on some of the principles which I have enunciated in earlier chapters. The draft version of the credo was distributed in September 1990 and it was developed from two national workshops in October 1989 and February 1990 which were sponsored by the MIT Hazardous Substances Management Programme, the Wharton Risk and Decision Processes Center and the MIT–Harvard Public Disputes Programme. The credo comprises ideal operational principles and mechanisms which might be incorporated into siting approaches by local and regional governments. It is argued that if the various stakeholders adopt the Credo then 'we might – as a nation – be able to deal with siting disputes in a fashion that produces fairer, wiser, and more efficient outcomes'. (1990: 1) In a word the thirteen principles which are enunciated seek to develop trust among the affected parties. The principles are:

1. Seek consensus through a broad-based participatory process.
2. Work to develop trust.
3. Get agreement that the status quo is unacceptable.
4. Choose the facility design that best addresses the problem.
5. Seek acceptable sites through a volunteer process.
6. Consider a competitive siting process.
7. Work for geographic fairness.
8. Keep multiple options on the table at all times.
9. Guarantee that stringent safety standards will be met.
10. Fully compensate all negative impacts of a facility.
11. Make the host community [of a noxious facility] better off.
12. Use contingent agreements.
13. Set realistic timetables.

7.2 Consensus: views from political science and sociology

Graham (1984: 89) argues that consensus plays a central role in the development of political theory and he offers a very detailed survey of the use of the term. He recognizes that the idea of consensus and the act of consent as 'shared public agreement' have been used in conflicting ways to serve prescriptive ends of political theorists. A clear statement and review of the debate on the so-called consensus–conflict theories of society is given by Bernard (1983). This will be reviewed later in this section.

The treatment of consensus as a concept in the study of politics embraces normative as well as prescriptive analyses and has attracted attention of classical writers (e.g. Plato and Aristotle) and modern ones (e.g. Machiavelli, Hobbes and Locke) as well as those who adopt a systematic approach (e.g. Easton and Parsons). In the light of a broad survey of classical and modern political philosophies, as well as contemporary usages in political science, Graham (1984: 111) seeks to identify the basic characteristics which appear to be central to most of the conceptions of the term. This he manages to do in a set of detailed points which can be collapsed into the following definitions of consensus as a 'state of agreement, which varies in intensity and scope over time, incorporating the goals for society, the procedures for decision-making, and the particular policies'. It must be clearly recognized and acknowledged, certainly for the sort of siting policies examined in this book, that the degree and intensity of a consensus will depend on a society's degree and intensity of commitment to shared norms. More particularly we must be aware that 'society' explicitly comprises proponents of a siting plan and other advocates, groups and individuals who may be opposed, those who are indifferent, and the regulators and decision-makers who have executive authority. All are stakeholders in the planning process. Credibility and more particularly legitimacy of the process must enjoy consensual support as a prerequisite for claiming that a reasonable and fair system is operating.

Anglade (1986) recognizes that legitimacy and consensus are key concepts of political science which unfortunately are least easily defined. There is a close functional relationship between authority and legitimacy. Authority to make and enforce siting decisions can be derived from the mere position of authority which gives access to monopoly use of coercion to obtain compliance. For a siting problem this can involve, for example, the use of instruments such as laws and regulations pertaining to information, demonstrations and hearings, as well as direct use of coercive force, such as policing agencies to protect a facility which some feel is particularly noxious and unwelcome. Anglade (1986: 1) claims that 'every government or regime is concerned about making the minimum possible use of coercion and prefers to rely instead on consent that will tend to be forthcoming if authority is seen to be legitimate'. The ongoing use of force by the Japanese government at Narita airport 56 km east of Tokyo is, according to McGill (1991), 'probably the biggest single blunder committed by a government that prides itself on consensus . . .'. The dispute between the government and local farmers continues unabated after almost thirteen years and violence has frequently broken out in this dispute.

Anglade goes on to argue that legitimacy as consensus is a relatively recent historical phenomenon, for as Jordan (1985: 107) has noted: 'In the European tradition, . . . the state was a cohesive force, purposefully unifying society, and its legitimacy was derived from this, rather than from the implicit or explicit consent of individual citizens. . . . The legitimacy of the state was thus moral, not utilitarian.' Recent political events which diminish sovereign authority of states and make transfers to supranational bodies through trade agreements (e.g. the USA–Canada Free Trade Agreement), or to quasi-federal agencies that issue directives to member states (e.g. the environmental directives issued under the Treaty of Rome to EC members), impinge on the traditional moral authority of a state and move towards administrative, managerial styles of utilitarianism. The two examples cited above have consequences on facility siting issues, first in the case of Canada and the USA with respect to the debate on universality of social programmes, especially health care, for example. Canada enjoys universality, and hospitals and other health care facilities are essentially *public* facilities which respond to a large degree on concerns with equity. The USA does not have a universal health care programme and hospital locations are influenced to a large extent by market forces. In the second example, there is an ongoing debate in Europe on the search for unified standards to manage waste to conform to agreed standards. There is a critical locational dimension to this work, especially with respect to the selection of sites for radioactive waste and the identification of existing waste sites which are hazardous and need to be decommissioned.

The rule of law can now be seen to represent the fundamental source of legitimacy following the evolution, especially in Western Europe, of the declining religious ethos of the seventeenth and eighteenth centuries through what Anglade (1986: 4) calls

> . . . the humanist, individualist and rationalist opposition which developed against the divine source of legitimacy of absolutist rule: . . . In the rationalistic European societies [and their colonies] *Reason* had become the most perfect form of legitimacy available for every form of political authority and, through the philosophy of the Enlightenment, it had found its most material expression in the rule of law.

In an attempt to establish a normative foundation for the legitimacy of authority in a state, there has developed a functional linkage among reason, law and state as a new basis unlike the previous one in which legitimacy was derived from a supernatural origin of both power and law. The functional linkages continue to develop and the nature of the linkages as they relate to facility planning depends on the level of consensus regarding the ways reason, law and state are interpreted to deal with a specific noxious or salutary facility siting problem. In a word a balance is sought which involves, *inter alia*, technical studies, managerial and bureaucratic procedures as well as legal and regulatory systems. This balance is the necessary consensus needed to ensure that planning is legitimate within a state.

Earlier in this section reference was made to the 'Consensus–conflict debate'. This phrase refers to a controversy which surrounds the view that social theories can be divided into two contrasting types. The consensual ones, it is argued, emphasize the persistence of shared values and norms based on tacit agreements about rules and practices as the fundamental characteristic of societies. Conflict theories are said to recognize that societies contain groups that dominate, and such powerful groups exercise control, for example, via education and the media. In such societies change occurs as new groups arise and successfully displace the powerful. By contrast change in the consensual societies occurs somewhat gradually as attitudes and beliefs evolve.

Bernard (1983) suggests that the consensual–conflict controversy arose in sociology in the 1950s, peaked some twenty years later and is now declining. Whereas Dahrendorf (1958: 115) concluded that, 'societies and social organizations are held together not by consensus but by constraint, not by universal agreement but by coercion of some by others'. Shils (1965: 4) stressed that: 'Modern society, especially in its latest phase, is characteristically a consensual society. . .'. Bernard (1983) systematically examines seven pairs of social theories, each pair comprising a consensual and a conflict theory. The form and content of the theories are analysed and a classification derived which dichotomizes human nature (HN) as either consensual or conflictual, a similar dichotomy is provided for contemporary societies (CS). In sum this yields four basic categories:

1. Conservative: consensual HN
                            consensual CS
2. Radical: consensual HN
                            conflictual CS
3. Sociological consensus: conflictual HN
                            consensual CS
4. Sociological conflict: conflictual HN
                            conflictual CS

It is exceedingly difficult to obtain empirical evidence or to develop an analytical argument which allows us to state categorically that individuals defined as HN, and groups defined as CS are either consensual or conflictual. Bruton and Nicholson (1987) suggest that consensual and conflictual perspectives on the ways in which social interaction takes place should be complemented by those that are pluralist. This latter perspective recognizes the diversity of group interests and the fact that planning is a political activity with politicians as the final arbiters. To give legitimacy it is necessary that all stakeholders have an opportunity to be represented, and to reduce social problems it is suggested that participation be used as a channel to influence decision-makers, with the planner acting in the role of an advocate. Whether public participation offers a framework to articulate conflicts rather than a device to achieve consensus is a moot point according to Bruton and Nicholson (1987).

A pervasive view is one that embraces consensus, conflict and pluralism as social processes that characterize the way a Regulatory State functions. However, the specific consensus–conflict debate has perhaps heightened general awareness and it is clear that politicians, regulators, proponents and opponents of siting projects all seek to achieve outcomes with which they feel comfortable. Inevitably conflicts arise, and in order to manage these a variety of strategies and tactics have been developed as mentioned in earlier chapters with reference to negotiations. The specific aim of such negotiations is to seek a functional consensus, and comments on negotiations will be made in section 7.4.

In summary, while it is virtually impossible to measure consensus in a technical way it is clear that the concept is generally thought to be highly significant and one that should be included as a necessary condition in successful collective choice planning. In section 7.3 support for this assertion will be offered by drawing on material extracted from newspaper articles.

7.3 What the papers say

The word 'consensus' appears frequently in the press, and this suggests that it has relevance to the contemporary world as a reflection of contemporary values and attitudes. Specifically the term is often included as an indication of a reasonable, acceptable, decent compromise position among competing interests. The lack of consensus suggests trouble and continuing strife, though this is not a unanimous opinion as noted earlier. Occasionally consensus is referred to as a necessary condition to enhance the chances of economic progress and hence social betterment and political stability. This is the view espoused by Gillies (1986) in his book on economic development in Canada in the next century. Important as the formation of consensus is to successful public policy-making Gillies makes it abundantly clear that 'it is not enough simply to forge consensus on national objectives – it is essential to create mechanisms which can meaningfully discriminate amongst real strategic options . . . and can force choice amongst them . . .'. (Gillies 1986: xi). Consensus and choice must be linked in an accountable political system as is stressed in this book.

Two questions appear to dominate the *realpolitik* of consensus as perceived by those who follow closely the activities of the men and women who are in positions of power and authority. First is consensus a lowest common denominator, a minimum position or a set of values and attitudes to which all can ascribe? As such is it a limiting force on the manœuvrability, imagination and initiative of a political leader and as a consequence on the collectivity? The second question, posed as the corollary, asks if consensus has a positive dynamic connotation which is perhaps suggestive of strength, conviction and solidarity?

In order to try to unravel some of these points this section reports on a selection of press cuttings over the period 1985–90. The followers referred to earlier are the reporters, with all their biases, prejudices and political preferences, and the range of newspaper sources can be categorized as broadly centre, rather than extreme left or right.

The comments on consensus have been culled from the following sources:

The Guardian Weekly (GW) UK
The Guardian UK
The Independent UK
The Observer UK
The Times UK
The Times Higher Education Supplement (THES) UK
The Telegraph Weekend Magazine (TWM) UK
The Irish Post Ireland
The New York Times (NYT) USA
The Globe and Mail (G&M) Canada
The Report on Business Magazine (ROBM) Canada
The Toronto Star (TS) Canada
The Jerusalem Post (JP) Israel
The Economist UK (international)

During the six-year period these papers were perused in a non-systematic fashion and a set of eighty specific references to consensus were identified. A sample of selected references with the contextual sentence (S) and title (T) are given below, and they have been ordered chronologically.

1. THES   May 1985

   T.   A wooden signpost, not a milestone.

   S.   Regrettably, this was not an attempt to seek common ground, or, to use a dirty word, consensus, about the future of higher education, despite the consultation, particularly with the University Granit Commission (UGC) and the National Academic Board (NAB), and the work of Lindop, Jarratt and others.

2. *The Times*   Feb. 1986

   T.   The Portuguese election: Soares supporters celebrate as he dons the crown.

   S.   Dr Soares's appeal to his countrymen that he could best fulfil the role of a conciliator and help to bring social consensus as Portugal takes its place within the European Community appeared to have succeeded.

3. *The Times* Feb 1986

 T. Chunnel: the Tory challenge.
 S. Or it may have been simply that, unlike Stansted or Sizewell, there is a national consensus supporting the tunnel.

4. *The Times* Feb. 1986

 T. Commentary.
 S. Sir Geoffrey, on the other hand, seems to sense the current public taste for 'a moderate, more consensual form of Conservatism'.

5. *The Observer* Jan. 1987

 T. A chill warning for the Chancellor.
 S. For many years the post-war consensus in Britain was that investment in education, health and the environment was beneficial to all, and that it was more efficacious to rely on a publicly funded safety net than the whims of private donors to provide charitable relief for the victims in our society.

6. *GW* May 1987

 T. A breath of democracy as Mexico adjusts to the end of consensus.
 S. A breath of democracy as Mexico adjusts to the end of consensus.

7. *G&M* June 1987

 T. The Meech accord strengthens bonds that link Canada.
 S. This will not result in continual stalemate but in a more creative and dynamic process of change – one that will place a premium on seeking consensus.

8. *The Independent* Sept. 1987

 T. Labour plan to abolish inner-city corporations.
 S. The only people who quite deliberately stand outside that consensus is the Government because they have an obsessional antipathy to local government.'

9. *THES* Sept. 1987

 T. Beyond the social counter-revolution.
 S. The breakdown of the consensus over social values in Western society has had at least one fortunate consequence (intended or otherwise): the re-examination of those fundamental principles on which a free and civilized society rests.

10. *The Economist* Oct. 1987

 T. The new threat from Japan is patience.

S.   Mr Takeshita [Japan's next prime minister] carries Japan's tradition of consensus to unusual lengths.

11.   *The Observer*   Nov. 1987

T.   Japan can't afford to fold up US umbrella.

S.   'He [Japanese Prime Minister Noburu Takeshita] has built his reputation as a man who knows how to build up a patient consensus on an issue, to get support for a policy,' argues Yoichi Masuzoe, Professor of Politics at the University of Tokyo.

12.   *NYT*   Jan. 1988

T.   Reagan's Search for New Year's Diplomatic Resolutions.

S.   How long can a President hold to a concept that contradicts the national consensus?

13.   *G&M*   Jan. 1988

T.   Coming of age: China may not be ready to make some needed foreign policy decisions.

S.   There is no consensus among Chinese leaders and policymakers on crucial issues such as whether Mr Gorbachev's apparently conciliatory foreign policy is merely a superficial shift in tactics or a more fundamental change.

14.   *The Times*   Feb. 1988

T.   The end of society?

S.   The puzzle is a deep one for Marquand since he thinks that the post-war consensus provided an approximation to the sort of political consensus on which social democracy rests: the abandonment of the post-war consensus must therefore be explained on this account within a larger interpretation of British history.

15.   *GW*   June 1988

T.   New fears of famine stalk Vietnam.

S.   Politically, the watchword seems to be consensus at any price.

16.   *THES*   June 1988

T.   Compromised health: a bargain system?

S.   Thus, far from the NHS [National Health Service] emerging out of a consensus which had its roots in the interwar period, Webster shows how it was a product of a series of political negotiations and compromises between parties with opposing views.

17.   *ROBM*   July 1988

T.   Breaking eggs.

S.   Thatcher has rejected the very idea of the consensus that has ruled British politics since the Second World War.

18. *The Independent* Oct. 1988
    T. Forging a new political vocabulary.
    S. As long as national [British] politics operated within a broad, consensual framework, awkward philosophical questions about 'freedom' were avoided.

19. *The Independent* Oct. 1988
    T. Fossil fuels pose tough dilemmas.
    S. Now a consensus is emerging among the experts that global temperatures are rising and will continue to do so, because of the increasing concentration of 'greenhouse' gases in the atmosphere which block the escape of infra-red radiation from the earth into space.

20. *The Guardian* Nov. 1988
    T. A long road back for the Liberals
    S. Hawke [Australian PM] came to office with a promise of 'consensus', of bringing the nation together after the division of the Fraser years.

21. *TWM* Nov. 1988
    T. Charity begins at Oxford.
    S. In the softer, consensual days of the mid-twentieth century it [Oxford] came to rely, like other universities, on the state.

22. *The Irish Post* Nov. 1988
    T. Consensus cracks up: early election in republic looks likely.
    S. The consensus which underpinned Charles Haughey's minority government has cracked and there now emerges the likelihood of an early general election in the [Irish] Republic.

23. *The Guardian* Dec. 1988
    T. A new consensus for a new era.
    S. Gorbachev heralds 'the birth of a new world order through a universal human consensus' in a UN speech which announces big unilateral Soviet troop cuts.

24. *The Guardian* Dec. 1988
    T. The charter of despair.
    S. Walter Bagehot's 'deliberate assembly of moderate politicians', determined 'never to press the tenets of their party to impossible conclusions' has been replaced by a [British] government which is explicitly opposed to consensus and led by a Prime Minister who despises compromise.

25. *The Guardian* Dec. 1988
    T. Losing freedom in the fog.

S. This was the time of the 'consensus' which meant that social tinkering made Britain appear less divisive and which held great benefits for the ruling order, whose power it reinforced.

26. *The Guardian* Jan. 1989

T. A politics of consensus.

S. David Basnett was *par excellence* the trade union leader [for Britain] crafted and shaped for the age of political consensus.

27. *JP* Jan. 1989

T. World pledges to eliminate chemical weapons.

S. The declaration [to eliminate chemical weapons] , adopted by consensus, marked a diplomatic triumph for France, which, with Finland, led efforts to find common ground between major powers and the Third World.

28. *The Guardian* Feb. 1989

T. Humiliation in the House for Mr Hurd.

S. For the shocking feature of Mrs Thatcher's decade in office is not just the havoc it has wrought on nice, easy-going, consensus-loving Britain.

29. *The Independent* Feb 1989

T. Gonzalez checks his European dream.

S. 'My [Spanish Prime Minister Felipe Gonzalez Marquez] job is to seek consensus.'

30. *JP* Mar. 1989

T. No peace without 'historic' compromise, says Peres.

S. At the beginning of his speech Peres [Vice Premier of Israel] asserted that there was a consensus in Israel on the necessity of electoral reform.

31. *JP* Mar. 1989

T. The solidarity conference and Soviet Jewry.

S. This week as 1700 Jewish leaders from all over the world – many more than even optimists expected – gathered in Jerusalem to re-emphasize the basic unity of the state, it was shown that the Jewish consensus on the vital issues is much wider and stronger than we sometimes feel.

32. *The Guardian* Apr. 1989

T. Hong Kong seeks MP's aid on rights.

S. Hong Kong's various interest groups are now all agreed on the need for eventual universal suffrage, even though they have still not reached consensus on the timetable towards its implementation.

33. *The Independent* Apr. 1989

T. Sunday trading changes 'depend on consensus'.
S. But we are in no hurry to finish it until we have consensus which commands the maximum support in this House, and throughout the country [Britain].

34. *THES* Apr. 1989

T. Legacies of war.
S. He [Elisha Efrat, author of the book, *Geography and Politics in Israel since 1967*] is right, of course, though ideological politics has a hard grip, and the necessary consensus to make such planning possible seems far off.

35. *The Economist* Apr. 1989

T. A tidy little man.
S. What Mr Takeshita [Japan's next prime minister] may deliver is a form of consensus-building caution that Mr Nakasone's five years in office had begun to make seem a thing of the Japanese past.

36. *The Independent* May 1989

T. 'Treachery' by Thatcher over 1992 EC market
S. Kinnock [leader of the opposition] 'They know that long-term competition requires that the market is managed, and they know that economic success is built on consensus not on conflict.'

37. *The Economist* May 1989

T. Green, greener, greenest?
S. Businesses are bound to suffer as nations strive for an environmental consensus.

38. *TS* May 1990

T. Politicians will solve Meech mess.
S. Consensus has been a rare commodity in this country [Canada] of late.

39. *THES* Oct. 1990

T. The land of missed opportunity.
S. The two most familiar cliches applied to British history in the forty-five years following the Second World War are those of 'consensus' and of 'decline'.

The set of eighty articles, all of which focus on broadly defined collective choice problems, can be categorized with respect to two dimensions as shown in Fig.7.1. The first dimension attempts to provide an assessment of the general thrust of the article and specifically as to whether consensus is seen as a positive concept or one that somehow will hinder constructive collective choice. Some 20 per cent of the articles fall into this category. The second dimension seeks to identify the level of organization. Fifty-two articles deal with problems at the level of the state, whereas twenty-five focus on international issues. Only three articles address local issues. Clearly it is at the state level that the greatest attention to consensus is focused and the breakdown between positive and negative suggests a balance of about 75 and 25 per cent respectively. Of course definitive conclusions based upon numerical frequency data should be tempered by knowledge of the data base. More particularly it is clear that in the set of articles there are quite a number which report the views of Mrs Thatcher about consensus, as she enjoyed a high public profile during the period of study. However, I believe the survey does give a clear indication that the press reflect public views regarding the generally supportive positive attributes of consensus and more particularly collective choice planning at the level of the state should, in a normative sense, be based on consensus.

7.4 Group judgement, mediation and consensus

The final section of this chapter will comment on selected approaches which have been developed to tackle the general problem of seeking consensus from a group. In recent years a variety of procedures have been devised and the most widely known are the Delphi technique, the nominal group technique (NGT) and social judgement analysis (SJA). Details of each of these will not be given as they are widely available in the literature, for example, Delphi (Linstone and Turoff 1975), NGT (Delbeeq, Van de Ven and Gustafson 1975), SJA (Brehmer 1976). With the growth of MCDA–DSS and its use in decision-conferencing a further class of techniques is emerging, as mentioned in Chapter 6, under the title group decision support systems (GDSS). This is reviewed in de Sanctis and Gallupe (1987). In essence the proponents of all these approaches argue that they are superior to the so-called conventional discussion groups. This assertion has rarely been tested systematically, not least because of the difficulty in defining a

| | SCALE | | |
	International	State Level	Local
Positive	19	42	3
Negative	6	10	

ATTITUDE

Fig. 7.1 Categories of views of consensus

measure to reflect the quality of a group decision or the degree of consensus which obtains.

A further point that must be made concerns the size and composition of the group which is involved in the consensus-building exercise. Generally speaking the smaller the group the easier it is to reach a consensus; however, this naïve assumption does not address squarely the fact that collective choice problems for public facilities typically involve stakeholders who hold widely divergent opinions about estimates of the magnitude and importance of impacts associated with alternative location choices for a facility. Also, it is not the easiest task to identify all the stakeholders, and ascertain that they are legitimate and acceptable representatives of a set of constituents who will accept the final outcome of the group's decision. Some of the stakeholders occupy key positions by virtue of their status as a proponent or a member of a regulatory body, for example. In the case of the latter accountability is readily identified, but for many other stake-holders this is often problematic as has been stressed in Chapter 5. Initially it can be argued that an effective approach to group decision-making is one that will not only reduce disagreement among the members, but also yields an accurate judgement. There is a body of literature that has examined this latter aspect and Reagan-Cirincione (1992: i) notes that: 'Interacting groups fail to make judgements as accurate as those of their most capable group members. . . .' It should be noted that the studies which yield this kind of result tend to focus on the general problem of predicting an outcome, then observing the actual outcome and measuring the deviation. With respect to facility siting it can be argued that estimates of the outcomes are predicted by 'technical experts' and these people can be seen as the 'most capable group members'. Hence a group decision approach would not generally be used to tackle this part of the problem.

The focus then turns to the matter of assessing the significance of the outcomes and the trade-offs, and this is the issue that stakeholders are forced to struggle with, and it is the part of the facility siting problem where specific attention should be placed on the reduction of disagreement among members of a group and hence consensus-building. Reagan and Rohrbaugh (1990: 21) draw attention to the fact that 'any assessment of the effectiveness of a group decision process requires directing primary attention to the process itself, not to subsequent outcomes'. They identify four perspectives concerning effective decision processes which are listed as follows:

1. *Consensual:* participatory process: supportability of decision.
2. *Political:* adaptable process: legitimacy of decision.
3. *Empirical:* data based process: accountability of decision.
4. *Rational:* goal-centred process: efficiency of decision.

All of these capture the essential requirements of an approach for tackling a facility siting collective choice problem.

Rohrbaugh and his co-workers have undertaken a series of systematic studies comparing the effectiveness of the Delphi technique, NGT, SJA and GDSS. In 1979 Rohrbaugh noted that SJA appeared to be superior to Delphi for reducing disagreement among group members, and five years earlier van de Ven (1974) undertook a comparative study of the effectiveness of Delphi and NGT, compared to a conventional discussion group. He concluded that this latter approach is the least effective way of generating imaginative solutions and allowing them to be elaborated and compared. The preferred approach is the NGT which is based upon the four steps of first, silent generation of ideas in writing, second, presentation and recording of independent ideas, third, discussion and classification of ideas and fourth, the independent ranking of priorities. All of this occurring in an open setting. The Delphi approach tends to rely on anonymity and interactions via mail responses to questionnaires. Several rounds may be involved in the search for a consensual outcome. De Loe (1991: 20) reminds us that 'the aim of the conventional Delphi has been to create a consensus' and while it may be cheaper to administer than arranging meetings which stakeholders have to attend there are serious criticisms of the approach. Bardecki (1984) infers that stakeholders with strong and divergent views may drop out, and consensus may be partly due to attrition, and Chan (1982: 440) notes that consensus may represent 'collective bias rather than wisdom'.

In the light of these comments it is not surprising that a clearly preferred and practical group decision approach has not yet emerged which can be readily applied to help stakeholders reach a consensus. However, the search continues and attempts are now being made to develop an integrated approach that takes the best of each. Reagan-Cirincione (1992) argues that the integration of group facilitation, decision modelling and information technology can overcome problems associated with interaction processes and cognition. The format is similar to that of decision-conferencing described in Chapter 6; however, if it is to be used to tackle public choice facility siting problems then the closed-room approach will have to be modified to allow stakeholders to assemble in a large space which is more like an auditorium than either a court-room setting or a specially designed high-tech room. Overall the thrust is toward a mediation approach for achieving consensus.

In 1989 a two-day symposium was held at Kingston on the topic of consensus and conflict resolution as related to planning. The keynote speaker was Lawrence Susskind, the founder of the Programme on Negotiation at the Harvard Law School and a Professor of Urban Studies and Planning at MIT. He is also the editor and publisher of the newsletter *Consensus* of the Public Disputes Programme at Harvard. Susskind drew attention to a number of initiatives by private and public agencies in the USA in the late 1970s which focused on the need for consensus-building as an alternative to litigation. The newsletter *Consensus* is distributed to 40 000 elected officials in the USA and Susskind argues that a market in the public sector for dispute resolution services has grown considerably and the business now involves over 3000 professionals. He recognizes that while 'conflict is the engine of social change' (Bowering 1989: 3) there is a constant need to refine consensus-building techniques which involve negotiation strategies and tactics that will achieve, 'the fairest, most efficient, most stable, wisest agreements'. And it is these which can be viewed as the consensual solutions because they not only yield outcomes which are technically efficient but more particularly the solutions are acceptable to stakeholders and citizens at large. The ideal agreement outlined above is a direct translation of the ideal negotiation process which was referred to in Chapter 2. In summary Susskind noted that consensus-building or conflict resolution has to be seen within a political milieu and he contrasted the litigation milieu of the USA with an administrative approach in Canada.

Some jurisdictions have attempted to pass legislation that mandates public participation in siting problems. For example, in 1981, the state of Illinois legislature passed Senate Bill 172, which mandated that the local jurisdictional unit hold public hearings and approve all applications to site hazardous and solid waste facilities. Regulatory agencies, for example the Environmental Assessment Board in Ontario, also typically inquire about the nature and level of public participation in a siting process.

Conflicting opinions and the related dilemmas can lead to judicial review or, according to Lake (1980) they can be channelled into administrative processes that directly involve opposing interest groups. This latter process involves mediation which Lake concludes is a feasible and appropriate alternative to litigation in solving disputes relating to siting problems. She also reminds us that '. . .justice does not rest with the courts, but in the minds and hearts of us all'. (Lake 1980: 36) And it is this view which mediated, negotiated settlements seek to achieve.

As information technology improves and MCDA–DSS become more acceptable to stakeholders so mediation can draw on expert opinions easily, and this could contribute towards the search for solutions which satisfy the four perspectives of an effective group decision process noted earlier, namely, consensual, political, empirical and rational. This is the ideal definition of a collective choice process and a goal that is sought by all who wish to see improvements to the processes for selecting sites for public facilities.

8

Epilogue

*How we allocate our country's resources is a
reflection of our faith in the future.*
        Government of Canada (1987: xiv)

The selection of a location for a public facility is an example of a specific
solution to a particular kind of collective choice problem in which the rights
of individuals with different opinions are confronted, and conflicts are
resolved. The resolution, if it is to be seen as acceptable to the collectivity,
should satisfy certain conditions concerning fairness and wisdom. Unfortunately these terms rarely lend themselves to formal technical definitions
which are entirely satisfactory to all parties, though it is hoped that the
process of resolving differences operates within a consensual milieu, and
thus a stable acceptable solution will be found.

The thesis of *The Right Place* extends the argument of Trakman (1991:
7) in which he 'cogently reminds us, democracy is not about right answers,
but the opportunity for everyone to seek answers to the right questions'
(quoted in Hutchinson 1992). Simon (1983: 105) extends the argument by
recognizing that self-interest is a powerful motivating force of individuals in
determining their behaviour and hence:

> a major task of any society is to create a social environment in which
> self-interest has reason to be enlightened. If we want an invisible hand
> to bring everything into some kind of social consonance, we should be
> sure, first, that our social institutions are framed to bring out our better
> selves, and second, that they do not require major sacrifices of self-
> interest by many people much of the time.

The title of the book includes 'responsibility', and this term draws on the
two essentially philosophical and human dimensions which have been
identified by Fingarette (1967: 6): 'One is that of acceptance, of
commitment, care and concern, and of the attendant elements of choice and
of creativity in choice; the other dimension is that of the "focus of life",

initially socially given and ultimately socially realized, which constitute the form and content of responsibility.'

These dimensions provide the focus for a wide ranging discussion on the concept of responsibility which draws on the work of psychotherapists and lawyers as well as those who have studied classical literature and the social sciences. All share a concern for the genesis of the concept and a clearer understanding to assist in the improved functioning of society. One of the classic books on the topic of responsibility is by Morris (1961: iii) who grounds his study in extensive philosophical and legal writings. He claims that, 'Our notions of responsibility are in flux, especially in the law, and we have serious reservations about our conceptual apparatus.' More recently Horosz (1975) squarely indicates that responsibility must be closely linked to accountability by arguing firmly for the view that the problems of modern society must be tackled in, what he calls, a human manner. The emphasis is on the search for purposive being.

I suggest that the emerging Regulatory State provides the contemporary context within which bureaucratic, legislative and political procedures operate to include technical evaluations and opinions of stakeholders in the search for responsible solutions to complex facility siting problems. Further, I argue that the concept of a successful planning process, as one that seeks to avoid mistakes, is a useful one to provide a measure of appropriateness of a particular process.

The complexities associated with collective choice and facility siting, and the notions of fairness and wisdom which are implicit and explicit in successful negotiations, have been elaborated in the first two chapters. Chapters 3 and 4 look specifically at formal evaluation procedures which are embraced under the term MCDA–DSS. It is clear that the use of formal techniques can help in the organization and analysis of data about the distribution of costs and benefits, expressed as expected impacts, which are associated with alternative sites for a facility. Also, because the assumptions about the data have to be clearly defined and the analysis can be replicated, the opportunity to scrutinize the evaluation is afforded to stakeholders. In a word, professional judgement, intuition and experience of those who evaluate options can be complemented and placed on a firmer basis if a traceable process for generating and comparing alternative sites is available. Further, I recognize and fully acknowledge that the use of formal MCDA–DSS techniques can only go part way to improve responsibility and to inform debate on facility siting, as acceptable locations can only be identified if the planning process enjoys legitimacy within a state and the credibility of the constituents, especially the stakeholders. For this reason those involved in the generation, evaluation and comparison of alternative sites as the preferred strategy and tactic for handling a collective problem, must bear responsibility for their actions. This quite explicitly requires clear definitions of lines of responsibility and accountability, and the monitoring of performance. This topic is addressed in Chapter 5.

Perhaps the most fundamental set of concepts that underlie the search for fair and wise solutions to siting problems concern choice. Choice lies at the heart of evaluation and accountability, and in Chapter 6 a review of this field is offered. While progress has been made on the development of rational choice models which are based on axioms of behaviour, the fact of the matter is that with respect to collective choice and facility siting the strict rational choice approach is found wanting. Unfortunately we still lack a good understanding of the explicit necessary and sufficient conditions of collective choice that will yield fair and wise outcomes. The search for this Holy Grail continues, and as new techniques, such as MCDA–DSS, become more widely available and understood, and as they are incorporated into monitoring and performance assessment exercises so mistakes will be identified. Once the recognition of the possibility of making siting mistakes becomes more widely acknowledged perhaps those in positions of executive authority, who are accountable to well-defined constituents, will seek to participate actively in the sharing of evaluation data, possibly via decision-conferencing and open negotiation processes, so that their decisions are placed on as firm a basis as possible.

The credence and legitimacy attached to a collective choice decision depend on the level of consensus which the planning process enjoys. While it must be freely recognized that consensus is a somewhat nebulous term it is used quite frequently and the appropriate literature is reviewed in Chapter 7. Formal methods of the axiomatic variety to calculate indices of consensus among individual sets of preferences do exist, but they play a relatively minor part in the overall definition of the term as understood by social scientists as they examine the functioning of a state. Further, it appears that politicians use the term with either negative or positive connotations and media reports comment on the advantages and disadvantages of searching for consensus. The preponderance of opinions attests to the advantages of seeking consensus and the benefits that flow from such an approach. In essence the benefits are legitimacy and credibility, and more importantly the notion of acceptance and shared responsibility for a collective choice decision.

Raiffa (1985) has examined a number of facility siting problems and he is firmly of the opinion that a new mind set is required, and this is a necessary condition so that proponents are not pitted against opponents, but rather mutual problem-solving is the order of the day. The aim is to build a planning process which seeks win–win outcomes and solutions to collective choice facility siting problems in which all the stakeholders participate in ways they find acceptable, and ultimately the responsibility for the siting decision is shared among those who are clearly accountable, so that over time the chances of making siting mistakes are reduced. This long-term goal is a worthy one, and if *The Right Place* makes a contribution to this end then its *raison d'être* will have been realized.

References

Ad hoc Committee (1965) *The science of geography.* NAS–NRC publication No. 1277, Washington, DC

Alemi F (1987) Subjective and objective methods of evaluating social programs. *Evaluation Review* **11**: 765–74

Allen J R (1982) *Step one: measure municipal productivity.* Ministry of Municipal Affairs and Housing, Province of Ontario, Toronto

Alonso W (1971) Equity and its relation to efficiency in urbanization. In Kain J F, Meyer J R (eds) *Essays in regional economics.* Harvard University Press, Cambridge, Massachusetts, pp 40–56

Alter S L (1980) *Decision support systems: current practice and continuing challenges.* Addison-Wesley, Reading, Massachusetts

Alterman R, Carmon N, Hill M (1984) Integrated evaluation: a synthesis of approaches to the evaluation of broad–aim social programs. *Socio-Economic Planning Sciences* **18**: 381–9

Ambrose P (1986) *Whatever happened to planning?* Methuen, London

Angell R C (1964) Consensus. In Gould J, Kolb W L (eds) *A dictionary of the social sciences.* Tavistock, London, p 128

Anglade C (1986) *Sources of legitimacy in Latin America: the mechanism of consensus in exclusionary societies.* Department of Government, University of Essex, Essex Papers in Politics and Government, No. 38

Anthony R N (1965) *Planning and control systems: a framework for analysis.* School of Business Administration, Cambridge, Massachusetts

Armour A M (1988a) Facility siting: a no–win situation? *Canadian Environmental Mediation Newsletter* **3**: 1–6

Armour A M (1988b) Impact compensation: presentation to Atomic Energy of Canada Ltd. Mimeo, Faculty of Environmental Studies, York University, North York

Armour A M (1991) *The siting of locally unwanted land uses: towards a cooperative approach.* Progress in Planning, Pergamon Press, Oxford

Armstrong M P et al. (1986) Architecture for a microcomputer based spatial Decision Support System. In Marble D E (ed) *Proceedings, 2nd International Symposium on Data Handling,* 120–31

Armstrong M P et al. (1990) A knowledge-based approach for supporting locational decision-making. *Environment and Planning B: Planning and Design* **17**: 341–64

Arrow K J (1951) *Social choice and individual values*. John Wiley, New York

Arrow K J (1967) Public and private values. In Hook S (ed) *Human values and economic policy*. New York University Press, New York, pp 3–21

Askew I (1985) *Research into community participation in family planning projects: summary of progress 1981–85*. Institute of Population Studies, University of Exeter

Askew I (1989) Organizing community participation in family planning projects in South Asia. *Studies in Family Planning* **20**: 185–202

Askew I, Carballo M, Rifkin S, Saunders D (1989) *Policy aspects of community participation in maternal and child health and family planning programmes*. WHO and UNFPA, Geneva

Askew I, Snowden R (1985) *Community participation in family planning: the rhetoric and the reality*. Institute of Population Studies, University of Exeter

Atkinson T (1981) *Evaluations of neighborhood conditions and municipal services in Metropolitan Toronto and its boroughs*. Institute for Behavioural Research, Report No. 3, York University, North York

Axelrod R (1980) More effective choice in the Prisoner's Dilemma. *Journal of Conflict Resolution* **17**: 379–403

Axelrod R (1984) *The evolution of co–operation*. Penguin, London

Ayeni B *et al.* (1987) Improving the geographical accessibility of health care in rural areas: a Nigerian case study. *Social Science and Medicine* **25**: 1083–94

Barde J-P, Pearce D (eds) (1991) *Valuing the environment*. Earthscan Publications Limited, London

Bardecki M (1984) *Wetland conservation policies in Southern Ontario: a Delphi approach*. Monograph 16, Department of Geography, Atkinson College, York University, North York

Barker E (trans) (1962) *The politics of Aristotle*. Oxford University Press, New York

Barry B (1990) Chance, choice and justice. Public lecture, London School of Economics, 25 April

Barry N (1990) *Welfare*. Open University Press, Milton Keynes

Bates R H (1981) Public choice processes. In Russell C S, Nicholson N K (eds) *Public choice and rural development*. Resources for the Future, Washington, DC, pp 81–117

Batty M (1974) *Plan generation*. Geographical Papers, Department of Geography, University of Reading

Batty M (1985) Formal reasoning in urban planning: computers, complexity, and mathematical modelling. In Breheny M, Hooper A (eds) *Rationality in planning: critical essays on the role of rationality in urban and regional planning*. Pion, London, pp 98–119

Beanlands G E, Duinker P N (1983) *An ecological framework for environmental impact assessment in Canada*. Ministry of the Environment, Ottawa

Bell D E, Keeney R L, Raiffa H (eds) (1977) *Conflicting objectives in decisions*. John Wiley & Sons, New York

Bennett V L *et al.* (1982) Selecting sites for rural health workers. *Social Science and Medicine* **16**: 63–72

Berkhout F (1991) *Radioactive waste: politics and technology*. Routledge, London

Bernard T J (1983) *The consensus–conflict debate: form and content in social theories*. Columbia University Press, New York

Bernardo J J, Blin J M (1977) A programming model of consumer choice among multi-attributed brands. *Journal of Consumer Research* **4**: 111–18

Berson J A (1971) The human values of city planning. *Journal of Environmental Systems* **1**: 283

Blair D H, Pollak R A (1983) Rational collective choice. *Scientific American* **249**: 88–95

Bloom A (1975) Justice: John Rawls vs. the tradition of political philosophy. *American Political Science Review* **69**: 648–62

Blowers A, Lowry D (1991) Trouble in store. *The Times Higher Education Supplement*, 5 July p 15

Borda J-C de (1781) Mémoire sur les élections au scrutin. *Histoire de l'académie royale des sciences*, Paris

Bosch–Domenech A, Escribano C (1988) Regional allocation of public funds: an evaluation index. *Environment and Planning A* **30**: 1323–33

Bowering A (ed) (1989) *Consensus: proceedings of the symposium*. The Canadian Centre for Livable Places, Heritage Canada, Ottawa

Bracken I (1981) *Urban planning methods: research and policy analysis*. Methuen, London

Bradshaw J (1972) The concept of social need. *New Society* **19**: 640–3

Brans J P, Vincke P, Mareschal B (1986) How to select and how to rank projects: the PROMETHEE method. *European Journal of Operational Research* **24**: 228–38

Braybrooke D, Lindblom C E (1963) *A strategy of decision*. Free Press, New York

Brehmer B (1976) Social judgment theory and analysis of interpersonal conflict. *Psychological Bulletin* **62**: 985–1003

Brill E D (1979) The use of optimization models in public sector planning. *Management Science* **25**: 423–32

Brill E D, Flach J M, Hopkins L D, Ranjithan (1989) *MGA: a Decision Support System for complex, incompletely defined problems*. Department of Mechanical and Industrial Engineering, University of Illinois, Urbana

Brown C A, Valenti T (1983) *Multi-Attribute Trade-off System: user's and programmer's manual*. Bureau of Reclamation, US Department of the Interior, Denver, Colorado

Brown P, Mikkelsen E J (1990) *No safe place, toxic waste, leukemia and community action*. University of California Press, Berkeley

Bruton M, Nicholson D (1987) *Local planning in practice*. Hutchinson, London

Bui T X (1988) *Co-op: a group decision support system for co–operative multiple criteria group decision making*. Lecture Notes in Computer Science, Vol. 290, Springer Verlag, New York

Bullock A, Stallybrass O (eds) (1980) *Dictionary of modern thought*. Fontana, London

Burstajn H, Feinbloom R I, Hamm R M, Brodsky A (1990) *Medical choices, medical chances*. Routledge, New York

Calabresi G, Babbitt T P (1978) *Tragic choices*. W. W. Norton, New York

Carter N, Klein R, Day P (1992) *The performance of government*. Routledge, London

Casper D E (1988) *Consensus in public decisions: analysis, 1981–1987*. Public Administration Series: bibliography, Vance Bibliographies, Monticello, Illinois

Catlow J, Thirlwall C G (1976) *Environmental impact analysis*. Department of the Environment, Research Report 11, London

Chalmers L, MacLennan M (1990) *Expert systems in geography and environmental studies*. Department of Geography Occasional Paper No. 10, University of Waterloo, Waterloo

Chan S (1982) Expert judgments under uncertainty: some evidence and suggestions. *Social Science Quarterly* **63**: 428–44

Churchman C W (1967) Wicked problems. *Management Science* **4, B**: 141–2

Cochrane J L, Zeleny M (eds) (1973) *Multiple criteria decision making*. University of South Carolina Press, Columbia

Cohen E, Ben-Ari E (1989) Hard choices: a sociological analysis of value incommensurability. Mimeo, Department of Sociology and Social Anthropology, the Hebrew University, Jerusalem

Conacher A (1988) Resource development and environmental stress: environmental impact assessment and beyond in Australia and Canada. *Geoforum* **19**: 339–52

Condorcet M (1785) *Essai sur l'application de l'analyse à la probabilité des décisions rendues à la pluralité des voix*. Paris

Cook W D, Golan I, Kazakor A, Kress M (1988) A case study of a non-compensatory approach to ranking transportation project. Journal of the Operational Research Society **39**(11): 901–10

Cook W D, Kress M (1984) Relationships between l' metrics on linear ranking spaces. *SIAM, Journal of Applied Mathematics* **44**: 209–20

Cook W D, Kress M (1992) *Ordinal information and preference structures: decision models and applications*. Prentice-Hall, Englewood Cliffs

Cook W D, Seiford L M (1978) Priority ranking and consensus formation. *Management Science* **24**: 1721–32

Cook W D, Seiford L M (1982) On the Borda–Kendall consensus method for priority ranking problems. *Management Science* **28**: 621–37

Cook W D, Seiford L M (1984) An ordinal ranking model for the highway corridor selection problem. *Complex Environmental Urban Systems* **9**: 271–6

Cooke P (**1990**) *Back to the future*. Unwin Hyman, London

Copeland A H (1951) A 'reasonable' social welfare function. Mimeo, Seminar on Applications of Mathematics to the Social Sciences, University of Michigan

Couch W J (1985) *Environmental assessment in Canada, 1985: summary of current practice*. Canadian Council of Resource and Environment Ministers, Minister for Supply and Services, Ottawa

Council for the Environment (1988) *Integrated environmental management in South Africa*. Council for the Environment, Pretoria

Cox K R (1979) *Location and public problems: a political geography of the contemporary world*. Maaroufa Press, Chicago

Cragg W (ed) (1987) Contemporary moral issues. McGraw-Hill Ryerson, Toronto

Dahrendorf R (1958) Out of utopia: toward a reorientation of sociological analysis. *American Journal of Sociology* **64**: 115–27

Danielson P (1986) The moral and ethical significance of TIT FOR TAT. *Dialogue* **XXV**: 449–70

Danielson P (1988) Review of Gauthier D (1986) *Morals by agreement*. Oxford University Press, Oxford, in *Canadian Journal of Philosophy* **18**: No. 2

Davidoff P, Reiner T A (1962) A choice theory of planning. *Journal American Institute of Planning* **28**: 103–15

Davies D H (1988) Spatial analysis a non–event? The case of Zimbabwe's development planning. *Professional Geographer*, **40**: 140–8

Davies D H (1989) Reply to Rushton's comments. *Professional Geographer* **41**: 205

Dawes R M, Delay J, Chaplin W (1974) The decision to pollute. *Environment and Planning A* **6**: 3–10

Day I F S (1987) Perceived contingency and air pollution in the Junction Triangle, Toronto. MA thesis, Department of Geography, York University, Toronto

Day P, Klein R (1987a) The business of welfare. *New Society* **19**: 11–3

Day P, Klein R (1987b) *Accountabilities: five public services*. Tavistock, London

Day P, Klein R (1990) *Inspecting the inspectorates*. Centre for the Analysis of Social Policy, University of Bath

Delbeeq A L, Van de Ven A H, Gustafson D H (1975) *Group techniques for program planning*. Scott, Foresman & Co., Glencoe, Illinois

De Loe R C (1991) The policy Delphi: a hindsight evaluation. *The Operational Geographer* **9**: 20–5

Densham P, Rushton G (1988) Decision support systems for locational planning. In Golledge R, Timmermans H (eds) *Behavioral modelling in geography and planning*, Croom Helm, New York, pp 56–90

De Sanctis G, Gallupe R B (1987) A foundation for the study of group decision support systems. *Management Science* **33**: 589–609

Dixon J, Welch H G (1991) Priority setting: lessons from Oregon. *The Lancet* **337**: 891–4

Dolan L W, Wolpert J, Seley J E (1987) Dynamic municipal allocation analysis. *Environment and Planning A* **19**: 93–105

Dooley J E, Byer P (1982) Decision-making for risk management. In Burton I, Fowle C D, McCullough R S (eds) *Living with risk: environmental risk management in Canada*. Environmental Monograph No. 3 (EM–3), Institute for Environmental Studies, University of Toronto, Toronto, pp 71–84

Douglas M (1970) *Natural symbols: explorations in cosmology*. Barrie & Rockliff, London

Douglas M (1978) *Purity and danger: an analysis of concepts of pollution and taboo*. Routledge & Kegan Paul, London

Douglas M (1986) *Risk acceptability according to the social sciences*. Russell Sage Foundation, New York

Downs A (1970) Uncompensated costs of urban renewel. In Margolis A (ed) *The analysis of public output*. Columbia University Press, New York, pp 68–106

Duinker P N (1985) Biological impact forecasting in environmental assessment. In Whitney J B R, Maclaren V W (eds) *Environmental impact assessment: the Canadian experience*. Institute for Environmental Studies, University of Toronto, Toronto, pp 115–27

Dunn N (1981) *Public policy analysis: an introduction*. Prentice-Hall, Englewood Cliffs

Dushnik B, Miller E W (1941) Partially ordered sets. *American Journal of Mathematics* **63**: 600–10

Dworkin R (1985) *A matter of principle*. Harvard University Press, Cambridge, Massachusetts

Dyer J S (1990) A clarification of 'Remarks on the analytical hierarchy process'. *Management Science* **36**: 249–58

Economist, The (1990) Goodbye to the nation state? Editorial comment, 23 June, pp 11–12

Edwards W (1971) Social utilities. *Engineering Economist*, Summer Symposium Series, No. 6

Edwards W (1977) Use of multiattribute utility measurement for social decision making. In Bell D E, Keeney D L, and Raiffa H (eds) *Conflicting objectives in decisions*, John Wiley & Sons, New York, pp 247–76

Elam J J, Huber G P, Hurt M E (1986) An examination of the D.S.S. literature (1975–1985). In McLean E, Sol H G (eds) *Decision Support Systems: a decade in perspective*. North-Holland, New York, pp 1–17

Elster J (1983a) *Sour grapes*. Cambridge University Press, Cambridge

Elster J (1983b) *Explaining technical change*. Cambridge University Press, Cambridge

Elster J (ed) (1986) *Rational choice*. Basil Blackwell, Oxford

Emond D P (1987) Waste management and the NIMBY syndrome. *Canadian Environmental Mediation Newsletter* **2**: 5–8

Environmental Assessment Branch (1989) *Interim guidelines on environmental assessment planning and approvals*. Ontario Ministry of the Environment, Queen's Printer for Ontario, Toronto

Environment Canada (1984) Facility siting and routing '84. *Energy and Environment*, Vols 1 and 2, *Proceedings*, 15–18 April 1984, Banff, Alberta

Etzioni A (1967) Mixed scanning: a third approach to decision making. *Public Administration Review* **27**: 385–92

Faludi A, Voogd H (eds) (1985) *Evaluation of complex policy problems*. Delftsche Vitgevers Maatsohappij BV, Delft

Fandel G, Spronk J (eds) (1985) *Multiple criteria decision methods and applications*. Springer-Verlag, New York

Fedra K, Reitsma R F (1990) *Decision support and geographical information systems*. Report RR–90–9, International Institute for Applied Systems Analysis, Laxenburg, Austria

Fekete–Szues L (1991) Decision conference for strategic issues: theory in practice. In

Sol H, Vecsenyi J (eds) *Environments for supporting decision processes*. Elsevier, Amsterdam, pp 308–18

Fingarette H (1967) *On responsibility*. Basic Books, New York

Fischer J (1973) Is casework effective? *Social Work* **17**: 5–20

Fischer J (1978) Does anything work? *Journal of Social Service Research* **1**: 215–43

Fishburn P C (1971) A comparative analysis of group decision methods. *Behavioral Science* **16**: 538–44

Fishburn P C (1974) Simple voting systems and majority rule. Behavioral Science **19**: 166–76

Fisher R, Brown S (1988) *Getting together: building relationships as we negotiate*. Penguin, New York

Fisher R, Ury W (1981) *Getting to yes: negotiating agreement without giving in*. Penguin, New York

Fitzgibbon J (1987) Environmental impact assessment in Ontario. *The Operational Geographer* No. 13, pp 35–8

Frankena W K (1963) *Ethics*. Prentice-Hall, Englewood Cliffs

French S, Hartley R, Thomas L, White D (1983) *Multi-objective decision making*. Academic Press, London

Freund P J (1986) Health care in a declining economy: the case of Zambia. *Social Science and Medicine* **23**: 875–88

Friend J, Hickling A (1987) *Planning under pressure: the strategic choice approach*. Pergamon Press, Oxford

Friend J, Jessop W N (1969) *Local government and strategic choice: an operational research approach to the processes of public planning*. Tavistock, London

Fuggle R F (1988) Integrated environmental management: an appropriate approach to environmental concerns in developing countries. Paper delivered at the International Association for Impact Assessment Conference, 5–9 July, Brisbane

Fukuyama F (1989) The end of history? *The National Interest* **16**: 3–18

Gablentz O H (1968) Responsibility. In Sills D L (ed) *International encyclopedia of the social sciences, vol 13*. Collier-Macmillan, London

Gardiner P C, Edwards W (1975) Public values: multiattribute-utility measurement for social decision making. In Kaplan M F, Schwartz S (eds) *Human judgement and decision processes*. Academic Press, New York, pp 1–37

Gil Y (1987) Criteria for the location of solid waste transfer stations in Israel. MA thesis, Department of Geography, Bar–Ilan University, Ramat Gan (Hebrew)

Gil Y, Kellerman A (1989) A multicriteria model for the location of solid waste transfer stations: the case of Ashdod, Israel. Mimeo, Department of Geography, University of Haifa, Israel

Gilles H M (1976) The ecology of disease in the tropics. In Cahill K M (ed) *Health and development*. Orbis, New York, pp 67–84

Gillies J (1986) *Facing reality: consultation, consensus and making economic policy for the 21st century*. Institute for Research on Public Policy, Montreal

Goodin R E (1987) Ethical principles for environmental protection. In Cragg W (ed) *Contemporary moral issues*. McGraw-Hill Ryerson, Toronto

Gorry A, Scott-Morton M (1971) A framework for information systems. *Sloan Management Review*, fall issue

Gould J, Kolb W L (eds) (1964) *A dictionary of the social sciences*. Tavistock, London

Gould P (1990) *Fire in the rain: the democratic consequences of Chernobyl*. Johns Hopkins University Press, Baltimore

Government of Canada (1987) *Sharing the responsibility*. Report of the Special Committee on Child Care, Ottawa

Graham G J (1984) Consensus. In Sartori G (ed) *Social science concepts: a systematic analysis*. Sage, London, pp 89–124

Gregg S R, Mulvey J M, Wolpert J (1988) A stochastic planning system for siting and closing public facilities. *Environment and Planning A* **20**: 83–98

Grima A P *et al.* (1986) *Risk management and EIA: research needs and opportunities*. Canadian Environmental Assessment Research Council, Ottawa

Gulliver P H (1979) *Disputes and negotiations: a cross-cultural perspective*. Academic Press, London

Gummer J S (1988) The freedom to choose that makes us human. *The Independent*, 8 Oct.

Haefele E T (1973) *Representative government and environmental management*. Resources for the Future, Washington, DC

Haigh N (1987) *E.E.C. environmental policy and Britain*. Longman, 2nd edition, London

Halfon E (1989) Comparison of an index function and a vectorial approach method for ranking waste disposal sites. *Environmental Science and Technology* **23**: 600–9

Hall P (1980) *Great planning disasters*. Weidenfeld & Nicolson, London

Hansen P, Thisse J-F (1981a) Outcomes of voting and planning: Condorcet, Weber and Rawls locations. *Journal of Public Economics* **16**: 1–15

Hansen P, Thisse J-F (1981b) The generalized Weber–Rawls problem. In Brans J P (ed) *Operations Research*. North-Holland, Amsterdam, pp 1–15

Hansen P, Thisse J-F, Wendell R E (1980) *Weber, Condorcet and plurality solutions to network location problems*. Research Programme Paper No. 14, SPUR, Université Catholique de Louvain, Belgium

Hardin G (1968) The tragedy of the commons. *Science* **162**: 1243–8

Harker P T, Vargas L G (1990) Reply to Dyer J S, Remarks on the Analytic Hierarchy Process. *Management Science* **36**: 269–75

Hartley D A (1972) Inspectorates in British central government. *Public Administration* **50**: 447–66

Hatry H P (1972) Issues in productivity measurement for local governments. *Public Administration Review* **32**: 776–84

Hatry H P (1991) Accountability for service quality, performance measurement, and closeness to customers. Paper presented at the UN University Conference on Decentralization and Alternative Rural–Urban Configurations, 9–13 April, Barcelona

Hatry H P, Millar A P, Evans J H (1984) *Guide to setting priorities for capital investments*. Guides to Managing Urban Capital, Vol. 5, The Urban Institute Press, Washington, DC

Healey P, McDougall G, Thomas M J (eds) (1982) *Planning theory: prospects for the 1980s*. Pergamon Press, Oxford

Heiman M K (1986) Review of Seley (1983). *Annals Association of American Geographers* **76**: 135–8

Henderson J C (1987) Finding synergy between decision support systems and expert systems research. *Decision Sciences* **18**: 333–47

Heseltine M (1987) *Where there's a will*. Hutchinson, London

Hill J (ed) (1990) *The state of welfare: the welfare state in Britain since 1974*. Clarendon Press, Oxford

Hill M (1968) A goals–achievement matrix for evaluating alternative plans. *Journal of the American Institute of Planners* **34**: 19–29

Hill M (1985) Decision-making contexts and strategies for evaluation. In Faludi A, Voogd H (eds) *Evaluation of complex policy problems*. Delftsche Vitgevers Maatschappij BV, Delft

Hindess B (1987) *Freedom, equality, and the market: arguments on social policy*. Tavistock, London

Hindess B (1988) *Choice, rationality, and social theory*. Unwin Hyman, London

HMSO (1981) Select committee on the European communities. Session 1980–81, 11th Report, *Environmental Assessment of Projects*, London

HMSO (1991) *The citizen's charter: raising the standard*. HMSO, Cm 1599, London

Hobbs B F (1985) Choosing how to choose: comparing amalgamation methods for environmental impact assessment. *Environmental Impact Assessment Review* **5**: 301–19

Hodgart R L (1978) Optimizing access to public facilities: a review of problems, models and methods of locating central facilities. *Progress in Human Geography* **2**: 17–48

Hodgson M J (1988) A hierarchical location–allocation model for primary health care delivery in a developing area. *Social Science and Medicine* **26**: 153–61

Hollis M, Sugden R, Weale A (1985) Riddles of public choice. *Times Higher Education Supplement*, 25 Nov., p 15

Holmes J, Williams F B, Brown L A (1972) Facility planning under a maximum travel restriction: an example using day-care facilities. *Geographical Analysis* **4**: 258–66

Horn M. O'Callaghan J, Garner B (1988) Design of integrated systems for spatial planning tasks. *Proceedings Third International Symposium on Spatial Data Handling*, 17–19 August, Sydney, pp 107–16

Horosz W (1975) *The crisis of responsibility: man as the source of accountability*. University of Oklahoma Press, Norman

House E R (1980) *Evaluating with validity*. Sage, New York

Humphreys P C, Wisudha A D (1987) *Methods and tools for structuring and analysing decision problems*. Technical Report 87–1, Decision Analysis Unit, London School of Economics and Political Science, London

Hutchinson A (1992) Legal wizardry. *The Literary Review of Canada* **1**: 5–7

Hutchinson B G (1974) *Principles of urban transport systems planning*. Scripta, Washington

Hwang C-L, Yoon K (1981) *Multi attribute decision making*. Springer-Verlag, New York

ISR (1990) The greening of Toronto: public opinion back environmentalists. *Newsletter*, Institute for Social Research, York University, North York

Jaakson R (1984) Recreational planning for a small urban lake. *Town Planning Review* **56**: 90–111

Jaques E (1990) In praise of hierarchy. *Harvard Business Review* **Jan.–Feb.**: 127–33

Jarke M, Jelassi M T, Shakun M F (1987) Mediator: toward a negotiation support system. *European Journal of Operational Research*, No. 3: 40–7

Johnson W C (1984) Citizen participation in local planning in the U.K. and U.S.A.: a comparative study. *Progress in Planning* **21**: 153–221

Jones K, Kirby A (1982) Provision and well being: an agenda for public resources research. *Environment and Planning A* **14**: 297–310

Jordan B (1985) *The state-authority and autonomy*. Basil Blackwell, Oxford

Joseph A E, Phillips D R (1984) *Accessibility and utilization: geographical perspectives on health care delivery*. Harper & Row, New York

Kahneman D, Tversky A (1979) Prospect theory: an analysis of decision under risk. *Econometrica* **47**: 263–91

Kahneman D, Tversky A (1984) Choices, values, and frames. *American Psychologist* **39**: 341–50

Kallen, H-M (1931) In Seligman E R A (ed) *Encyclopedia of the social sciences*. Vol. IV. Macmillan, New York, pp 225–7

Kanaroglou P S, Rhodes S A (1990) The demand and supply of child care: the case of the City of Waterloo, Ontario. *The Canadian Geographer* **34**: 209–24

Karski A (1985) *Strategic planning: some lost lessons from British planning methodology*. Planning Studies No. 16, Polytechnic of Central London, School of Planning

Kartez J D (1989) Rational arguments and irrational audiences: psychology, planning and public judgment. *American Planning Association Journal* **Autumn**: 445–56

Kasonde J M, Martin J D (1983) Moving toward primary health care: the Zambian experience. *World Health Forum* **4**: 25–30

Kasonde J M, Martin J D (eds) (in press) *Primary health care in Zambia*. World Health Organization, Geneva

Kasperson R G, Breitbart M (1974) *Participation, decentralization and advocacy planning,* commission of college geography. Resource Papers No 25, Association of American Geographers, Washington DC

Katz Y (1989) Public participation in the Danish planning system –a cybernetics approach. *Environment and Planning A* **21**: 975–82

Kavanagh D (1987) *Thatcherism and British politics: the end of consensus*. Oxford University Press, Oxford

Keen P G W, Scott-Morton M S (1978) *Decision support systems*. Addison-Wesley, Reading, Massachusetts

Keeney R L (1972) Utility functions for multi-attributed consequences. *Management Science* **18**: 276–87

Keeney R L (1981) Siting major facilities using decision analysis. In Brans J P (ed) *Operational research*. North-Holland, Amsterdam, pp 355–78

Keeney R L, Nair K (1977) Selecting nuclear power plant sites in the Pacific Northwest using decision analysis. In Bell D E, Keeney R L, Raiffa H (eds) *Conflicting objectives in decisions*. John Wiley & Sons, New York, pp 298–322

Keeney R L, Raiffa H (1976) *Decisions with multiple objectives: preferences and value tradeoffs*. John Wiley & Sons, New York

Keeney R L, Winterfeldt D V (1988) The analysis and its role for selecting nuclear repository sites. In Rand G K (ed) *Operational research '87*. Elsevier, Amsterdam, pp 686–701

Keeney R L, Winterfeldt D V, Eppel T (1990) Eliciting public values for complex policy decisions. *Management Science* **36**: 1011–30

Kemp R (1990) Why not in my backyard? A radical interpretation of public opposition to the deep disposal of radioactive waste in the United Kingdom. *Environment and Planning A* **22**: 1239–58

Kendall M (1962) *Rank correlation methods*. Hafner, New York

Kerr C, Dunlop J, Harbinson F, Myers C (1973) *Industrialism and industrial man*. Penguin, Harmondsworth

Kirby A (1982) *The politics of location: an introduction*. Methuen, London

Klein R (1991) On the Oregon trail: rationing health care. *The British Medical Journal* **302**: 1–2

Lake L M (ed) (1980) *Environmental mediation: the search for consensus*. Westview Press, Boulder

Lake R W (ed) (1987) *Resolving locational conflict*. Rutgers University, New Jersey

Lang R (ed) (1990) *Integrated approaches to resource planning and management*. University of Calgary Press, Calgary

Langley P (1974) *Evaluating the effectiveness of alternatives in structure planning*. Department of the Environment, Planning Techniques Paper 1/74, London

Langone J (1981) *Thorny issues: how ethics and morality affect the way we live*. Little, Brown and Co., Boston

Leiserson A (1964) Responsibility. In Gould J, Kolb W L (eds) *A dictionary of the social sciences*. The Free Press of Glencoe, New York, pp 599–601

Leopold L, Clarke F E, Hanshaw B B, Balsley J R (1971) *A procedure for evaluating environmental impact*. Geological Survey, Circular 645, Washington, DC

Levy J M (1991) *Contemporary urban planning*. Prentice-Hall, Englewood Cliffs

Lewandowski A (1989) SCDAS – Decision Support System for group decision making: decision theoretic framework. *Decision Support Systems* **5**: 403–23

Lichfield N (1970) Evaluation methodology of urban and regional plans: a review. *Regional Studies* **4**: 151–65

Liebman J C (1976) Some simple-minded observations on the role of optimization in public systems decision making. *Interfaces* **6**: 102–8

Lindblom C E (1979) Still muddling, not yet through. *Public Administration Review* **39**: 517–26

Linstone H A (1984) *Multiple perspectives for decision making*. North-Holland, Amsterdam

Linstone H A, Turoff M (1975) *The Delphi method: techniques and applications*. Addison-Wesley, Reading, Massachusetts

Lloyd W F (1833) *Two lectures on the checks to population*. Oxford University Press, Oxford

Lofti V (1989) An Aspiration-Level Interactive Method (AIM) for decision making. *Operations Research Letters* **8**: 113–15

Lofti V, Stewart T J, Zionts S (1989) *An Aspiration-Level Interactive Model for multiple criteria decision making*. Working Paper No. 711, Department of Management Science and Systems, School of Management, State University of New York at Buffalo

Logan B I (1985) Evaluating public policy costs in rural development planning: the example of health care in Sierra Leone. *Economic Geography* **61**: 144–57

Lootsma F A, Meisner J, Schellmans F (1986) Multi-criteria decision as an aid to the strategic planning of energy R & D. *European Journal of Operational Research* **25**: 216–34

Lynn J, Jay K (1986) *Yes Prime Minister: the diaries of the Rt. Hon. James Hacker*. BBC Publications, London

McBride G (1990) Rationing health care in Oregon. *The British Medical Journal* **301**: 355–6

McCartt A T, Rohrbaugh J (1989) Evaluating Group Decision Support System effectiveness: a performance study of decision conferencing. *Decision Support Systems* **5**: 243–53

McGill P (1991) Japan looks to grovel out of the Narita nightmare. *Observer* 29 Dec., London

McHarg I (1969) *Design with nature*. Doubleday, New York

Mackie J L (1977) *Ethics: inventing right and wrong*. Penguin, Harmondsworth

Maclaren R (1984) *Consensus: a Liberal looks at his party*. Mosaic Press, Oakville

Maclean D (1982) Risk and consent: philosophical issues for centralized decisions. *Risk Analysis* **2**: 59–67

McLean I (1987) *Public choice: an introduction*. Basil Blackwell, Oxford

McLeod R (1986) *Management information systems*. Science Research Associates Inc., Chicago

Macmillan W D (1987) The measurement of efficiency in multiunit public services. *Environment and Planning A* **19**: 1511–24

McQuaid-Cook J (1986) Yes! In my backyard – managing special wastes in Alberta. In *Environment Canada*, 8th Canadian Waste Management Conference, Halifax, 3–5 Sept., Environment Canada, Ottawa.

Maegrith B G (1973) *One world*. Athlone, London

Malczewski J (1990) *Locational decision-making and decision support systems*. Department of Geography, York University, North York

Malczewski J (1991) Central facility location and environmental health. *Environment and Planning A* **23**: 385–95

Malczewski J, Ogryczak W (1990) An interactive approach to the central facility location problem: locating pediatric hospitals in Warsaw. *Geographical Analysis* **22**: 244–58

Management Board of Cabinet (1982) *Accountability*. Queen's Printer, Toronto

March J G (1978) Bounded rationality, ambiguity, and the engineering of choice. *Bell Journal of Economics* **9**: 589–608

March J G, Simon H A (1958) *Organizations*. Wiley, New York

Marchet J-C, Siskos J (1979) Aide à la décision en matière d'environnement: application au choix de trace autoroutier. *Sistemi Urbani* **1**: 65–95

Marshall D *et al.* (1985) *Environmental management and impact assessment: some lessons and guidance from Canadian and international experience.* Federal Environment and Assessment Review Office, Ottawa

Maslow A H (1954) *Motivation and personality.* Harper & Row, New York

Massam B H (1975) *Location and space in social administration.* Edward Arnold, London

Massam B H (1980) *Spatial search: applications to planning problems in the public sector.* Pergamon Press, Oxford

Massam B H (1982) The search for the best route: an application of a formal method using multiple criteria. *Sistemi Urbani* **4**: 183–94

Massam B H (1984) The site location problem. *The Operational Geographer* **5**: 16–19

Massam B H (1986) The need for sensitivity tests in multicriteria plan evaluation. *The Operational Geographer* **10**: 28–30

Massam B H (1988a) *Multi-criteria decision making (MCDM) techniques in planning.* Progress in Planning, Vol. 30, Pergamon Press, Oxford

Massam B H (ed) (1988b) *Complex location problems: interdisciplinary approaches.* Institute of Social Research, York University, North York

Massam B H (1988c) *Evaluation and implementation: the location of health centres in Zambia, a study in consensus.* Occasional Paper No. 8, Institute of Population Studies, University of Exeter, Exeter, UK

Massam B H (1991a) A methodological study of need assessment: the spatial allocation of resources for day care in Ontario. *Computers, Environment and Urban Systems* **15**: 229–38

Massam B H (1991b) The location of waste transfer stations in Ashdod, Israel, using a multi-criteria Decision Support System. *Geoforum* **22**: 27–37

Massam B H, Askew I D (1982) Methods for comparing policies using multiple criteria: an urban example. *OMEGA The International Journal of Management Science* **10**: 195–204

Massam B H, Askew I D (1984) A theoretical perspective on rural service provision: a systems approach. In Lonsdale R E, Enyedi G (eds) *Rural public services: international comparisons.* Westview, Boulder, pp 15–38

Massam B H, Askew I, Singh C P (1987) Location patterns of health centres in Salcetta, Goa. *Annals, National Association of Geographers, India* **7**: 13–26

Massam B H, Malczewski J (1990) Complex location problems: can Decision Support Systems help? *The Operational Geographer*

Massam B H, Manahan A, Askew I D, Singh C P (1984) The location of health care facilities in Salcetta, Goa. *Annals of the National Association of Geographers, India* **IV**: 66–75

Massam B H, Skelton I (1986) *Application of three plan evaluation procedures to a highway alignment problem.* Transportation Research Record, Transportation Research Board, National Research Council, No. 1076, Washington, DC, pp 54–8

Mayer A J (1979) *Madame Prime Minister.* Newsweek Books, New York

Megaw J (1985) Life is a risky business. *York Science*, Vol. 6, No. 1, pp 3–5, York University, North York

Midgley J, Piachaud D (eds) (1984) *The fields and methods of social planning.* Heinemann, London

Miller C (1987) Efficiency, equity and pollution: the case of radioactive waste. *Environment and Planning A* **19**: 913–24

Minford P (1984) State expenditure: a study in waste. *Supplement to Economic Affairs.*

Ministry of Community and Social Services (1987) *New directions for child care.* Government of Ontario, Toronto

Ministry of Energy, Mines and Resources (1987) *Siting process task force on low-level radioactive waste disposal.* Government of Canada, Ottawa.

Ministry of the Environment (1990) *Computer-based Decision Support Systems (DSS): their role in environmental assessment.* Government of Ontario, Toronto

Ministry of Municipal Affairs and Housing (1981) *Performance measurement for municipalities.* Government of Ontario, Toronto

Ministry of Municipal Affairs and Housing (1982) *Monitoring guidelines: an approach to monitoring official plans.* Government of Ontario, Toronto

Minsky M (1975) A framework for representing knowledge. In Winston P H (ed) *The psychology of computer vision.* McGraw-Hill, New York

Mishra R (1984) *The welfare state in crisis.* Wheatsheaf Books, Brighton, England

Mitchell J K (1984) Hazard perception studies: convergent concerns and divergent approaches during the past decade. In Saarinen T, Seamon D, Sell J L (eds) *Environmental perception and behaviour: an inventory and prospect.* Department of Geography, Research Paper 209, Chicago

Morris H (ed) (1961) *Freedom and responsibility: readings in philosophy and law.* Stanford University Press, Stanford

Moser C O N (1989) Community participation in urban projects in the Third World. *Progress in Planning* **32**: 77–133

Mounfield P R (1991) *World nuclear power.* Routledge, London

Munn R E (1975) *Environmental impact assessment: principles and procedures.* Scientific Committee on Problems of the Environment, Toronto

Nagel S S (1986) Policy/goal percentaging analysis: a personal computer program to aid assessment. *Impact Assessment Bulletin* **5**: 88–92

Nagel S S (1989) *Teach yourself decision-aiding software.* Decision Aids Inc., Champaign, Illinois

Nagel S S (1990) *Decision-aiding software: skills, obstacles and applications.* Macmillan, London

Nelkin D (ed) (1984) *Controversy: politics of technical decisions.* Sage, London

Nesbitt J (1984) *Megatrends.* Warner, New York

Newman E, Turem J (1974) The crises of accountability. *Social Work* **19**: 5–16

Nijkamp P (1979) *Multidimensional spatial data and decision analysis.* John Wiley, New York

Nijkamp P (1989) Quantity and quality: evaluation indicators for our cultural–architectural heritage. Research Memorandum, Free University, Amsterdam.

Nijkamp P, Spronk J (1981) *Multiple criteria analysis.* Gower, Aldershot

Nowlan D M (1975) The use of criteria weights in rank ordering techniques of project evaluation. *Urban Studies* **12**: 169–76

Nutt P C (1979) Comparing methods for weighting decision criteria. *OMEGA The International Journal of Management Science* **8**: 163–72

Observer (1988) Tories plan 'Green' bill. 2 October, p 1

Odum E P, Bramlitt G A, Zieman J C, Shugart H H (1976) *Totality indexes for evaluating impacts of highway alternatives.* Transportation Research Record, No. 561, pp 57–67

Ogryczak W *et al.* (1988) Dynamic interactive network analysis system-DINAS, version 2.1. *User's Manual*, WP-88-114, Ilasa, Laxenburg

O'Hare M, Bacon L, Sanderson D (1983) *Facility siting and public opposition.* Van Nostrand, New York

Olson M (1965) *The logic of collective action public goods and the theory of groups.* Harvard University Press, Cambridge, Massachusetts

Ontario Waste Management Corporation (1985) *Annual report.* Toronto

Openshaw S (1986) *Nuclear power: siting and safety.* Routledge & Kegan Paul, London

Openshaw S, Carver S, Fernie J (1989) *Britain's nuclear waste: safety and siting.* Belhaven, London

Ostrom V, Ostrom E (1971) Public choice: a different approach to the study of public administration. *Public Administration Review* **31**: 203–16

O'Sullivan E (1985) Decision support systems: an introduction for program evaluators. *Evaluation Review* **9**: 84–92

Patton C V, Sawicki D S (1986) *Basic methods of policy analysis and planning.* Prentice-Hall, Englewood Cliffs

Peelle E, Ellis R (1986) Hazardous waste management outlook: are there ways out of the 'not-in-my-backyard' impasse? *Journal of Water Pollution Control Federation,* January: 1–4

Peet R (1991) The end of history . . . or its beginning? *Professional Geographer* **43**: 512–19

Phillips L D (1979) *Introduction to decision analysis.* Tutorial Paper 79–1, Decision Analysis Unit, London School of Economics

Phillips L D (1983) A theoretical perspective on heuristics and biases in probabilistic thinking. In Humphreys P C, Svenson O, Vari A (eds) *Analysing and aiding decision processes.* North-Holland, Amsterdam, pp 525–43

Phillips L D (1984) A theory of requisite decision models. *Acta Psychologica* **56**: 29–48

Phillips L D (1986b) Computing to consensus. *Datamation,* Oct., pp 2–6

Pinch S (1985) *Cities and services: the geography of collective consumption.* Routledge & Kegan Paul, London

Plott C R (1967) A notion of equilibrium and its possibility under majority rule. *American Economic Review* **57**: 787–806

Prentice R (1976) The social welfare function: beacon or diversion. *Area* **8**: 231–3

Price Waterhouse Management Consultants (1985) *A study of management and accountability in the Government of Ontario.* Queen's Printer, Toronto

Province of British Columbia (1980) *Environment and social impact compensation/ mitigation guidelines.* Environmental Land Use Committee Secretariat, Victoria

Pushchak R (1985) Political and institutional context of EIA. In Whitney J B K, Maclaren V W (eds) *Environmental impact assessment: the Canadian experience.* Institute for Environmental Studies, University of Toronto, Toronto, pp 75–87

Radford K J (1980) Categories of decision problems and their resolution. *Infor* **18**: 82–8

Radford K J (1986) *Strategic and tactical decisions.* Holt McTavish, Toronto

Radford K J (1988) Complex decision situations. In Massam B H (ed) *Complex location problems: interdisciplinary approaches.* Institute for Social Research, York University, North York, pp 36–54

Raiffa H (1968) *Decision analysis: introductory lectures on choices under certainty.* Addison-Wesley, Reading, Massachussetts

Raiffa H (1982) *The art and science of negotiation.* Harvard University Press, Cambridge, Massachussetts

Raiffa H (1985) Creative compensation: maybe 'in my backyard'. *Negotiation Journal,* July, **1**: 197–203

Rawls J (1971) *A theory of justice.* Harvard University Press, Cambridge, Massachusetts

Reagan P, Rohrbaugh J (1990) Group decision process effectiveness. *Group and Organization Studies* **15**: 20–43

Reagan-Cirincione P (1992) Combining group facilitation, decision modeling, and information technology to improve the accuracy of group judgment. Mimeo, Center for Policy Analysis, SUNY, University of Albany

Reiner T A (1990) Choices and choice theory revisited. In Shefer D, Voogd H (eds) *Evaluation methods for urban and regional plans.* Pion, London, pp 65–78

Rietveld P (1980) *Multiple objective decision methods and regional planning*. North-Holland, Amsterdam

Rietveld P (1984) Public choice theory and qualitative discrete multicriteria decision methods. In Bahrenberg G, Fischer M, Nijkamp P (eds) *Recent developments in spatial data analysis*. Gower, Aldershot, pp 409–26

Relman A S (1990) The trouble with rationing. *New England Journal of Medicine* **323**: 911–13

Richard D, Beguin H, Peeters D (1990) The location of fire stations in a rural environment: a case study. *Environment and Planning A* **22**: 39–52

Richards A (1989) Managing a site selection process to minimize conflict. *Canadian Environmental Mediation Newsletter* **4**: 1–4

Richardson A (1983) *Participation*. Routledge & Kegan Paul, London

Richelson J (1978) A comparative analysis of social choice functions. *Behavioral Science* **23**: 169–76

Rivett B H P (1977) Policy selection by structural mapping. *Proceedings, Royal Society*, 354, London, pp 367–79

Rivlin A M (1971) *Systematic thinking for social action*. Brookings Institute, Washington, DC

Robertson A F (1984) *People and the state: an anthropology of planned development*. Cambridge University Press, London

Robinson V B (1983) *Urban Data Management Software (UDMS) package – user's manual*. UN Centre for Human Settlements (Habitat), Nairobi, Kenya

Rohrbaugh J (1979) Improving the quality of group judgment: Social Judgment Analysis and the Delphi technique. *Organizational Behavior and Human Performance* **24**: 73–92

Romzek B S, Dubnick J (1987) Accountability in the public sector: lessons from the Challenger tragedy. *Public Administration Review* **47**: 227–38

Rosenbaum S P (ed) (1975) *The Bloomsbury Group*. University of Toronto Press, Toronto

Rosenman R, Fort R, Budd W (1988) Perceptions, fear, and economic loss: an application of prospect theory to environmental decision making. *Policy Sciences* **21**: 327–50

Roy B, Bouyssou D (1986) Comparison of two decision-aid models applied to a nuclear power plant siting example. *European Journal of Operational Research* **25**: 200–15

Roy B, Present M, Silhol D (1986) A programming method for determining which Paris metro stations should be renovated. *European Journal of Operational Research* **24**: 318–24

Roy B, Sussmann B, Benayoun R (1966) A decision method in presence of multiple view-points: ELECTRE. Study Session on Methods of Calculation in the Social Sciences, Rome

Rushton G (1975) *Optimal location of facilities*. Dartmouth College, New Hampshire

Rushton G (1989) Spatial analysis in development planning. *Professional Geographer* **41**: 203–4

Rushton G, McLafferty S, Ghosh A (1981) Optimum locations for public services: individual preferences and social choice. *Geographical Analysis* **13**: 196–202

Rushton G, Armstrong M P, Densham P J, De S (forthcoming) *Spatial decision support systems: principles and applications*. Oxford University Press, New York

Saaty T L (1980) The analytic hierarchy process. McGraw-Hill, New York

Saaty T L (1990) An exposition of the AHP in reply to the paper 'Remarks on the analytical hierarchy process'. *Management Science* **36**: 259–68

Sager T (1981) Evaluation methods in local participatory planning. *Town Planning Review* **52**: 417–32

Schuman S P, Rohrbaugh J (1991) Decision conferencing for systems planning. *Information and Management* **21**: 147–59

Schwartz W B, Aaron H J (1990) The Achilles heel of health care rationing. *New York Times*, 11 July

Seley J E (1983) *The politics of public-facility planning*. Lexington Books, Lexington, Massachussetts

Seo F, Sakawa M(1988) *Multiple criteria decision analysis in regional planning: concepts, methods and applications*. D Reidel Publishing Co, Dordrecht

Shils E (1965) The calling of sociology. In Parsons T, Shils E, Naegele K D, Pitts J R (eds) *Theories of sociology*. The Free Press, New York, pp 1405–48

Shils E, Lipsitz G (1968) Consensus. In Sills D (ed) *International encyclopedia of the social sciences*. Macmillan, New York, Volume 3, pp 260–71

Shim J P (1989) Bibliographic research on the Analytic Hierarchy Process (AHP). *Socio-economic Planning Science* **23**: 161–7

Shipley L S, Shubik M (1954) A method for evaluating the distribution of power in a committee system. *American Political Science Review* **48**: 787–92

Shopley J B, Fuggle R F (1984) A comprehensive review of current environmental impact assessment methods and techniques. *Journal of Environmental Management* **18**: 25–47

Shrivastava P (1987) *Bhopal: anatomy of a crisis*. Ballinger, Cambridge, Massachusetts

Shrybman S (1986) Environmental mediation. In Lang R (ed) *Integrated approaches to resource planning and management*. University of Calgary Press, Banff, pp 81–98

Siemens H G, Schalit L M, Nieuwboer H W (1985) Who pays for waste site clean-up costs? *Industrial Development* **March/April**: 349–52

Simon H A (1983) *Reason in human affairs*. Stanford University Press, Stanford

Siting Process Task Force on Low-Level Radioactive Waste Disposal (1987) *Opting for cooperation*. Energy, Mines and Resources Canada, Ottawa

Skaburskis A (1988) Criteria for compensating for the impact of large projects: the impact of British Columbia's Revelstoke Dam on local government services. *Journal of Policy Analysis and Management* **7**: 668–86

Skaburskis A, Bullen J (1987) Measuring the impact of waste disposal sites. *Impact Assessment Bulletin* **5**: 25–33

Skeffington A M (1969) *People and planning*. HMSO, London

Skelton I (1990) Multicriteria decision aid in social planning: allocating child care resources in Ontario. PhD thesis, York University, Department of Geography, Toronto

Smith L G (1987) Impact assessment in Canada: current practice and future directions. *The Operational Geographer*, No. 13, pp 12–14

Smith L G (1989) Evaluating Canadian impact assessment provisions. Paper presented at the 8th Annual Meeting of the International Association for Impact Assessment, 24–28 June, Montreal, Quebec

Smith L G (1991) Canada's changing impact assessment provisions. *Environmental Impact Assessment Review* **11**: 5–9

Solomon B D, Haynes K E (1984) A survey and critique of multiobjective power plant siting decision rules. *Socio-Economic Planning Sciences* **18**: 71–9

Spezzarro C (1986) Decisions, decisions. *Macworld*, April, pp 102–5

Steiss A W (1978) *Local government finance: capital facilities planning and debt administration*. Lexington Books, Lexington

Stevens H (1989) A needs analysis approach to setting funding priorities for human services. Mimeo, Social Planning Council of Winnipeg, Winnipeg

Stewart T J (1981) A descriptive approach to multiple-criteria decision making. *Journal Operations Research Society* **32**: 45–53

Susskind L, Babbitt E (1987) *Resolving public disputes: interactive teaching of negotiation and dispute resolution in the public sector*. MIT–Harvard, Cambridge, Massachusetts

Tausig C (1991) Accountability takes on new meaning. *University Affairs, Canada*, March, pp 3–5

Taylor J, Taylor W (1987) Searching for solutions. *PC Magazine* **16**: 311–37

Taylor-Gooby P (1991) Public spending. Review of Hills J (1990) *Times Higher Education Supplement*, 3 March

Teitz M (1968) Toward a theory of urban public facility location. *Papers, Regional Science Association* **21**: 35–51

Thiriez H, Zionts S (eds) (1976) *Multiple criteria decision making*. Springer-Verlag, New York

Thisse J-F, Zoller H G (eds) (1983) *Locational analysis of public facilities*. North-Holland, Amsterdam

Thom R (1972) Stabilité structurelle et morphogénèse. Benjamin, New York

Town and Country Planning Association (1987) *Sizewell Report, a new approach for major public inquiries*. TCPA, London

Trakman L E (1991) *Reasoning with the Charter*. Butterworth, Toronto

Truelove M I (1989) Pre-school day care and public facility provision: a case of Metropolitan Toronto. PhD thesis, University of Toronto, Department of Geography, Toronto

Turney J (1988) Out of tune with the rest of the group. *Times Higher Education Supplement*, 25 Nov., pp 11–13

Tversky A, Kahneman D (1981) The framing of decisions and the psychology of choice. *Science* **211**: 453–8

Ullmann-Margalit E, Morgenbesser S (1977) Picking and choosing. *Social Research* **44**: 757–85

US Department of the Interior (1980) Public involvement manual. US Government Printing Office, Washington, DC

US Water Resources Council (1983) *Economic and environmental principles and guidelines for water and related land resources implementation studies*. US Government Printing Office, Washington, DC

Van Dyke V (1964) *Pride and power: the rationale for the space program*. University of Illinois Press, Urbana

Van de Ven A H (1974) *Group decision making and effectiveness*. Kent State University, Kent, Ohio

Vari A (1991) Argumatics: a text analysis procedure for supporting problem formulation. *Quality and Quantity* **25**: 1–17

Vari A, Vecsenyi J (in press) Experiences with decision conferencing in Hungary. *Interfaces* (special issue on risk and decision analysis)

Vincke P (1986) Analysis of multicriteria decision aid in Europe. *European Journal of Operational Research* **25**: 160–8

Vizayakumar K, Mohapatra P K J (1989) An approach to environmental impact assessment by using cross impact simulation. *Environment and Planning A* **21**: 831–7

Vlek C, Cvetkovich G (eds) (1989) *Social decision methodology for technological projects*. Kluwer Academic Publishers, London

Von Neumann J, Morgenstern D (1947) *Theory of games and economic behavior*. Princeton University Press, Princeton, New Jersey

Voogd H (1983) *Multicriteria evaluation for urban and regional planning*. Pion, London

Wagner C (1980) The formal foundations of Lehrer's theory of consensus. In Bogdan R J (ed) *Keith Lehrer*. Reidel, Dordrecht, pp 165–80

Wald M L (1989) US will start over on planning for Nevada nuclear waste dump. *New York Times*, 29 Nov.

Walsh K (1991) Quality and public services. *Public Administration* **69**: 503–14

Warnock M (1988) Biblical authority lacking in humility. *The Independent*, 8 Oct.

Warrington J (trans) (1963) Aristotle: *Ethics*. Dent, London

Weber A (1909) *The theory of the location of industries* (English translation). Chicago University Press, Chicago

Welch H G, Larson E B (1988) Dealing with limited resources: the Oregon decision to curtail funding for organ transplantation. *The New England Journal of Medicine* **319**: 171–3

Welsh I (1991) Boundaries of control. *Times Higher Educational Supplement*, 14 June

Whitney J B R, Maclaren V W (eds) (1985) *Environmental impact assessment: the Canadian experience*. Institute for Environmental Studies, University of Toronto, Toronto

Wierzbicki A P (1982) A mathematical basis for satisficing decision making. *Mathematical Modelling* **3**: 465–85

Williams E A, Massa A K (1983) *Siting of major facilities: a practical approach*. McGraw-Hill, New York

Won J (1990) Multicriteria evaluation approaches to urban transportation projects. *Urban Studies* **27**: 119–38

Woods S (1986) *Her Excellency Jeanne Sauve*. Macmillan, Toronto

Wooler S (1987) *Analysis of decision conferences: interpretation of decision makers' activities in problem identification, problem expressing and problem structuring*. Technical report 87–2, Decision Analysis Unit, London School of Economics and Political Science, London

York R O (1988) *Human service planning: concepts, tools, and methods*. University of North Carolina Press, Chapel Hill

Young H (1989) *One of us*. Macmillan, London

Zeiss C (1991) Community decision-making and impact management priorities for siting waste facilities. *Environmental Impact Assessment Review* **11**: 231–55

Zeleny M (1976) The theory of displaced ideal. In Zeleny M (ed) *Multi criteria decision making*. Springer-Verlag, New York, pp 153–206

Zeleny M (1982) *Multiple criteria decision making*. McGraw-Hill, New York

Zeleny M (ed) (1984) *MCDM: past decade and future trends, a sourcebook of multiple criteria decision making*. Jai Press, London

Index